Shame the Devil

To Anneget and Berkeley,

In sincere friendship,
and a special shout out
to BR, a model for us all
in the writing trade.

Love,
Wayne

Shame the Devil

How Critics Keep
American Journalism Honest

Wayne J. Guglielmo

ROWMAN & LITTLEFIELD
Lanham • Boulder • New York • London

Published by Rowman & Littlefield
A wholly owned subsidiary of
The Rowman & Littlefield Publishing Group, Inc.
4501 Forbes Boulevard, Suite 200, Lanham, Maryland 20706
www.rowman.com

86-90 Paul Street, London EC2A 4NE

British Library Cataloguing in Publication Information Available

Library of Congress Cataloging-in-Publication Data Available

ISBN 978-1-5381-7481-4 (cloth) | ISBN 978-1-5381-7482-1 (epub)

To Maria, *sensa di chi*, *niente*, and the loving memory
of my mother and father, Mary and Tony

And I can teach thee, coz, to shame the devil
By telling truth. Tell truth and shame the devil.

            —Hotspur, *Henry IV, Part I*

There can be no higher law in journalism than to tell
the truth and to shame the devil.

      —Walter Lippmann, *Liberty and the News*, 1920

Contents

Preface

I began writing this book when the American press was under attack. People who work in journalism are no strangers to denunciation, of course, and occasionally that denunciation has turned violent. Several years ago, for instance, a man carrying a shotgun and smoke grenades stormed into the newsroom of *The Capital*, an Annapolis-based daily newspaper, and killed five staff members and wounded two others. Most attacks on the media do not reach this extreme, thank goodness. But even verbal denunciations from those seeking to consolidate their authority poison the atmosphere, sow distrust, and cause otherwise well-meaning citizens to doubt what they read, hear, or see. And when such doubt and distrust reach a critical mass—as they have in both the past and more contemporary times—the minimal consensus required for democracy is itself placed in jeopardy. It is, alas, a much-reenacted authoritarian scenario.

But there is another history of press criticism. Unlike the more violent one, this one does not typically trade in denunciation or physical threat, although those who have contributed to it can be merciless when they think the press has become too slanted in one direction, or has fallen short of some ideal, or is too concentrated for its own good, or seems to be underreporting or ignoring altogether some critical story. At times, some of the harshest criticism has been hurled from inside the profession, by active or former reporters and editors who know the inner workings of journalism; at other times, criticism has come from the outside, by academic critics who try to make sense of the vital connections between the press and wider social and political trends.

Such criticism deserves our attention and, I would argue, our gratitude. For whether it comes from the inside or outside, whether it seeks to upend the prevailing system or simply to reform it, it is rarely nihilistic. It almost never forgets that a free and independent press is, as Justice Felix Frankfurter said in the early 1950s, "not an end in itself but a means to the end of a free society." And precisely for this reason, our most thoughtful press critics have continued to respect the institution, even when strenuously insisting that it needs to mend its ways.

Introduction

Toward a Modern American Press Criticism

In fact, there is no colorless newspaper, though a few approximate it; every news report has some point of view, expresses some mission of God or of the Devil.

—Will Irvin, "The American Newspaper," 1911

Criticism of the press is almost as old as the institution itself. In America, the modern origins of the press are often traced to the rise of the penny papers, those cheap, mass-produced publications that began circulating in the 1830s. Untethered from political parties, as the earliest newspapers were, these penny papers were commercial enterprises built on a base of expanding circulation and advertising. To be sure, "popularization and commercialization were long-term developments that had been under way for decades before the penny press emerged," Paul Starr points out in *The Creation of the Media: Political Origins of Modern Communications.* Still, "the penny papers were an editorial and entrepreneurial innovation of singular importance." In their efforts to boost circulation, they were the first US papers to expand local news coverage and turn news itself into a form of entertainment.[1]

Both editorial policies proved significant, especially the emphasis on entertainment. Indeed, if the penny press ushered in an era of independent journalism, less beholden to the whims of party politics, it also introduced a form of tabloid reporting in which facts could be manipulated in order to craft a compelling story.[2] For historians, a revealing instance of this trend was the April 1836 murder of Helen Jewett, a prostitute who worked in a New York City brothel run by a madam named Rosina Townsend.

Jewett was bludgeoned to death and set on fire in her bed by one of her clients, who was later tried and acquitted, apparently because powerful interests intervened. The *New York Herald*, the penny paper founded on a shoestring the year before by James Gordon Bennett, provided the most extensive coverage of the crime and subsequent trial. In his dual roles as publisher and reporter, Bennett appeared dogged. If his claims were to be believed, he had visited the scene of the crime almost immediately after the killing, thereby allowing him to describe the partially charred corpse in vivid if florid prose and to land an interview with the brothel owner herself. Initially, his apparent journalistic pluck was applauded. Over time, though, a backlash set in, and some historians came to suspect that Bennett may have taken creative license in crafting his report. Among other things, he was accused of imaginatively embellishing his description of the murdered Jewett and of fabricating entirely, perhaps, his interview with her onetime madam.[3] Nevertheless, such fact-bending sensationalism won over his contemporary readers. Soon, other penny publishers like Benjamin Day of the *New York Sun* would join Bennett in pioneering a new journalistic model. Firmly wedded to commercialism, it sought to attract consumers through a variety of strategies, not least of which was a reliance on an unapologetic sensationalism.[4]

In the post–Civil War period, the model took even firmer hold, and commentators of the period took notice: while they remained generally effusive about a press putatively independent from political parties, some began to fault, on the one hand, its commercially driven reliance on sensation, sex, and crime and, on the other hand, its "willful perversion of facts."[5] Few commentators seemed more exasperated by those twin errors than Mark Twain, a onetime newspaperman himself. In a speech before the Hartford's Monday Evening Club, on March 31, 1873, for instance, he decried the burgeoning effect of newspapers on the nation's moral decay, noting with typical comic exaggeration, "The more newspapers, the worse morals." He was especially incensed, or so he insisted, by the rise of the tabloid press, which he thought had become as popular as it had "because the virtuous newspapers long ago nurtured up a public laxity that loves indecency and never cares whether laws are administered or not."[6]

In Twain's sense of the term at least, neither Joseph Pulitzer's *New York World* nor William Randolph Hearst's *New York Journal* were tabloids. Certainly, each published its share of serious reporting, as even some of their severest critics acknowledged. At the same time, the *World* as well as the *Journal* were leading avatars of the so-called yellow press, a class of circulation-hungry newspapers that featured exaggerated reporting, often lurid stories, scare headlines, and graphic photos. Toward the end of the nineteenth century, Pulitzer and Hearst used precisely these techniques in their battle for dominance in the competitive New York newspaper market.

Their tactics caught the attention of critics, including some veterans of the profession. One was George Washburn Smalley, a former Civil War reporter and current US correspondent of the London *Times*. Writing in *Harper's Magazine* in 1898, Smalley made no secret of his fondness for the profession, especially as a career for promising young men. Still, while gingerly sidestepping the issue of yellow journalism, he acknowledged that newspapers that "trade in filth" sometimes flourished, as did those that "trade in sensation, and the supply of what is called news without much regard to its accuracy or truth." Some might be blind to it, but the sensationalistic, commercial press was an unfortunate but undeniable fact of contemporary life.[7]

Other critics voiced even stronger sentiments. They not only decried the commercial press for distorting news content but for mirroring the excesses and corporate greed of the Gilded Age, that period of accelerated economic growth in the United States between 1870 and 1900.[8] In the October 1897 edition of *Scribner's Magazine*, for example, journalist and future muckraker Lincoln Steffens, at this point employed by the *New York Evening Post*, spoke of the "new journalism" as being the product "of a strictly commercial exploitation of the market."[9] After listing some of the "tricks of the trade" that wily publishers and their editorial hires employed to drive circulation, he noted how those on the editorial side were now being abetted by those on the business side, including that newest member of the team, the circulation manager: "As the manager of a high office building goes forth in search of tenants, and as the bank president, in more dignified mien, invites depositors to patronize his institution, so the circulation man in the newspaper business sends out his agents to 'drum up' readers."[10]

Even the harshest critics were forced to acknowledge, of course, that the push for circulation was not necessarily incompatible with quality journalism, as both Pulitzer and Hearst had partially demonstrated in New York City. But, as critics came to see, those twin goals often clashed, and when they did publishers more often than not permitted their commercial instincts to run roughshod over their journalistic ones.

Critics in the Progressive Era continued to take note. Even the so-called muckraking press was, they believed, not immune from the temptation to give commercial values precedence. While praising certain newspapers and magazines for helping to root out economic corruption and political malfeasance, two key progressive goals, such critics worried that some of these same publications had hid behind the muckraking banner in order to traffic in scandal and sensationalism, in much the same way that the yellow press had.[11] Among the commentators calling attention to this and other issues of the day was William "Will" Henry Irvin, one of the most influential reporters of the era and something of a muckraker himself.

Will Irwin was born in upstate New York in 1873. After spending his early childhood in Colorado, he was educated at Stanford University and began his career in journalism at the *San Francisco Chronicle*. In 1904, he headed east again, working first as a reporter for the *Sun* (where he wrote about the 1906 San Francisco earthquake in absentia); next as managing editor and then editor of *McClure's Magazine*; and, finally, in a return to what he liked best, as an investigative reporter for *Collier's*, the national weekly founded in 1905.[12] It was on *Collier's* that, in late September 1909, he began an investigation of the American newspaper—in effect, a muckraker muckraking the press. The research occupied him over the next ten months, culminating in a fifteen-part series titled "The American Newspaper," which appeared in *Collier's* from January to June 1911.[13]

From the outset, Irwin made clear the contemporary power of newspapers, now second only to religion as an "extrajudicial force." The source of this power, he emphasized, was not the editorial side of the newspaper, as in the past when papers were party aligned, but the news side. It was this side of things, in fact, that served up "the raw material for public opinion." And yet, if publishers were capable of educating the public with vital information, they were just as capable of coarsening it with scandal, gossip, sensationalism, and trivia. And nowhere was this dichotomy better illustrated than on the papers owned by William Randolph Hearst. At the heyday of yellow journalism at the turn of the twentieth century, Hearst had perfected a new business model, which was initially designed to build circulation through scandal, gossip, and related techniques. Then, with circulation on his largest dailies secured, "Hearst journalism responded to a sounder taste on the part of its public," giving readers public interest investigations and the like. This was not to say that Hearst's shady tactics suddenly disappeared. Certain sordid practices were still very much in evidence, Irwin reminded his readers. In the tenth installment of his series, "The Unholy Alliance," he documented one especially nasty practice. Between 1908 and 1909, it seemed, Hearst newspapers, in particular the *New York Journal* under Arthur Brisbane, a close friend of the publisher, routinely slanted editorial matter in exchange for bigger advertising dollars. Hearst was not alone in this, although as in so many other areas of newspapering he had brought it to a fine burnish.[14]

A MODERN PRESS CRITICISM

In its complicated view of the press as at once a public good and a commercial undertaking, Irwin's "The American Newspaper" was the culmination of much of the commentary that preceded it. A similar conundrum haunted the criticism that followed Irwin. But this newer criticism was also forced, by both circumstances and changes in thought, to address a different set of issues. One brought on by the US entry into World War I in April 1917, was the question of the role of the press during wartime. Suddenly, newspapers were not only called on to be the primary medium for keeping the home front informed, typically about events taking place thousands of miles away. They were also responsible for amusing and distracting it through a variety of extra-news departments, including light features, advice columns, horoscopes, and comics.[15] In time, the government also enlisted newspapers in the war effort itself. As passive participants, newspapers voluntarily agreed to restrict any information that might impede that effort, such as news reports on troop strength, shipping routes, or base locations. But government officials soon realized that newspapers could also play a more active war role, especially as propaganda tools in Washington's effort to build and sustain support for the American involvement abroad.

The major arm of this campaign was the Committee on Public Information (CPI), also known as the "Creel Committee." Named after George Creel, a former investigative journalist, onetime Denver police commissioner, and candidate Woodrow Wilson's campaign strategist, CPI was a multifaceted operation. Fully operational, it comprised numerous divisions, including the Division of Pictorial Publicity, the News Division, and the Censorship Board. Under Creel's determined leadership, CPI attracted scores of talented artists, speakers, and publicists.[16] Perhaps the most brilliant of the latter group was Edward Bernays, an Austrian-born former medical editor and press agent who was hired to pump up public support for the war, with a special emphasis on American businesses operating in Latin America.[17]

CPI and Creel had their critics, though. One of the fiercest was the brilliant young journalist who ironically had been instrumental, at the outset of the war, in persuading Wilson to form a pro-war propaganda committee in the first place. The young man was Walter Lippmann, who in 1913, at the still callow age of twenty-four, had been one of the founding editors of the *New Republic*, the progressive magazine of political and cultural commentary. Lippmann had become especially skeptical of CPI's London-based work in Europe, charging that Creel's staff knew little about European politics or British journalism.[18] At the same time, his experience of the war—and government efforts at propaganda—awakened him to a harsh truth: news was subjective and almost infinitely malleable. Through it, opinion could be manufactured and truth itself manipulated.

After the war, Lippmann and a coauthor tested his hypothesis by examining how the nation's most preeminent newspaper, the *New York Times*, had permitted extra-journalistic concerns to distort its coverage of the Bolshevik Revolution, in late October 1917. In many ways, this was a new form of press criticism—keenly alert to editorial sleights of hand, skeptical of journalistic shibboleths, and at once conscious and wary of the uneasy link between public opinion and democracy. For these reasons and others, historians have often regarded Lippmann as the first modern press critic, someone whose work introduced novel terms, raised new psychological concerns, and proved essential as both a model to emulate and oppose. For these reasons, we will begin our study of modern American press critics with Walter Lippmann.

In a brief but impressive outpouring of books on the media and public opinion, Lippmann's thinking on the press and its role in a democratic society gradually evolved. In *Liberty and the News* (1920), written in the aftermath of the war, he was still in a reformist frame of mind, critical of the war-time press for its clumsy partisanship and propagandizing but nevertheless hopeful that, with the proper corrections, the postwar press could once again become a beacon of truth and liberty. His subsequent books revealed, though, a more skeptical frame of mind. In *Public Opinion* (1922), his most famous book, he argued that even a reformed press would prove an inadequate instrument for ensuring an enlightened public, historically regarded as the cornerstone of a democracy. Modern society in all its facets was, after all, simply too inaccessible, the public too distracted, and the tendency of both citizens and journalists to reduce the world's complexity to convenient "stereotypes" too irresistible. Better that, in the larger realms of domestic and world affairs, the public cede its truth-seeking to a cadre of experts who by training, position, and inclination were up to the task. In his follow-up book, *The Phantom Public* (1925), he went further still, dismissing as fiction the very idea of a sovereign public. What was regarded as the "public" was, instead, a revolving cast of agents and bystanders, actors and spectators, insiders and outsiders. Certainly, these were controversial, seemingly undemocratic proposals, and they put Lippmann at odds with some of the leading thinkers of his day.

Following Lippmann, the study will move through the twentieth century and early twenty-first century via other key press critics—George Seldes, A. J. Liebling, Ben Bagdikian, Reed Irvine, Neil Postman, and

Noam Chomsky. It will arrive, finally, at the contemporary scene, which, in comparison with the past, is significantly more diverse in gender, sexual orientation, minority representation, and political affiliation. This diversity has been key to today's critics raising new issues, while revisiting older ones in novel ways.

HISTORY, DEMOCRACY, AND THE PRESS

For anyone studying how critics have tried to keep the press honest, two impressions seem unavoidable. First, in framing their critiques, critics have by necessity responded to the salient events of their times—the social movements, wars, economic milestones and dislocations, intellectual changes. For the young Walter Lippmann, for instance, World War I and the pivotal role played by newspapers of the day proved crucial to his earliest critical formulations. For A. J. Liebling, it was his tour as foreign correspondent during World War II that led him to question press performance. For Neil Postman, it was mass entertainment's rise that colored his views of media, including TV news. For Noam Chomsky, it was America's foreign involvements and continuing economic inequality that fueled his propaganda model. And for many contemporary press critics, it has been the Trump era and its aftermath that have shaped some of their press thinking. In short, critics have had little choice historically but to ground their more abstract thoughts in real-world events.

At the same time, these more abstract ideas have not been ignored. Key among them is the question of the role of the press in a democratic society. Since the earliest days of the republic, the answer to this question has typically included a view of the institution as a source of public information—information vital to a deliberative democracy. The institution has often carried out this mission successfully, but not always. When the press falters, as it has in the past and today, it may be rightly labeled, as Liebling once colorfully described it, "the weak slat under the bed of democracy."[19] The press may also falter, though, when public mistrust in the key institutions of society, including the institution of journalism, has become so endemic, so unyielding, that even forthright efforts at truth telling are marginalized, dismissed, labeled fake. At such times, press critics must contend not only with a journalistic crisis but an epistemic one as well.

A FINAL WORD

The following chapters are based on a pair of assumptions. The first is that modern press critics are best understood not only in the context of their biographies, some of which are singularly eventful, but through a sampling of their non-press books. In regard to the latter, even when these books range far afield, they serve to illuminate a writer's broader vision of the world. The second premise is that the core of what modern critics have had to say is best grasped through a close reading of their written works on the press. Certainly, speeches, radio commentaries, interviews, and conferences also yield useful insights, and, whenever appropriate, they have been included here as source material. It is in their books and articles, though, that press critics from Lippmann to the present have most clearly articulated their thinking.

In this sense, the chapters that follow may be regarded as parts of an illuminating if highly selective intellectual history of the twentieth century and the early twenty-first century. To some readers, this may seem like a strange characterization, given how wary most journalists are of seeming too abstract. Leave that airy stuff to the academics, some are inclined to say. Still, many of the critics included here—Lippmann, Postman, Chomsky, James Fallows, McChesney, among others—are properly understood as intellectuals, whatever their current or former journalistic status. As for others for whom the label of intellectual fits uncomfortably, the fact remains: ideas evolve and assemble, often in spite of ourselves. Our task as students of history is to be alert to them when they do.

NOTES

1. Paul Starr, *The Creation of the Media: Political Origins of Modern Communications* (New York: Basic Books, 2004), 134–35.

2. Ibid., 134.

3. Starr, *Creation*, 133; see also Andie Tucher, *Froth and Scum: Truth, Beauty, Goodness, and the Axe Murder in America's First Mass Medium* (Chapel Hill: University of North Carolina, 1994), 35–36, 38; for the story of Jewett, see Patricia Cline Cohen, *The Murder of Helen Jewett: The Life and Death of a Prostitute in Nineteenth-Century New York* (New York Knopf, 1998).

4. Yasmine Tarrek Dabbous, "'Blessed Be the Critics of Newspapers': Journalistic Criticism of Journalism: 1895–1930 (PhD diss., Louisiana State University, 2010, LSU Digital Commons, https://digitalcommons.lsu.edu/cgi/viewcon tent.cgi?article=2189&context=gradschool_dissertations, 38.

5. Ibid., 29.

6. Mark Twain, *Speeches*, vol. 24, *The Complete Works of Mark Twain* (New York: Harper, 1923), 46–52.

7. George W. Smalley, "Notes on Journalism," *Harper's Monthly*, July 1898, 219, The Unz Review, https://www.unz.com/print/Harpers-1898jul-00213/.

8. Dabbous, "Blessed," 66.

9. Lincoln Steffens, "The Business of a Newspaper," *Scribner's Magazine*, October 1987, *Lincoln Steffens Collection*, 6, The Archive of American Journalism, http://nebula.wsimg.com/89745ffea8abed717cb0d9cada53211a?AccessKeyId=94 861742399A59C7B18A&disposition=0&alloworigin=1.

10. Ibid., 8.

11. Dabbous, "Blessed," 95.

12. Robert V. Hudson, *The Writing Game: A Biography of Will Irwin* (Ames: Iowa State University, 1982), 3–56.

13. Ibid. 69–70.

14. Will Irwin, "The American Newspaper," a series first appearing in *Collier's*, January–July 1911, with comments by Clifford F. Weigle and David G. Clark (Ames: Iowa State University, 1969), 18, 20, 57–63; See also Hudson, *Writing Game*, 71.

15. Michaela Smith, "Hot Off the Presses: Newspapers during WWI," Remembering WWI, Villanova Digital History, https://rememberingwwi.villanova.edu /newspapers/.

16. Among the many books on George Creel and the Committee on Public Information are Alan Axelrod, *Selling the Great War: The Making of American Propaganda* (New York: St. Martin's, 2009); Celia M. Kingsbury, *For Home and Country: World War I Propaganda on the Home Front* (Lincoln: University of Nebraska, 2010); and John Maxwell Hamilton, *Manipulating the Masses: Woodrow Wilson and the Birth of American Propaganda* (Baton Rouge: Louisiana State University, 2020).

17. See, for example, Edward Bernays's own forthright discussion of his role on the committee, *Propaganda*, with an introduction by Mark Crispin Miller (1928; repr., Brooklyn: IG Publishing, 2004).

18. Ronald Steel, *Walter Lippmann and the American Century* (Atlantic Monthly Press, 1980), 145.

19. A. J. Liebling, *The Press*, in *Liebling: The Sweet Science and Other Writings*, ed. Pete Hamill (New York: The Library of America, 2009), 742.

Walter Lippmann, c. 1920
Source: Library of Congress

Chapter One

Walter Lippmann

The Evolution of a Press Skeptic

*[The press] is too frail to carry the whole burden of popular sover-
eignty, to supply spontaneously the truth which democrats hoped was
inborn.*

—Walter Lippmann, *Public Opinion*, 1922

At a time when it was still possible for a single journalistic voice to
command the nation's attention and shape its thinking—when radio was
as yet in its infancy and TV news a thing of the distant future—Walter
Lippmann, born in New York City into an upper-middle-class German
Jewish family in 1889, was on his way to becoming what his *New York
Times* obituary eighty-five years later would call "the dean of American
political journalism in the 20th Century."[1]

Lippmann's outsized influence at the height of his fame was captured
with grim humor by the *New Yorker*'s James Thurber. In a cartoon in
1943, two years after the United States entered World War II, Thurber
pictured one of his classic domestic scenes: Sitting in an overstuffed chair
in their comfortable living room, a woman turns to her bow-tied, bespectacled husband and says flatly, "Lippmann scares me this morning."[2] At
the time, Lippmann had been writing his influential syndicated column
for the *New York Herald Tribune*, "Today and Tomorrow," for twelve
years; both before and during this period, he was also the author of topi-
cal articles and essays for other publications and a steady flow of closely
researched, deeply reflective books on a range of subjects.

"Lippmann scares me this morning."

James Thurber cartoon, "Lippmann Scares Me This Morning," *The New Yorker*, 1943

One of those subjects was his own profession. His preeminent status aside, Lippmann was in many ways his still-evolving profession's first and fiercest modern critic.[3] In a series of increasingly pessimistic books, *Liberty and the News* (1920), *Public Opinion* (1922), and *The Phantom Public* (1925), he went from arguing that the press of his day had shirked its truth-telling mission in favor advocacy and propagandizing, especially during World War I, to the view that even a reformed press, should it emerge, would be an inadequate instrument of public enlightenment in the increasingly complex world of the early twentieth century. To think otherwise was so much wishful thinking, thought Lippmann. Given its reliance on stereotypes, "pseudo environments," and other simulacra of the truth, journalism was simply not up to that monumental task. And even if it did a better job of informing than it did, how many working men and women had the time or inclination to devote hours reading their local paper or the better national ones? There were other remedies for how a deliberative democracy might function, Lippmann thought. And these would become the focus of an intense contemporary debate that has lasted until today.

A SKEPTIC'S EDUCATION

Lippmann's press skepticism can be traced, at least in part, to his background and early years in the profession. Neither of these was typical of the journalists of his day. An only child, he was raised in urban comfort on the Upper East Side, thanks to his father, Jacob Lippmann, who prospered in the family's clothing company, and his mother, Daisy Lippmann, née Baum, who was the recipient of a sizable inheritance from her parents, immigrants who had begun life in America living in relatively modest circumstances.

Together, the Lippmanns ensured that their son was "brought up to be a gentleman," as his biographer explains.[4] In 1896, at age six, he was taken on a transatlantic trip aboard the luxurious ocean liner the RMS *Etruria*, built in Scotland for the Cunard Line.[5] This trip would be the first in a series of annual family excursions to Europe and points farther east, including Moscow and St. Petersburg. That September, a few days before turning seven, he entered the Sachs School for Boys, a private elementary school that catered to the children of the city's "German-Jewish establishment," as well as to "rich Catholics who didn't want their children to mingle with the poor Irish in the parochial schools."[6] The Sachs School was demanding, with large segments of its weekly curriculum devoted to Latin and Greek. The young Walter excelled, though, both academically and socially, and eventually matriculated to the school's upper division, the Sachs Collegiate Institute, which had a reputation for placing its graduates either directly into business or into top-tier universities like Harvard.[7] More interested in art history than business, Lippmann took the latter route.

At Harvard in fall 1906, he soon discovered a world that was socially stratified and largely off-limits to Jews, nonathletes, or anyone else who seemed different. Still, it was an intellectually stimulating environment. A student in the A.B. degree program, one of two degrees offered to Harvard undergraduates at the time, he could largely design his own curriculum, a freedom he took full advantage of. He enrolled in courses in psychology, English, French literature, comparative literature, languages, philosophy, economics, history, and government. He also became acquainted with several of the school's most celebrated teachers and lecturers, three of whom—William James, George Santayana, and the visiting English political scientist Graham Wallas—exerted an especially strong influence on him.[8]

Lippmann never took a formal course from William James, who by 1907 was officially an emeritus professor of philosophy. Outside the classroom, though, the pair struck up an unlikely friendship. The catalyst was a Lippmann essay James read lampooning a former faculty colleague, the English Department's Barrett Wendell, "an Anglophile defender of gentility."[9] A bond was instantly formed. Thereafter, in a series of weekly teas at the James house on Irving Street, across from Harvard Yard, the impressive sophomore and arguably America's most important philosopher ranged widely over topics both speculative and practical. Gradually, James's qualities as a man and a thinker—and especially his intellectual tolerance, deep democratic instincts, and insistence on applying a pragmatic test to any truth—cast their optimistic spell. Learning of James's death in summer 1910, the recent graduate eulogized his friend and intellectual mentor, noting that the man he knew was "a democrat. He gave all men and all creeds, any idea, any theory, any superstition, a respectful hearing."[10]

And yet it was James's former student and colleague, George Santayana, who made the more lasting intellectual impression on Lippmann. In many ways James's philosophic and temperamental opposite, the Spanish-born thinker and polymath had recently completed his five-volume *The Life of Reason* (1905–1906) when Lippmann enrolled in his introductory course in Greek philosophy. In that wide-ranging work, Santayana had made clear his distrust of democracy, and especially American democracy, which in its emphasis on equality and majority rule, he believed, both imperiled individual self-realization and spirituality and enforced a slavish public uniformity.[11] "There is no greater stupidity or meanness than to take uniformity for an idea," Santayana wrote in his book.[12] More interested in individual than collective development, Santayana envisioned the role of the state as safeguarding the right of the individual to flourish intellectually, morally, and spiritually. The state should also enlist the most able to serve as part of a natural aristocracy or governing class. For Lippmann, who during his senior year would take advanced courses in philosophy with Santayana, such democratic skepticism clashed head-on with Jamesian pluralism and optimism. And yet it was the Spaniard's skepticism that would eventually win Lippmann over, especially after his dispiriting experiences in World War I. Ten years after leaving Harvard, he would write, "I love James more than any great man I ever saw, but increasingly I find Santayana inescapable."[13]

Lippmann learned still other lessons from the third in the triumvirate of his Harvard teachers. Born in Sunderland, England, in 1858, Graham Wallas had earned a degree in classics at Oxford after a strict religious upbringing; entered the teaching profession after graduation; and, in 1895, accepted a position at the newly formed London School of Economics, which he had helped to establish along with fellow socialists Sydney and Beatrice Webb and George Bernard Shaw. In 1896, he followed their example and joined the Fabian Society, devoted to the cause of democratic socialism in Great Britain. It was an association that would last until 1904, when Wallas split from the group over policy differences.

In spring 1910, Wallas taught the first of several Harvard politics seminars, which Lippmann eagerly attended.[14] The awkward scholar's storied association with the Fabians was certainly an attraction for the upperclassman, who for several years now had "come around to Socialism as a creed."[15] Even more appealing, though, was Wallas's iconoclastic ideas on politics.

In *Human Nature in Politics* (1908), Wallas had argued for why political science, as commonly practiced, had underestimated the psychological and irrational elements in political institutions and decision making. Such qualitative elements or impulses—"personal affection, fear, ridicule, the desire of property, etc."— were often, he believed, just as or more determinative of a final outcome than other more quantifiable elements.[16] Even in established democracies, where the free access to the facts was taken for granted, the outcomes of elections or the currents of public opinion were frequently baffling and disappointing, a theme that Lippmann would later develop in *Public Opinion*.

During his Harvard seminar, Wallas also raised other ideas linked to the new political science. Among these were the psychological problems created by a sprawling and variegated mass industrial society, which Walls would elaborate on in *The Great Society* (1914), dedicated to Lippmann. Later, the pupil would return the favor, building on his teacher's seminal insights in his own series of works on society and public opinion. In a 1932 letter to Wallas's widow, the former student made clear his debt:

"He was the greatest teacher I have ever known, and already I believe he has altered the course of Anglo-American political thinking. . . . For myself[,] I owe everything to him that enables me to understand at all the human problems of the Great Society."[17]

JOURNALISTIC TRAINING GROUNDS

The influence of Wallas, James, and Santayana might have prepared Lippmann for an academic career, perhaps one in philosophy or art history. By his senior year, though, he had grown weary of academia and was eager to seek out another line of work. Several journalists had advised him that writing for publication was especially well suited to his verbal talents. One of these was the muckraker Lincoln Steffens, who as editor of *McClure's Magazine* had gained widespread fame for his series on metropolitan corruption.[18] Lippmann worried, though, that his scant journalistic experience would prove fatal. As a partial remedy, and after consulting Steffens, he considered an offer from the publisher of the newly formed *Boston Common*, a small weekly paper that leaned Progressive and adopted an upbeat and optimistic tone.[19] In May 1910, while still enrolled in college, Lippmann accepted an entry position on the weekly, hopeful, as Steffens had suggested, that the unsophisticated startup would nevertheless serve as a worthy journalistic training ground.

The novice reporter's hopes were almost immediately dashed. "I have been with the paper since the beginning," Lippmann wrote to Steffens two weeks after starting, "and I see clearly that it would be a waste of time on my part to stay with it after the summer." The work was simply too mechanical and uninspiring.[20] What Lippmann really wanted to do was to work for Steffens himself. "There is no position I should go at with more eagerness, because there is no kind of work that appeals to me as much as yours does," he wrote to his confidant and adviser, who had come out of semiretirement to join the editorial board of *Everybody's Magazine*, the New York publication that several years earlier had published a series of muckraking articles on American finance.[21] "Money does not happen to be an important consideration for me at the present time," he added reassuringly. "Opportunity to work and learn is what I am looking for."[22]

The magazine's editors were understandably wary. Steffens persisted, though, even wagering he could turn the novice into a real writer within his first year. Lippmann worked hard to justify his mentor's faith in him. Together, they set out on several local investigations, along with a banking industry project with national implications.[23] Such an investigation was exhilarating for the young writer, although Lippmann was less content than the older muckrakers, including Steffens himself, to let things stand at descriptive reporting and exposé. He also had his eye on actual reform, on redirecting money and political power toward the public good, as he would later argue in his second book, *Drift and Mastery* (1914).[24] Still, after a year under Steffen's tutelage, Lippmann was eager to express his gratitude. In an April 2011 letter, he wrote to his mentor, now in England: "You gave me a chance to start—you know what that means to a fellow who has an indifferent world staring him in the face."[25]

Lippmann at this point still regarded himself as a socialist, a stance his muckraking work under Steffens may have kept from cooling completely. Nevertheless, his academic influences and practical experience had left him with an abiding wariness of the inherent goodness or wisdom of the masses. In socialist publications like the *International* and the *Masses*, he voiced his skepticism, which was apparently shared by enough others on the political left so that he remained "in demand as a speaker and writer of political tracts."[26]

HUMAN NATURE AND POLITICS

In late 1911, Lippmann took a temporary detour from journalism and accepted a position as special assistant to the newly elected socialist mayor of Schenectady, New York, the Reverend George Lunn. The switch to electoral politics started off well. At last, he was able to address issues directly. He soon grew disillusioned, though, by what he regarded as Lunn's too-cautious approach to the city's problems. Overcoming for the moment his political wariness, Lippmann joined Lunn's other socialist backers and pushed for bolder measures, including the city takeover of public utilities. His efforts failed to result in the desired change, however. "I fought as hard as I could within the 'organization' without any result," he wrote to Wallas, his former teacher, several months after quitting his special assistant post. "When I saw that the policy and program were settled . . . I resigned and attacked the administration in a socialist paper"—the *New York Call*.[27]

In this same letter to Wallas, Lippmann mentioned in passing that he was working on "what may be a little book—at least a series of essays, and no small part of it is aimed at popularizing your 'Human Nature and Politics,'" the book in which Wallas had urged social scientists to more closely calibrate the psychological and irrational aspects of political behavior.[28] Lippmann's "little book" turned out to be his first full-length publication, *A Preface to Politics* (1913).

Here, Lippmann took note, as he had promised Wallas, of the changing direction in political thinking: "When we recognize that the focus in politics is shifting from a mechanical to a human center, we shall have reached what is, I believe, the most essential idea in modern politics." If the older model of politics was to "harness mankind to abstract principles, the new effort proposes to fit creeds and institutions to the wants of men, to satisfy their impulses as fully and beneficially as possible."[29] For Lippmann, the new effort was, in short, a long-overdue attempt by both theorists and politicians to place human needs and desires first. In time, the "impetus of Freud" would move this program still further. In the meantime, though, while the precise contours of a human-centered politics remained murky, he was eager to sketch a gradualist program that went beyond traditional Progressivism or other merely reformist agendas.[30]

A Preface to Politics was neither an original book nor a coherent contribution to political philosophy. It was, rather, a rehash in many ways of other thinkers' ideas, preeminently Wallas's. Still, it was at once sufficiently irreverent toward older modes of political thinking and amply supportive of newer ones to attract an appreciative readership.

One such reader was Herbert Croly, an editor and political analyst whose influential first book, *The Promise of American Life* (1909), had argued for a "New Nationalism," an enhanced federal government, to offset the unchecked power of big business. At a lunchtime meeting in New York City in fall 1913, Croly explained to Lippmann that he had received four years of guaranteed funding to start a new magazine, which besides covering politics and the arts would champion editorially the notion of a more robust federal government. Would Lippmann, Croly asked, like to be in on the ground floor of the new startup, tantalizingly named, the *New Republic*? Excited to resume his career in journalism—and on a magazine sure to place him in the center of the political action—Lippmann readily accepted the invitation. A little over a year later, on November 7, 1914, the first issue of the *New Republic* appeared, with "Walter Lippmann" listed prominently in the staff box as one of the six founding editors.[31]

A CRISIS IN JOURNALISM:
LIBERTY AND THE NEWS (1920)

Lippmann's official association with the *New Republic* would continue for the next seven years. For much of that time, he was in fact very much at the vital center of things, as he had hoped. His tenure on the magazine was broken, though, by an extended leave of absence from 1917 to 1919. During this two-year period, he took part in the war effort, serving first as assistant to the secretary of war, Newton Baker; then as part of a member of a secret "inquiry" tasked with formulating what would become President Wilson's Fourteen Points, the intended blueprint for peace negotiations to end World War I; and finally, under diplomat Edward M. House, aka Colonel House, as the author of the principal commentary on the terms of peace.[32]

In early 1919, the now thirty-year-old Lippmann returned to the *New Republic*. While resuming his editorial duties, he also began reflecting on his war experience, and in particular on his "experiences with the official propaganda machines"—those methods used by the government to gin up public support during the war. "Opinion can be manufactured," Lippmann had more than ever come to realize, and that was a fact, he believed, worth exploring in depth. In a pitch letter to Ellery Sedgwick, the editor of the *Atlantic Monthly*, he explained his idea: "My hope is to attempt a restatement of the problem of freedom of thought as it presents itself in modern society under modern conditions of government and with a modern knowledge of how to manipulate the human mind."[33] Sedgwick liked what he read, offering Lippmann a freelance assignment that resulted in two articles that ran in successive year-end issues of the magazine. In time, Lippmann appended a third introductory essay and collected all three essays in a monograph titled *Liberty and the News*, published in early 1920.

At the outset, Lippmann framed his theme in terms that may well have struck his contemporary readers as hyperbolic. "For in an exact sense," he explained, "the present crisis of western democracy is a crisis in journalism."[34] Given the recent global war, how could this be? How could the seemingly benign institution of journalism be at the very center of a postwar crisis, even in the heyday of such rapacious media moguls as William Randolph Hearst? Lippmann devoted the remainder of his monograph to answering these questions, and in particular the need for supporters of democracy to rethink not only traditional notions of journalism but classic ideas of freedom of thought.

Modern conditions of government had changed, Lippmann began, echoing Wallas. Whereas in the not-too-distant past the locus of power and decision making tended to reside in the legislative and executive branches of government, with the public playing a decidedly secondary role, modern politics had reversed this paradigm. Now it was public pressure, especially that exerted by special-interest groups on the executive branch, that was instrumental in what got done and what did not. "Government tends to operate by the impact of controlled opinion upon administration," he wrote. And because of "this shift in the locus of sovereignty," those with the capacity to "manufacture consent" or, in the case of propaganda, to "manipulate the human mind," wield the power. Writing before the rise of true mass media, he nevertheless cited the outsized influence of big newspapers: "No wonder that the most powerful newspaper proprietor in the English-speaking world [i.e., Hearst] declined a mere government post" (*Liberty*, 37). Journalism, not politics, was Hearst's platform of choice.

Journalism was failing its responsibility, though. Instead of telling the truth and shaming the devil, editors, especially since World War I, "have come to believe that their highest duty is not to report but to instruct, not to print news but to save civilization." Even at the lower ranks of the profession, "the work of reporters has . . . become confused with the work of preachers, revivalists, prophets and agitators" (*Liberty*, 3–4). Certainly, such editorializing also played a role in a free society. In the modern world, though, journalism's core mission was to inform public opinion, not to shape it.

Lippmann was hopeful this could be done, assuming the profession might adopt the necessary changes, both theoretical and practical. On the theoretical side of things, this would mean rethinking the classic definition of liberty, and this in turn meant a reconsideration of foundational English texts: John Milton's *Areopagitica* (1644) and John Stuart Mill's *On Liberty* (1859).

At first glance, both Milton and Mill seemed to be championing an expansive idea of liberty, a near sacred tolerance for an unfettered expression of opinion. And yet, as Lippmann explained, at some point in their respective arguments each set about defining the limits of liberty by raising what Milton regarded as the "notion of indifference." In this formulation, liberty was permitted as long as "differences are of no great moment," pose no great danger. And so it was one thing to tolerate the insignificant hairsplitting and denominational infighting of certain Protestant sects, and quite another thing to permit heresies like "Popery, and open superstition." The former was permitted because it posed no real threat to the established religious order of the day; the latter was not permitted precisely because it did (*Liberty*, 16–21).

The utilitarian Mill argued, Lippmann believed, for a roughly similar exception to liberty. Though he like Milton not only championed freedom of opinion but the freedom to act upon opinion, he also drew the line at the point where the consequences of an action exceeded the individual and affected society more broadly. And so, once again, it was tolerable for an individual man to transgress a religious norm, since the risk he ran was limited to his social and possibly personal condemnation. It was not tolerable, however, for this same man to make clear his disdain for private property by inciting a mob to seize another man's farm. In the first instance, the man was placing himself in potential jeopardy; in the second, both his belief and his actual speech were imperiling the prevailing social order. The moral for Mill and Milton was clear: in matters of indifference to society, liberty has nearly free rein; but where matters cease to be indifferent—where they seem or can be made to appear seditious or otherwise dangerous—"tolerated indifference is no longer tolerable because it has ceased to be indifferent." This was a slim reed on which to hang the concept of liberty, Lippmann believed, especially in times of stress like war and especially in a society "where public opinion has become decisive." (*Liberty*, 21).

Lippmann knew of what he spoke, of course. World War I had ushered in a time of stress like few others, and, in this climate of fear and foreboding, the government had censored certain ideas and information as dangerous and even seditious, often calling upon newspapers to co-operate in the effort. In turn, a fearful public had come to accept that its freedom of expression was not inviolate and that certain statements and ideas were, for the moment at least, off-limits.

This state of mind did not suddenly end with the end of the war. In fact, in its aftermath, as Lippmann saw, both the impulse among leaders to manipulate public opinion and the tools for doing so became more power-ful. More things counted now than ever before, and the more they did the more they were susceptible to being shaped, controlled, and exploited. For this reason, modern society was in dire need of a counterbalance, a new conception of liberty that provided a too easily manipulated public with the information necessary "by which to detect lies," form "true opinions," and "successfully organize human life." In short, as Lippmann put it, "lib-erty is the name we give to measures by which we protect and increase the veracity of the information upon which we act" (*Liberty*, 21, 40).

The press would have a key role to play in making such information available, but the press of course had lost its way both during and after the war. For it to function properly in the modern democratic society, it needed not only to embrace this new conception of liberty but to adopt reforms that would enable it carry out this conception. In many ways, the reforms that Lippmann was calling for seem self-evident or even tame by today's standards, but they were bold by the still developing standards of the day. Among other things, he wanted to see better sourced and labeled news, a stricter set of professional codes, a better articulated sense of mis-sion, and a clearer sense of what was trivial (the "flicker of events") and what truly mattered (*Liberty*, 45, 48–49, 51–52).

To this list, Lippmann added two tentative reforms. The first was the idea of expanding the number of journalism schools. At the time, the na-tion's first J-school, the University of Missouri School of Journalism in Columbia was just over a decade old and consisted of only one building, erected in 1919.[35] It would be useful, Lippmann thought, to see whether there was any value in endowing "large numbers of schools on the model of those now existing, and make their diplomas a necessary condition for the practice of reporting," although almost immediately he qualified his own proposal and raised, among other things, the risk of overspecializa-tion (*Liberty*, 48).

Lippmann embraced a second reform with fewer reservations, though he struggled to define the practice behind the principle. In principle, he was calling for something that sounds a lot like a private and journalistic version of what became the Government Accountability Office (GAO), established in 1921: an expert group of reporters whose mission is "to study statistics and orders and reports which are beyond the digestive powers of a newspaperman or of his readers." He had a number of ideas on how such an agency could be funded, including through a private trust. He also imagined an independent news agency—one funded at least in part by a foundation in the way that National Public Radio and the Public Broadcasting System are today. As with the GAO-like research agency, this entity would be editorially independent, although how that would be guaranteed is left unaddressed (*Liberty*, 54–61).[36]

Its critical tone aside, *Liberty and the News* was, on balance, a cautiously optimistic book. If Lippmann repeatedly faulted the press for conflating fact and opinion, he was nevertheless cautiously hopeful that it could be improved and that, when it was, a properly informed citizenry, at least partially insulated from insidious manipulation, might emerge. Lippmann knew he was engaged in a hard struggle. Among other things, the project required the selfless participation of labor and other groups that seemed to him more often focused on parochial issues than on the common good. Still, for the moment, he had a tentative faith that, however difficult, progress toward an informed citizenry, insulated to some extent against "fake news," was still possible.

A REAL-WORLD TEST OF THE NEWS

In *Liberty and the News*, Lippmann had complained about the pernicious effects of wartime boosterism on the ideals of truth and fairness. In service to the national interest and to save civilization from the barbaric "Huns," editors and reporters had jettisoned standard journalistic practices and behaved like preachers, prophets, and even dupes of the government. Lippmann at the time had offered relatively little evidence to back up his accusation. That supposed evidence came a half year later, when he and a colleague on the *New Republic*, Charles Merz, put out a special forty-eight-page supplement to the magazine titled "A Test of the News."

Published on August 4, 1920, it documented what the authors saw as the often incomplete, inaccurate, and slanted coverage of the Russian Revolution by one of the nation's and the world's great newspapers, the *New York Times*. Their study, detailed, nuanced, carefully argued, not only led to what contemporary industry commentators called "epochal results" in international reporting at the *Times* and other papers; it also prompted changes in Lippmann's own thinking that would culminate in the gloomy thesis at the heart of his next book, *Public Opinion*.[37]

"Test of the News" focused on a three-year period from March 1917 to March 1920. The period began with the abdication of Nicholas II, who had ruled Russia for nearly twenty-five years, and ended with the arrest of anti-communist commander Nikolai Yudenich and the dissolution of his White Army. At certain critical points along this time span, the authors contended, *Times* correspondents and editors had all but abandoned fairness and objectivity and allowed their hopes for the United States to dictate their news coverage. In so doing so, the *Times* had deprived its readers of the facts they needed to reach reasonable conclusions about urgent matters of public policy.

Early on, for instance, the dominant question before the nation was whether to enter World War I on the side of the Allies, including Russia. That question, in turn, raised a number of subsidiary ones, including "whether the Russians would continue to fight."[38] In weighing this issue, contemporary readers of the *Times* had every right to expect, indeed to demand, "reliable reports about the morale and strength of Russia's armies" ("Test," 4). Certainly, in the course of covering Russia, the paper had provided a number of such reports. One, on March 16, 1917, included a candid assessment of the situation by Leon Trotsky, the Ukrainian-Russian revolutionary who had been deported to the United States from Spain and was now in New York. From the safety of the United States, Trotsky made several claims: that the Provisional Government formed after Nicholas's abdication in no way represented the goals of the revolutionaries who had forced his removal; that the Russian masses revolted because they were discontent with, and suffering dreadfully in, the European war; and most tellingly, that, if the mass of Russian people did not favor Germany, they also had no desire to continue fighting against it. That very same day in the paper, however, a *Times* dispatch from London presented a more optimistic view of things.

Juxtapositions of this kind were not unusual, Lippmann and Merz discovered. In fact, sunnier reports were often given more editorial weight than gloomier ones. One practice was to attribute the optimistic stories to so-called authoritative sources, making them seem more credible to the average reader than those dispatches citing questionable sources, such as an exiled revolutionary with perhaps his own axe to grind. "This is characteristic of the news of the period we are considering," Lippmann and Merz pointed out. "The values placed on the news items were wrong, wrong by the ultimate test of battle"—that is, the Russian losses in the war, which up to this point were catastrophic. The *Times*'s news slant was also discredited a year later by the peace treaty between the Bolsheviks and the Central Powers, which officially brought Russia's disastrous participation in World War I to an end ("Test," 5).[39]

How could this sort of reporting occur, especially on a newspaper like the *New York Times*? Lippmann and Merz believed they had the answer:

> There was an initial desire, shared by the editors and readers of the *Times* to have Russia fight, to secure the military assistance of Russia without opening up contentious questions of war aims, to smother pacifist agitation. Conflicting estimates of Russian strengths and weaknesses came to the *Times* office. One series was optimistic. The other pessimistic. The optimistic series had the right of way. ("Test," 5)

To this apparent news breakdown, the authors cited six others during the period of their study. In all, as they saw it, reporters and editors at the nation's most important newspaper permitted personal bias to take precedence over their professional standards and ethics.

In a concluding section, Lippmann and Merz cautioned that future abuses of this kind would need to be curbed. They hesitated to forbid them by law, since that would not only invite a media backlash but also raise a host of constitutional issues. Instead, the authors placed their faith in other measures. One was for the profession to police itself, in much the same way that the "Bar Associations and Medical Societies" do their respective professions. The second was a proposal for newspaper readers to speak "through organizations"—like the Popular Government League and the Interchurch World Movement, both now defunct—"which will become centers of resistance." Lippmann and Merz foresaw the collective role of such groups as "a powerful engine of criticism" ("Test," 42).

Criticism of the press was a necessary first step, of course, but clearly there were even deeper issues involved. In the case of the *Times* reporting, for instance, how had the public permitted itself to be hoodwinked in the first place? This was a question worth probing, Lippmann decided. And so with his earlier reformist faith now partially shaken, he set out to examine the interplay between the press, on one hand, and the psychological underpinnings of public opinion, on the other. His next book would focus on this very issue.

DISTORTED PICTURES IN THEIR HEADS: *PUBLIC OPINION* (1922)

Lippmann began to set aside time for his new project. His first step was to reduce his workload at the *New Republic* (*NR*), where he had grown restless. Among other things, he convinced Croly, his *NR* editor, to let him hire a managing editor for the magazine. The new recruit was Edmund Wilson, the future literary critic, who at just twenty-five had already held the same managing editor post for the past two years at *Vanity Fair*, the society magazine. As part of his workload reduction, Lippmann also handed off his regular freelance assignments for the *Manchester Guardian*.

Lippmann was now free to take a six-month leave of absence from *NR*, beginning on April 21,1921. Joined by his wife of several years, the former Faye Albertson, he sought refuge from the hurly burly of Manhattan in a recently purchased beach house in the tiny village of Wading River, on Long Island's North Shore. By late August, he had decided not to return to *NR* when his leave of absence was over. Beginning that January, he would be the assistant director of the editorial page at the liberal *New York World*. By this date, he had also completed a long and ambitious manuscript, which he promptly turned over to his publisher, Harcourt Brace and Company.[40]

In its densely argued pages, *Public Opinion* advanced themes that Lippmann had only taken a sidelong glance at in *Liberty and the News*. In that earlier work, he had corrected "the popular theory of representative government," arguing that, in the modern state, decisions were mostly formulated not by the interaction of the legislative and executive branches of government but "by the impact of controlled opinion upon administration," that is, the executive branch. With this new "shift in the locus of sovereignty," considerable power had accrued to those individuals and institutions that could assist the public in formulating true opinions for the successful organization of human life. But what if many of the opinions the public had formed were based not on actual fact but on distortions? If this were the case, how could public opinion be relied on to exert a beneficial effect on governance?

In his new book, Lippmann illustrated this dilemma by comparing modern democracy with its early American version. In that more contracted world, communities typically hosted town meetings in which citizens could directly influence governance. For such citizens, participation in local civic affairs was not only direct but unmediated: in reaching their decisions, they more often than not relied on firsthand knowledge of the crucial issues, knowledge they had gleaned with their own eyes and ears, rather than from secondary news accounts. This was an example of democracy in its purest form, reminiscent of the ancient Athenian assembly. In the modern world, though, democracy of this sort was a quaint relic of the past: individual citizens had not only ceded governance to others, even at the local level; in gaining whatever knowledge they could about complex domestic and international issues, they were forced to rely on a variety of secondary sources, including of course newspapers.

Clearly, secondary sources had their uses, since they brought a remote world closer and provided people with knowledge that they might not otherwise have access to. They had their limitations too, however. Unlike firsthand sources of knowledge, secondary sources offered not the world itself but a mental simulacrum of it—what Lippmann referred to as "pseudo environments."[41] Despite their uses, these mental approximations of reality inevitably reduced complexity, thereby giving people the illusion that they know more than they actually did. But real comprehension had been sacrificed: "the pictures inside people's heads" were often poor representations of the world beyond their immediate one (*Public*, 19). This misalignment posed a real problem for the formulation of sound public policy. And that problem needed to be addressed.

But what were the dependable sources of actual rather than illusory knowledge? Earlier in his career, Lippmann had counted on the press to provide the facts for the formation of true opinions, which is why in

Liberty and the News he had argued so strenuously for its reform. Now he was skeptical, raising the more fundamental question of whether even a reformed press was a reliable instrument of truth. As he saw it, the problem was inherent in the very nature of the press. Too often, it casted about for news, sometimes significant, sometimes considerably less so. But the mere fact that some event drew press attention conferred a measure of importance on it, whether deserved or not. In this way, the press "is like the beam of a searchlight that moves restless about," he said, "bringing one episode and then another out of the darkness into vision." It might appear that this restless and intermittent light was a reliable source of real knowledge, but that was a dangerous illusion: "Men cannot do the work of the world by this light alone" (*Public*, 229).

More than this secondhand and random knowledge, the work of the world demanded the pursuit of actual truth. By this Lippmann meant, as his teacher Graham Wallas had taught him, the task of revealing "the hidden facts," of setting these facts "into relation with each other," and finally of making "a picture of reality on which men can act." In its analysis of events, the press was perhaps capable of providing such a picture of reality. But with the exception of stories that involved "a good machinery of record"—which is to say those that were quantitatively based like the fluctuations of the stock market or election returns—the press was usually set adrift in a subjective muddle when it departed from its news-gathering function and set out to analyze and make sense of the world. That was because, unlike disciplines such as medicine, engineering, law, and some of the social sciences, the press had no "fixed standards" to guide it, no methodology for sifting through data. For this reason, charged Lippmann, the press was simply "not constituted to provide from one edition to the next the amount of knowledge which the democratic theory of public opinion demands" (*Public*, 216, 226, 228–29).

There was, however, a viable alternative to the press. For Lippmann, this alternative was inspired by the work of Frederick W. Taylor, the American mechanical engineer who went on to become one of the leaders in the movement to improve industrial management and efficiency.[42] Some forward-thinking industrial leaders had already embraced the work of Taylor and his students, and so too had a few of "the more enlightened directing minds," that is, political administrative leaders: They "have called upon experts who were trained, or had trained themselves, to make parts of this Great Society intelligible to those who manage it" (*Public*, 233–34).

The movement was admittedly at a nascent stage. But Lippmann imagined how it could be incorporated into the federal government, with experts enlisted from the hard, applied, and even experimental social sciences to staff a series of "intelligence bureaus" embedded within the various government agencies and departments. The principal role of these bureaus would be straightforward—to offer hard data, analysis, and quality control to decision makers in both government and industry. Beyond their contributions to decision makers, though, these intelligence bureaus would also serve a vital societal role as the primary sources of real knowledge. Of course, these organizations and their staffs would need to be insulated from political and other outside meddling. But such insulation would only make it more likely that the intelligence bureaus would end up serving as worthwhile counterbalances to "the subjectivism of human opinion based on the limitation of individual experience" (*Public*, 249).

The sweep and depth of Lippmann's analysis won reviewers' praise. There was less enthusiasm, though, for the remedies he had proposed. In his review of *Public Opinion* in the *New Republic*, for instance, progressive philosopher and educational reformer John Dewey, Lippmann's senior by thirty years, applauded the book as "perhaps the most effective indictment of democracy as currently conceived ever penned." But after summarizing that indictment in some detail, Dewey concluded "that its critical position is more successful than it's constructive."[43]

Dewey had some constructive suggestions of his own: A key one flipped Lippmann's conception of "organized intelligence" around, proposing that it be directed not primarily to administrators and decision makers, an undemocratic project if there ever was one, but to the public via the press. It would be a difficult task, he acknowledged, since he essentially agreed with Lippmann's unflattering and pessimistic view of the institution. Still, he faulted the young author of *Public Opinion* for giving up on "the case for the press too readily"—for concluding, that is, "what the press is it must continue to be." Despite its faults, it remained a potentially valuable source of public education and enlightenment, assuming it could be augmented by something akin to Lippmann's intelligence bureaus.[44]

Dewey's review of *Public Opinion* was polite, at times deferential, but there was no mistaking his fundamental differences with Lippmann over the democratic role of not only the press but also education, Dewey's special area of interest. Both institutions had fundamental roles to play in the enterprise of democracy, an argument the progressive philosopher would lay out more fully in his later work, *The Public and Its Problems* (1927).

But the debate between the younger and older thinker was more than just a scholarly one. In an era disillusioned by the horrors of the "war to end all wars," that was witnessing the rise of radical movements on both the left and right, and that was living riotously but uneasily through what would be the false calm before a near-total economic collapse, their debate also centered on and how Americans saw not only themselves but their collective future. Were we, despite all, still a fundamentally optimistic nation, confident in our popular sovereignty and ready to embrace what lay ahead with a cautious but buoyant spirit? Or were we unsettled about both our own society and governance and the likely road ahead? Of the two men, Lippmann clearly tended toward the latter vision. And in his next book, he would turn darker still.

TWILIGHT OF THE PEOPLE:
THE PHANTOM PUBLIC (1925)

By mid-1923, Lippmann was firmly planted at the *New York World*. Here he wrote brilliant, elegantly argued editorials, albeit ones that did not always connect with the paper's essentially blue-collar readership. He refused to pander to the masses, however, just as in *Public Opinion* he had raised and dismissed certain democratic bromides. His pessimism in that book had verged on the antidemocratic, and yet he knew he had more to say on the subject of public opinion. In early June 1923, he and Faye once again left New York City for Wading River, where he would work on the follow-up to *Public Opinion*, while also phoning in his daily editorials. With few houseguests besides Graham Wallas, his former teacher and newest sounding board, he was able to write steadily each day. By summer's end, he had a manuscript in hand.[45] It pleased him generally, but he worried that its tone and argument were so pessimistic that he was "likely to be put on trial for heresy by his old liberal friends at *The New Republic*."[46] His fears were well-grounded.

The Phantom Public was, in fact, a heretical book in many ways. In it, Lippmann criticized "democratic reformers" whose effort to educate the citizenry for self-government was rooted in the idea "that the voter should aim to approximate as nearly as he can the knowledge and point of view of the responsible man."[47] But that was an impossible ideal, Lippmann believed, since the responsible man had obtained his training systematically—in law schools and offices and in the corridors of business—while the average man by contrast "has had no coherent political training of any kind." Progressive reformers like Dewey had placed their faith in such remedial institutions as the press and the schools. Each of these institutions was flawed, however. In the case of the press, how many citizens pursuing their busy lives had adequate time to read newspapers carefully? As for civic education in the schools, it "does not even begin to tell the voter how he can reduce the maze of public affairs to some intelligible form" (*Phantom*, 139).

Most citizens had been ill-prepared, in short, to influence much less direct public affairs. Their fate was to remain "outsiders"—a category of democratic man who "is necessarily ignorant, usually irrelevant and often meddlesome, because he is trying to navigate the ship from dry land." The "insider," meanwhile, is the democratic man's opposite—better, more rigorously trained but most of all savvy about the ways of government and how public policy is proposed, debated, and ultimately adopted (*Phantom*, 140).

Lippmann's inner elitist was clearly on full display here. If in his previous book he had defined the limits of public opinion, here he dismisses the very notion of public opinion as a phantom, a ghostly vestige of democratic sentimentalism, much like the idea that good ideas spring naturally from the heart of democratic man. In the modern era, even the expert is no match for the complexities of the Great Society. More relevant now was one's knowledge of, and position in, the centers of power, where decisions large and small were made. Despite its strangely tautological nature—insiders were distinguished by knowledge gained by being insiders—Lippmann's argument was strictly in keeping with his view that only an elite subset of the public was capable of running things. In his scheme, the public at large was relegated to the role of glorified referee, brought in during a "crisis of maladjustment" when the insiders were at loggerheads (*Phantom*, 189). At such moments, the public's duty was to decide which of the insiders were acting on behalf of the common good and lend them support. Otherwise, the public would do well to stop meddling and get of the way. This was, for Lippmann, "the essence of popular government" (*Phantom*, 116, 189).

Several reviewers of *The Phantom Public* found it even darker than *Public Opinion*. In a January 1926 review in the *American Mercury*, for example, H. L. Mencken, no stranger to pessimism himself, referred to "Mr. Lippmann's book . . . [as] extremely depressing stuff. He seems to have abandoned hope altogether."[48] Other reviewers were more temperate, although not by much. They too chided Lippmann for his gloomy conclusions. In the *New York Times*, for instance, after praising Lippmann for being at his best "in his critique of the limitations of the concrete public intelligence"—a critique that justified "the simple rules of public conduct" he had set out—the reviewer issued a caveat. Had the author stopped there, all would have been well. Since Lippmann had clearly not stopped there, he was guilty of overstating his case: "It was not necessary to deny the existence of the Public altogether. The book is called 'The Phantom Public,' whereas the Public is a very real thing."[49] The *Saturday Review*'s reviewer sounded a similar note. After praising Lippmann for his well-founded observations, he wondered why the author had felt compelled to banish the public to some shadowy netherworld, emerging ghostlike only in moments of crisis. Would the public even cede its popular sovereignty in this way? Not likely, thought the reviewer: "Unless we are to find some better authoritarian principle than democracy, we must still face the fact that men who have the vote are going to hold strong opinions about their right to opinions."[50]

CONCLUSION

A democratic at heart, albeit a skeptical one, Lippmann would not have disagreed with the reviewer from the *Saturday Review* about the dangers of authoritarianism. Given the history he lived through, how could he? Still, even in his final book, *The Public Philosophy* (1955), he reiterated his long-standing skepticism of popular sovereignty: while the people "can elect the government . . . , can remove it . . . can approve or disprove its performance," they cannot "administer the government . . . , cannot themselves perform . . . , cannot normally initiate and propose the necessary legislation." In a phrase, "a mass cannot govern."[51]

This conviction had not been arrived at casually. In a series of books beginning with *Liberty and the News*, he had struggled to maintain a Jamesian democratic faith in both the people and the press. His first book had identified the press's shortcomings and offered a menu of remedies, both theoretical and practical. By his next book, *Public Opinion*, though, he had become more pessimistic, concluding that even a reformed press was not up to the task of preparing a public to govern. The more reasonable alternative was to entrust such governance to a cadre of experts, leaving the public to its own domestic and professional affairs. By his final book in the series, even this diluted faith in popular sovereignty was further attenuated. In the Great Society, governance was best left to the insiders, savvy political players whose expertise and knowledge of the mechanisms of power would help to ensure a more functional and less irrational democracy. Except in moments of crisis, the people would be best left to tending their own gardens.

Certainly, Lippmann's skepticism toward popular democracy and his own profession was deeply rooted. In part a reflection of his character and patrician upbringing, in part the influence of early mentors like Santayana and Wallas, his skepticism forced even his detractors, and there were many, to consider seriously his examinations of the romantic shibboleths underlying the American press and American democracy. At the same time, there were paradoxes in Lippmann's life and work that may have confused even him. For one, despite his problems with modernism, he was in many ways our first modern press critic, attentive to questions and spheres of investigation barely noticed by earlier commentators. Educated early on in the role of the subjective in the press, politics, and the public sphere, he was keenly aware how paradigms of thought—those stereotypes and other mental constructs hovering just below consciousness—shaped what people read and heard and thus how they saw the world. Making explicit what was too often left unexplored was for him an act not only of personal but social liberation, one that belied his skeptical instincts and his middling faith in the masses.

There was another and equally curious paradox in Lippmann's life. Despite his tendency toward gloom, his actions as a journalist and public intellectual often betrayed a somewhat sunnier frame of mind. Indeed, throughout his life, he continued to write, continued to speak out on the issues of his day, continued to attempt to enlighten the public, whatever his misgivings. In the introduction to *The Public Philosophy*, Paul Roazen, a political scientist and well-regarded historian of psychoanalysis, sought to untangle this seeming paradox:

> No matter how trenchantly Lippmann dissected democracy, and populist faith in the people's wisdom, he still sought to study the world in order to help govern it. His constant flow of journalism was written with the educative intent of raising the level of the public's knowledge. He sought to instruct and clarify, in the democratic faith that he could elucidate the facts for the public's consumption.[52]

Evidence for Roazen's analysis is not difficult to uncover.

In 1959, on the occasion of his seventieth birthday, for example, Lippmann voiced a surprisingly idealistic, even sentimental, description of his profession in a speech before the National Press Club. The essence of good journalism, he said to the professional gathering, was to provide the vital information citizens needed to decide how they want to be governed: "This is our job. It is no mean calling. We have a right to be proud of it and to be glad that it is our work."[53] This was the democratic Lippmann speaking, a man who never fully cast off an early faith in the sacred mission of his profession.

This ambivalence is perhaps one reason that commentators on the right and left have consistently embraced Lippmann as their own. At a time in the 1990s when populism shaded left, for instance, a conservative commentator praised Lippmann for his "stubborn 'elitism'" and for skewering "the interactive gadgetry of 'direct democracy.'"[54] More recently, another conservative commentator applauded Lippmann for exploding the "journalistic myth"—the idea that "a national corps of journalists" can "supply a single 'public' with the knowledge to act as deliberating citizens."[55] Not so, the commentator insisted: just as the federal government needed to be decentralized, so too should the establishment press.

On the left, meanwhile, Lippmann has been congratulated for scolding the press during World War I. One journalist and former Washington official pointed to that wartime critique and speculated that, had Lippmann been alive during the run-up to the Iraq War, "he would have discovered a depressingly similar press corps on a bandwagon of jingoism, disseminating falsehoods leaked by government officials, engaging in ruthless self-censorship, and preening in careerist triumphalism."[56]

A reasonable case can be made to support either the conservative or neoliberal Lippmann profile. And yet perhaps his best claim to relevance today is not any one critique but his pioneering and persistent effort to raise difficult questions that still haunt us: What is the proper role of the press in a democratic society? What is the distinction between news and truth? What are the dangers of "fake news"? What are the mental constructs that shape and manipulate public opinion? How do the media self-police in order to sustain public trust? In his press criticism, as in much of his other writing, he responded to these and other key questions in a tone of omniscience, one that seemed calculated to ward off contradiction. Nevertheless, he was wise enough to know that he was not uttering the last word on any subject—that, in a continually evolving democracy and media landscape, each new generation of citizens, reporters, editors, and scholars would need to revisit the big issues and formulate its own responses. For each generation that does, Lippmann's inquisitive spirit serves to inspire.

NOTES

1. Alden Whitman, "Walter Lippmann, Political Analyst, Dead at 85," *New York Times*, December 15, 1974, Times Archives, https://www.nytimes.com/1974/12/15/archives/walter-lippmann-political-analyst-dead-at-85-walter-lippmann.html.

2. James Thurber, *Men, Women and Dogs*. Reprinted with Dorothy Parker's original preface and a new introduction by Wilfred Sheed (New York: Ballantine Books, 1977), 133.

3. Sean Wilentz, general editor's introduction to *Liberty and the News*, by Walter Lippmann. (1920; repr., Princeton: Princeton University Press, 2008), vii.

4. Ronald Steel, *Walter Lippmann and the American Century* (Boston: Little Brown, 1980), 3.

5. Wikipedia, s.v "RMS *Etruria*," last edited on June 7, 2018, https://en.wikipedia.org/wiki/RMS_Etruria.

6. Steel, *American Century*, 6.

7. Ibid., 14–17.

8. Ibid., 17–22.

9. Ibid., 18.

10. Walter Lippmann, "An Open Mind: William James," *Everybody's Magazine*, December 1910, in *Stories from Everybody's Magazine*. https://books.google.com/books?id=pgy8DgAAQBAJ&dq=walter+Lippmann+An+Open+Mind+Everbody%27s+magazine+1910&source=gbs_navlinks_s.

11. *Stanford Encyclopedia of Philosophy*, "George Santayana," revised August 8, 2018, https://plato.stanford.edu/entries/santayana/.

12. George Santayana, *The Life of Reason: Reason in Society*, in *The Works of George Santayana*, vol. 7, bk. 2, Marianne S. Wokeck and Martin A. Coleman, eds., with an introduction by James Gouinlock (Cambridge: MIT Press, 2013), 58.

13. Quoted in Steel, *American Century*, 21; see also César Garcia, "Walter Lippmann and George Santayana: A Shared Vision of Public Opinion, *The Journal of American Culture* 29, no. 2 (May 2006), 183–90.

14. Ibid., 26–27.

15. Walter Lippmann to Lucile Elsas, May 10, 1908, in *Public Philosopher: Selected Letters of Walter Lippmann*, ed. John Morton Blum (New York: Ticknor & Fields,1985), 4.

16. Graham Wallas, *Human Nature and Politics*, 3rd ed. (London: A. Constable & Co., 1908), Internet Archives, x, https://archive.org/details/humannatureinpol00walliala.

17. Walter Lippmann to Audrey Wallas, August 16, 1932, in Blum, *Public Philosopher*, 295.

18. See Lincoln Steffens, *The Shame of the Cities* (New York: McClure Philips & Co., 1904), Project Gutenberg eBook. https://www.gutenberg.org/files/54710/54710-h/54710-h.htm.

19. Steel, *American Century*, 32–34.

20. Walter Lippmann to Lincoln Steffens, May 18, 1910, Blum, *Public Philosopher*, 6.

21. Justin Kaplan, *Lincoln Steffens: A Biography* (New York: Simon & Shuster, 2004), 176.

22. Walter Lippmann to Lincoln Steffens, May 18, 1910, Blum, *Public Philosopher*, 6.

23. Kaplan, *Lincoln Steffens*, 177.

24. Ibid., 177–78.

25. Walter Lippmann to Lincoln Steffens, April 17, 1911, Blum, *Public Philosopher*, 7.

26. Quoted in Steel, *American Century*, 40.

27. Walter Lippmann to Graham Wallas, July 31, 1912, Blum, *Public Philosopher*, 11.

28. Ibid., 12.

29. Walter Lippmann, *A Preface to Politics* (New York: Mitchell Kennerley, 1913), Internet Archive, 83–84, https://archive.org/details/prefacetopolitic00lipp uoft/page/n7.

30. Ibid., 85.

31. See *The New Republic* (November 7, 1914), 28, Google Books, https://books .google.com/books?id=MN1AAQAAMAAJ&pg=PP9&lpg=PP9&dq=november +7,+1914+%2B+the+new+republic&source=bl&ots=LwLAk8ylnU&sig=pPbr4 a5FdSY7jFlF5JzX6DRrl2I&hl=en&sa=X&ved=2ahUKEwi9w9yx8d3eAhXrm -AKHciLCNsQ6AEwDnoECAgQAQ#v=onepage&q=november%207%2C%20 1914%20%2B%20the%20new%20republic&f=false.

32. Steel, *American Century*, 116–54.

33. Walter Lippmann to Ellery Sedgwick, April 7, 1919, Blum, *Public Philosopher*.

34. Walter Lippmann, *Liberty and the News* (1920; repr., Princeton: Princeton University Press, 2008). All further references will be to this edition and cited parenthetically in the text.

35. See "A Brief History," School of Journalism, University of Missouri, accessed November 18, 2018, https://journalism.missouri.edu/jschool/.

36. Created in 2004, the PBS Foundation seeks donations from individuals, corporations, and foundations) to support the work of the Public Broadcasting Service at the national level. The Corporation for Public Broadcasting, created in 1967 by an act of Congress, is an American privately owned nonprofit corporation funded by the federal government to promote and support public broadcasting and government contributions.

37. John J. McQuiston, "Charles Merz, a Former Times Editor, Is Dead at 84," *New York Times*, September 1, 1977, ProQuest Historical Newspapers, https://

www.documentcloud.org/documents/1391920-charles-merz-a-former-times-edi
tor-is-dead-at-84.html.

38. Walter Lippmann and Charles Merz, "A Test of the News." Supplement
to *The New Republic*, August 4, 1920, Internet Archive, 4. All further references
will be to this electronic edition and cited parenthetically in the text.

39. Among the many studies of this period, see Borislav Chernev, *Twilight
of Empire: The Brest-Litovsk Conference and the Remaking of Central Europe,
1917–1918* (Toronto: University of Toronto Press, 2017).

40. Steel, *American Century*, 173, 175–76.

41. Walter Lippmann, *Public Opinion* (1922; repr., New York: Free Press,
1997). All further references will be to this edition and cited parenthetically in
the text.

42. See, for example, Charles D. Wrege, *Frederick W. Taylor: The Father
of Scientific Management: Myth and Reality* (Homewood: Business One Irwin,
1991.)

43. John Dewey, review of *Public Opinion*, by Walter Lippmann, *The New
Republic* (May 3, 1922), The Unz Review, http://www.unz.com/print/NewRe
public-1922may03-00286.

44. Dewey, review of *Public Opinion*, 288.

45. Steel, *American Century*, 211–12.

46. Quoted in Steel, *American Century*, 212.

47. Walter Lippmann, *The Phantom Public* (1927; repr., New Brunswick:
Transaction Publishers, 1993), 136. All further references will be to this edition
and cited parenthetically in the text.

48. H. L. Mencken, review of *The Phantom Public*, by Walter Lippmann, *The
American Mercury* (January 1926), 125, The Unz Review, https://www.unz.com
/print/AmMercury-1926jan-00125/.

49. Simeon Strunsky, review of *The Phantom Public*, by Walter Lippmann,
New York Times Book Review, October 25, 1925, 1, Times Machine, https://
timesmachine.nytimes.com/timesmachine/1925/10/25/issue.html#.

50. W. Y. Elliott, review of *The Phantom Public*, by Walter Lippmann, *The
Saturday Review*, December 12, 1925, 407, The Unz Review, https://www.unz
.com/print/SaturdayRev-1925dec12-00406a02/.

51. Walter Lippmann, *The Public Philosophy*, with an introduction by Paul
Roazen (1955 repr., New Brunswick: Transaction Publishers, 1989), 14.

52. Paul Roazen, introduction to *The Public Philosophy*, xix.

53. Quoted in Michael Petrou, "Reexamining Lippmann's Legacy," *Nieman
Reports* September 20, 2018, https://niemanreports.org/articles/re-examining
-lippmanns-legacy/.

54. Wilfred M. McClay, introduction to *The Phantom Public*, by Walter Lippmann (New Brunswick: Transaction Publishers, 2006), xliv.

55. Ted McAllister, "Walter Lippmann and the Crisis in Journalism," *Public Discourse*, November 8, 2012, https://www.thepublicdiscourse.com/2012/11/6771/.

56. Sidney Blumenthal, afterword to *Liberty and the News*, by Walter Lippmann (Princeton: Princeton University Press, 2008), 68–69.

George Seldes, *Chicago Tribune* Press Photo, 1919.
Source: Courtesy of Rick Goldsmith

Chapter Two

George Seldes
The Last Muckraker

Nothing is sacred to the American press but itself.

—George Seldes, *The Lords of the Press*, 1938

Henry George Seldes was born on November 16, 1890, a year after Walter Lippmann. While the two contemporaries did not usually travel in the same circles, their biographies overlapped in significant ways: like Lippmann, Seldes was Jewish but nonpracticing; entered the profession of journalism at an early age; was a youthful admirer of Lincoln Steffens, among other muckrakers; attended Harvard, albeit for just a year as a "special student"; and gradually directed much of his mental energies to press criticism.

There, essentially, is where the similarities ended. In contrast to Lippmann's comfortable childhood on Manhattan's Upper East Side, Seldes and his younger brother Gilbert, the future writer and cultural critic, grew up in relatively modest circumstances across the Hudson in New Jersey. The sons of ethnic Russian émigrés Anna Saphro and George Sergius Seldes, the boys came of age in Alliance Colony, a Jewish agricultural community in the rural southern part of the state. Their mother died early, and they were brought up largely by their paternal grandparents, also residents of Alliance, and by their cigarette-smoking Aunt Bertha, their father's sister and a suffragette. Their opinionated and freethinking father was a law student before purchasing a Philadelphia drugstore, and he more than anyone was responsible for his sons' fierce independence of mind.[1] Gilbert entered Harvard on a scholarship after spending his senior year at Central High, in Philadelphia, but George, as he was known, dropped out of high school after his junior year. For a brief time, he worked with his father—becoming an "excellent soda jerk" and later "a qualified assistant pharmacist." Then, at nineteen years old, and with his country boy's head filled with romantic notions of starting out in "the greatest of all callings," he headed directly into journalism.[2]

The muckraking era was winding down, but Seldes dreamed of writing the kind of investigative journalism pioneered by practitioners like Ida Tarbell, Will Irwin, and Steffens. The author of *The Shame of the Cities* and other exposés had also served, of course, as the role model and mentor for the young Lippmann. But if Lippmann soon grew disillusioned with much of the muckraking enterprise, Seldes never did. For the rest of his reporting and writing life—one that stretched well into his nineties—the impulse to dig deeply into the muck remained strong. It was an impulse that drove not only his investigative work but also his press criticism.[3]

The overarching premise of that criticism was that the American press could no longer be considered free. Drawing from both his own experience as a domestic reporter and foreign correspondent and his acute if unforgiving observations of the news business itself, Seldes educed example after example to prove his point. Like Lippmann, he dated the beginning of the slide to the newspaper war propaganda during World War I. The downward trend continued, he believed, during the Depression and into the 1930s, when he saw the American public being fed a diet of slanted and often overly optimistic economic news. Compared with the fascist-dominated European press of the period, of course, the US press still retained a measure of its former integrity. Still, Seldes argued, there were ominous influences at work.

In his first major work of criticism, aptly titled *Freedom of the Press* (1935), he discussed what he viewed as the key outside forces corrupting the newspaper industry, including advertising, private utilities, big oil, and big business. His detailed, often personal reporting could be powerful, and yet his book was fairly standard muckraking fare. But his exposé hinted at other corrupting forces at work, those not external to newspapering but at its very core. In *The Lords of the Press* (1938), his next and arguably most central book of criticism, he explored how the pursuit of profits—the rampant commercialization of the press—had eroded the industry from the inside out. And nowhere was this better illustrated than the struggle between owners and labor, publishers and rank-and-file staff.

Seldes's juxtaposition of the two economic classes was intentional. A committed leftist who for a time may have been a secret member of the Communist Party of the United States of America (CPUSA), he saw both the fight for a free press and its eventual resolution as part of the larger class struggle.[4] If news was being suppressed, distorted, or colored to meet the spoken and implicit demands of special interests and advertisers; if publishers publicly touted their commitment to the common man while conspiring behind closed doors to weaken any laws or movements that threatened their hegemony; and if even a onetime socialist like Lippmann had now become a leading establishment figure—it was largely because newspapering was first and foremost a business, often a very lucrative one. "The press needs free men with free minds intellectually open," Seldes wrote in one of his many moments of high dudgeon in *The Lords of the Press*, "but its leadership consists of moral slaves whose minds are paralyzed by the specter of profits."[5]

A possible counterweight to commercialization was the American Newspaper Guild, the labor union to which he had dedicated *The Lords of the Press*. He had high hopes that, through its lobbying and example, it could bring about the sort of free press he envisioned. But when the Guild rebuffed one of his bolder suggestions—that it take steps to exert editorial control over newspapers—he grew disillusioned. Eventually, he broke with the Guild, putting forth a series of alternative proposals for wresting control of newspapers from their allegedly monarchical owners.

In 1940, at the instigation and perhaps assistance of CPUSA, Seldes and a partner started *In Fact*, an independent newsletter originally subtitled "For the millions who want a free press."[6] For the next ten years, *In Fact* became his platform not only for covering what he regarded as taboo news—the health dangers of cigarettes, among them—but for his unrelenting class-based critique of the media. He also wrote and occasionally self-published a steady series of books, including several additional critiques of the press.

Seldes's message and uncompromising tone won him scores of admirers, including progressive journalist I. F. Stone, who began publishing his own newsletter a few years after *In Fact* folded. Seldes's message and tone also earned him his share of detractors, especially after the norms of journalism had changed, and his fiery impatience with "balance" and "objectivity" fell out of fashion.[7] Even fellow writers who acknowledged the value of his unrelenting muckraking occasionally took exception to his tone. "He's about as subtle as a house falling in," wrote fellow press critic A. J. Liebling in an often-quoted passage from his 1947 book, *The Wayward Pressman*. "He makes too much of the failure of newspapers to print exactly what George Seldes would have printed if he were the managing editor."[8] For all its excesses, though, Seldes's critique of the press still resonates today, especially among commentators on the left who warn that hyper-commercialization and the concentration of media ownership pose a continuing threat to a free press and American democracy.

PITTSBURGH APPRENTICESHIP—1909–1912

Seldes's career as a working journalist started in Pittsburgh. His first job, begun on February 9, 1909, was at the *Pittsburgh Leader*, a civic-oriented newspaper that had recently been purchased from its longtime owners, the Nevin family. The new publisher and editor in chief was Alexander Pollock Moore, who had acquired the *Leader* with financial backing from William Flynn, a former political boss and construction magnate who had grown rich on city jobs. The Moore-Flynn allegiance struck many in the city as a threat to independent journalism. In his series on the American newspaper in *Collier's* magazine, muckraker Will Irwin, one of Seldes's journalistic heroes, was more tempered in his judgment, but he too was concerned about the newspaper's legacy: It was not only the likely strings attached to the Flynn loan that worried him but also Moore's abrupt change in "news policy"—one that measured "the worth of a story by the scandal it involved."[9]

As a cub reporter, Seldes was exposed to both the *Leader*'s new brand of "yellow journalism" and its reluctance to offend vested interests. In late 1910, for instance, he was assigned to report on the Andrew Mellon divorce case. The heir of Thomas Mellon, the founder with his sons of what became the Mellon National Bank, the center of a sprawling financial empire, Andrew Mellon was at the beginning of a divorce action with his wife, Nora, twenty-one years his junior. The trial promised to be messy, with allegations of extramarital affairs and other sordid business—in other words, just the kind of sensational story that was now the *Leader*'s stock in trade. When Seldes began covering the preliminary court proceedings, though, he was surprised "to find myself the only reporter present."[10] How could this be, he wondered? One of the most scandalous divorce cases of the young century, and there was virtually a news blackout in town? The answer was, not surprisingly, that Mellon's influence in the city and beyond extended to the major newspaper publishers, who not only feared his political clout but counted on his advertising dollars. Seldes's copy was censored by his editors, although before long Mellon took matters into his own hands to keep his divorce private.[11]

In 1912, Seldes accepted an invitation to join the *Pittsburgh Post* from his friend Ray Sprigle, the city editor and future Pulitzer Prize winner.[12] To the paper's owners, Seldes, like Sprigle, was suspect because of his support for labor and labor leaders, including William Dudley "Big Bill" Haywood, a founder and member of the Industrial Workers of the World (IWW), and the Swedish-born activist and balladeer known as "Joe Hill." If Seldes's and Sprigle's prolabor sentiments were viewed suspiciously on the *Post*, however, each was protected in large measure by his reputation, the latter as a great city editor, the former as the paper's star reporter. Seldes's status also guaranteed him a good salary and "some of the best assignments," including one in 1912 to cover evangelist William Ashley "Billy" Sunday when he came to town.[13]

A former major league baseball player who preached a mix of conservative Christianity and a no-nonsense brand of heartland Republicanism, Sunday was famous for his rousing sermons, stage theatrics, and carefully orchestrated revival meetings. His popularity gained him both financial success and influential friends but also the ire of critics, including Sinclair Lewis and Carl Sandburg, who regarded him as a charlatan and business toady. Despite warnings from his editors to remain neutral because of a potential religious backlash, Seldes sided with the critics when he wrote about one of Sunday's fake meetings, as he recalled years later:

> My report said that almost all the first hundred "sinners" to come forward were frauds. They were stooges. They were what circus men called "shills"— hired men, the first to come forward when the fakers make their spiel and offer tuberculosis cures and similar frauds for a dollar a bottle. Someone has to start buying or none would be sold. The shills are the first to buy.[14]

The story cost him his reporting job. Reassigned to the copy desk, he eventually rose from copy reader to chief copy editor. Sitting in the "slot," he was both responsible for catching any factual and stylistic errors and for crafting the paper's attention-grabbing headlines.

PITTSBURGH APPRENTICESHIP—1913–1916

The following year, 1912, Seldes took a leave of absence from the *Post* and enrolled as a "special student" at Harvard, where his brother, Gilbert, was beginning his junior year. Once in Cambridge, Seldes took full advantage of the opportunity, enrolling in courses with some of the university's most famous teachers and attending meetings of the Harvard Socialist Club, started several years earlier by Walter Lippmann. He also landed a spot on a new college magazine, the *Harvard Illustrated Monthly*. His initial job was to edit submissions, most of which he found to be "very high-schoolish."[15]

He was soon given a chance, however, to report on Harvard's vaunted tutorial system, under the direction of one W. W. Nolen, whose mandate among other things was to keep the school's championship football team from flunking out.[16] In his article, Seldes acknowledged Nolen's ability to work miracles, but he also exposed a system that, while not unique to Harvard, nevertheless seemed to him anti-academic. The magazine's editor, a college loyalist, read the piece and became irate. Calling Seldes into his office, he hurled the manuscript in his direction and called the story a work of "plain, outright treason."[17] But Seldes could not let a good investigative piece go to waste: in Boston one day, he presented his story to an independent magazine editor eager for an inside scoop on the university.

After a year, Seldes returned to Pittsburgh and the *Post*, where he was soon promoted to night editor. The new job meant a slight bump in pay and of course a shift change. But Seldes was happy: he had met Peggy Keith, a pretty if impecunious young woman from a traveling theater company, and they had begun living together in Seldes's apartment. He seemed established in Pittsburgh, perhaps for the rest of his career. He was in for a rude shock, however: by chance, he discovered that, during his overnight shifts, the seemingly innocent Keith had been practicing "the first and oldest profession." Splitting whatever money he had with her, he bought a single one-way train ticket to New York. It had been a painful but liberating episode, as he would later recall in his autobiography. "Were it not for Peggy Keith I would probably have remained in Pittsburgh for the rest of my life."[18] In a real sense, the city had not only catapulted his rise in the profession but also challenged his early romantic notions of it.

WAR CORRESPONDENT

Seldes was ready to make a new life for himself in New York. Renting a modest apartment in Washington Square, he began freelancing for the *New York World*, among other papers. Freelancing and the Village's bohemian culture suited him, and he felt as if he had finally found a place to call home. And yet once again, his life was upended by Peggy Keith, who had tracked him down in New York and now pleaded for a second chance, which he reluctantly granted her. History repeated itself, though, and she ended up betraying him once again, in this case with a successful bohemian writer who invited her to join him on vacation. Seldes had finally had his fill of Keith and of New York, which was no longer the home he had once imagined it. Obtaining a visa at the British consulate, he headed by ship to England, eventually making his way to wartime London and a job with United Press stretching World War I cables into news stories. He was suddenly making more money than he ever made back home, although the work itself was tedious.

An interim job on the Army edition of the *Chicago Tribune* followed, but Seldes's real break came next: eager to report directly on the war, he was accepted as one of the select members of G-2D, the designation of the Army Press Section under General John J. Pershing, the commander of the American Expeditionary Forces on the Western Front, the war's main battlefield. He now found himself among the most prominent journalists of the day—Irvin S. Cobb, Damon Runyon, William Allen White, Heywood Broun, Floyd Gibbons, and Peggy Hull, the first women accredited by the US War Department. Collectively, these distinguished correspondents covered many of the major post-1917 engagements—the Third Battle of the Aisne, the Battle of Belleau Wood, the Battle of Château-Thierry, the Battle of Saint-Mihiel, and the decisive Battle of the Argonne Forest. And yet if they did their best to report what they heard and saw to their various press organizations, they were nevertheless mindful that the military viewed their actual job as lending patriotic support to the war effort.[19]

Seldes's biggest scoop was his post-Armistice interview with Field Marshal Paul von Hindenburg, the commander of the German military during the second half of World War I and the future president of the doomed Weimar Republic. Flouting new regulations that prohibited travel into Germany, Seldes and four press corps companions drove from Luxembourg to Frankfurt, and then on to Kassel, where Hindenburg was now stationed. The field marshal was reluctant to talk at first, but, when he finally agreed, Seldes was diplomatic, asking through an interpreter why the four-year stalemate had finally come to an end. Hindenburg's response, candid and clearly heartfelt, cited both an underlying and proximate cause. Certainly, the British-led blockade of the country's food supply had over time weakened both civilian and military morale. But the decisive blow had been delivered fairly and squarely on the field of battle by the American infantry in the Argonne. The Field Marshal was equally careful not to point the finger of blame for Germany's loss at the "back-stabbing" socialists, communists, and Jews," as Hitler and the Nazi Party would do almost immediately after the war. An interview that might have mitigated the Nazi stab-in-the-back myth was, however, never published. Looking back, Seldes pointed his own finger of blame at what he regarded as Pershing's shortsighted and reflexive censors. He also accused a cabal of professionally jealous press corps members, correspondents who not only backed the Army's censorship but demanded that Seldes and his rule-bending colleagues be fired.[20]

CHICAGO TRIBUNE DECADE, 1919–1929

In September 1919, and now temporarily back in the States, Seldes accepted an invitation to join the fledgling foreign news service of the *Chicago Tribune*. Both the service and paper were owned and published by Robert R. "Colonel" McCormick, a staunchly conservative Republican who played an active role in the American Newspaper Publishers Association.[21] The *Tribune* returned Seldes overseas, where, in the aftermath of the war, he spent his first year on the paper "wandering and blundering around Europe" before landing his dream job, Berlin bureau chief.[22] Over the next five years, Berlin was the base from which he would travel throughout Europe and report on some of the major events and people of the period: the rise of Hitler and the Nazi Party, the efforts of the American Relief Administration to assist famine victims in the Soviet Union, the final days of Lenin, and the efforts of the Soviet "Cheka" to identify and root out counterrevolutionary activity.

In late 1924, Seldes was reassigned to Rome, where Mussolini was now in his second year as prime minister. Several months before Seldes had arrived, an Italian socialist named Giacomo Matteotti had been assassinated. There were whispers of Il Duce's involvement, but coverage of the murder up to this point, not to mention more general stories about Mussolini and his National Fascist Party, seemed to Seldes suspiciously accommodating, a sign perhaps that the fascists had more supporters among reporters and their publishers than he had realized. Nevertheless, Seldes decided to pursue the story, ignoring his colleagues' warnings that he tread carefully.

In his finished piece, Seldes implicated Mussolini and his Blackshirts in the Matteotti murder. Alert to the personal danger his story posed, he asked the Paris edition of the *Tribune*, sold throughout Europe, to omit the exposé, presumably until he was on safer ground. The story was printed anyway, and the Italian government first ordered Seldes to vacate the country; then granted him a reprieve; and finally sent a small contingent to escort him to the train station, where the Orient Express would take him to Paris. In the Italian city of Modena, though, the train came to an abrupt stop. After a short pause, he spotted some local club-wielding Blackshirts searching the sleeping cars and shouting, "*Dov'é Seldes?*" Frightened, he took refuge in the compartment of a group of British naval officers, whose leader loudly commanded the "*porci fascisti*" to get out. The Blackshirts grumbled but complied, and Seldes reached the French border unharmed.[23]

A year after his expulsion from Rome, Seldes's *Tribune* bosses made him the paper's unofficial roving correspondent for Eastern Europe and beyond. The new post was an exciting one, taking him regularly to various cities, including Vienna, Budapest, Belgrade, Athens, Bucharest, Istanbul, Damascus, and Baghdad. But one of his late assignments for the *Tribune* had nothing to do with Eastern Europe. Temporarily back in the states on sick leave, Seldes was tasked by McCormick, the paper's publisher, to cover what looked like an imminent declaration of war by the United States against its southern neighbor, Mexico, which had threatened to expatriate mineral rights that US corporations over the years had appropriated.[24]

The farther Seldes traveled in the country, though, the more the rumors of war seemed manufactured. The responsible parties were forces hostile to the current government, including oil interests and the American Embassy in Mexico City. His reporting assignment had evaporated. Still, his trip was not a total loss: while in the capital city, he unearthed documents that offered substantial proof that, more than a decade earlier, US diplomats had neither stopped nor warned of a right-wing plot to kill then Mexico President Francisco Madero and his vice president, both of whom were executed in 1913.[25] Seldes's plan, initially endorsed by the paper's managing editor, was to write a series of short columns on this plot and other Mexican issues, following a format that would give all sides their say. Returning to Europe, Seldes waited for the series to appear, but over time only those columns presenting the pro-oil, pro-American positions were published. Those presenting the Mexican side of things never made it through the editing process.

"This was total censorship and suppression," Seldes would later charge, [and] it had never happened to me in the more than eight *Tribune* years."[26] He suspected that the suppression, if that is what it was, was dictated by McCormick, who seemed to treat international news differently from news closer to home. Whatever the case, roughly two years later, and with an offer in hand from a new publishing house to write his first book, he sent the Colonel his resignation.

AN INSIDER'S VIEW OF NEWSPAPERING:
FREEDOM OF THE PRESS (1935)

Seldes was now an independent journalist and author, although one with a twenty-year track record as a daily reporter and foreign correspondent. Fueled by the frustrations, observations, and lessons learned over this period, he set out to share his experiences. In his first book, *You Can't Print That* (1929), he looked back on many of his assignments, filling in details and conversations that he believed had been censored or suppressed, including his interview with Hindenburg and the real story of "the Assassination of a Mexican President."[27] His second book, *Can These Things Be!* (1931), followed in much the same vein. Specifically, it focused on the post–World War I rise of dictatorship and terrorism and the efforts to counter them. In the last of his first three books, *World Panorama* (1933), he abandoned his typically episodic approach and tried his hand at a narrative history of the postwar years from the imperfect peace to "our terrible thirties."[28] The ex-newspaperman was by now an established author.

His next three books took on targeted subjects. In *The Vatican* (1934), he looked at the history of the Vatican State, including both its clerical and political influence in the modern world. In *Iron, Blood, and Profits* (1934), he exposed the wheeling and dealing of the worldwide arms industry. (A similar exposé, *Merchants of Death*, appeared the same year.) And in *Sawdust Caesar* (1934), he wrote what he termed the "untold" history of Mussolini and Italian fascism.

His books to this point had largely been concerned with filling in the blanks in contemporary history. As he saw it, the whole truth about certain people and events had largely been obscured, the result of a conspiracy of silence or worse by publishers, governments, the military, and other vested interests. As a former working journalist, he was especially interested in the hidden machinations of his own profession. And thus in his next two books, *Freedom of the Press* (1935) and *Lords of the Press* (1938), he not only set out to fill in the missing chapters of history but to probe why such chapters were missing from the pages of American newspapers in the first place.

The first of these books, *Freedom of the Press*, was partially autobiographical. Early on in it, he traced his personal evolution from eager novice to experienced reporter—from, that is, a starry-eyed idealist who imagined he was entering the greatest of all callings to seasoned veteran with few illusions about the hard realities of the newspaper business. The latter perspective dominated the book and defined its prevailing theme: despite the journalist's core mission to gather and present the facts "as truthfully as human frailty permits," there are "powerful forces which do not want the facts."[29] Acting on the press from the outside, and with the complicity of commercial-minded publishers, these forces too often succeeded in undermining the core journalistic mission. In part 2 of *Freedom*, Seldes named names, identifying not only the major corrupting influences of his day but how they operated, sometimes openly, sometimes behind the scenes.

He was not shy about identifying his favorite villain. "As a reporter my first hate was the advertiser," he pronounced at the top of the chapter, confident he could mitigate the charge of emotionalism by offering examples of advertiser malfeasance, especially in the area of news suppression he had himself witnessed (*Freedom*, 42). These examples were drawn in part from his early experiences on the *Pittsburgh Leader*, from the notorious Mellon divorce to the Billy Sunday takedown. In cases like the Mellon divorce and Billy Sunday's fake revivals, publishers had bowed to the inherent conservatism of their advertisers, which both individually and as a group sought to avoid any topic that might alienate and drive away customers.

A rung lower on Seldes's hate list was an assortment of other entities, ranging broadly across the American economy. Among these were the utilities. In the 1930s, the gas, electric, and water suppliers were the target of lawmaker efforts to exert greater governmental oversight. In order to tell the public their side of the story, the utilities had spent lavishly on paid newspaper advertising. Paid advertising was not their only weapon, however. They had also conducted a well-funded "propaganda" or public relations campaign, supplying the newspapers of the day with advertorials, press releases, selective fact sheets, staged photographs, cartoons, and the like. The bigger metropolitan papers resisted manipulation, often becoming the only outlets presenting "the claims of public [utility] ownership truthfully." The smaller news outlets were more compliant, claimed Seldes: "Rarely if ever was the public made aware of the fact that thousands of newspapers presenting the cause of private ownership were in the pay of private corporations" (*Freedom*, 84). (Despite this, lawmakers ushered in a new era of regulation with the Public Utility Holding Company Act of 1935, which remained on the federal books until its repeal and replacement in 2005.[30])

In the final part of his book, Seldes took aim at the so-called establishment press. While such newspapers often had the resources to be independent, they were inclined to buckle under it almost by instinct. He was especially infuriated by the *New York Times*, nearly everyone's favorite target, reiterating his earlier charge that it was "the organ of the men of the status quo." He also scolded it for a variety of editorial sins, including misrepresenting the current news out of Italy as badly as it had misrepresented news out of Russia more than a decade earlier, as documented by Lippmann and Merz in "A Test of the News" (*Freedom*, 224).

Other major news organizations fared little better. In the case of the dominant wire services (the Associated Press and the United Press), for example, Seldes repeated a charge he had leveled in his earlier books, namely that, in an era of dictatorial regimes, even putatively independent press services must toe the party line or risk expulsion or worse. Such a risk was intolerable for profit-making corporations, of course. But to the extent they served their bottom line and acquiesced to authoritarian states, complained Seldes, "the less do they serve us, the citizens of non-dictatorial lands, who are confronted with the problems of Fascism and Communism and . . . want to know the truth about them." If that truth was too often a rare commodity, it was precisely because the news coming out of "dictator countries is poisoned at the source" (*Freedom*, 239).

The prospects of a free press under all these circumstances seemed bleak. True, there were outlets that merited a place on "a roll of honor" for their dogged attempts to stay firm in their mission. Here he cited, among other news sources, the *Manchester Guardian*, the liberal British daily today known as the *Guardian*; Germany's *Frankfurter Zeitung*; the *St. Louis Post-Dispatch*; the *New York Post*; the *Raleigh News and Observer*; the *Baltimore Sun*; and the Scripps-Howard papers. But journalism more broadly needed to rise to these lofty standards. The question was how?

Seldes responded by considering several reforms endorsed by his fellow newspapermen. One was for an "ad-less newspaper," a radical proposal at a time when ad-based revenue was a leading driver of profits. The idea could still work, he thought, assuming that readers were willing to pay more for fewer pages with no ads and that these cheaper papers did not drive away good but comparatively expensive ones. Another idea for what ailed the industry was the endowed publication, a paper or group of papers financially supported with no strings attached by university trustees, philanthropists, or publishers. The idea may have seemed at the time fantastical, although Seldes took heart from the example of the *Frankfurter Zeitung*, the German-language paper that had remained stubbornly independent during the difficult days of the Weimar Republic.[31] Still, would such a paper succeed in the United States, where publishing "unwelcome" news would inevitably depress advertising revenue? Seldes had his doubts (*Freedom*, 358).

In the end, none of the reforms he considered seemed to him viable, with the exception perhaps of one: unionization. He had in mind the American Newspaper Guild (ANG), the professional association and future labor union established in 1933 by a group of newspapermen led by Heywood Broun of the *New York World-Telegram* and Jonathan Eddy of the *New York Times*.[32] Broun, Eddy, and others favored a trade-union model for the new national guild, while some other ANG members initially resisted. Despite this, most members agreed that freedom of the press was "one of the essential foundations of human liberty," which Seldes took as a sure sign of the Guild's "social conscience" as compared with publishers' all-consuming commercialism (*Freedom*, 358).[33]

In light of this, why not permit those who were actually putting out the papers—the editors, reporters, typographers, and other union members—to largely run them? Publishers would remain the custodians of the business side of things, of course. But whenever business and good journalism clashed, Guild members would ensure that conscience triumphed over profits. It was a utopian scheme to be sure, counting as it did on the powerful being willing to relinquish their power. In the immediate term, though, Seldes was content to have the Guild adopt the trade-union model and begin collective bargaining for its members.[34] The country was going through a Great Depression, after all. How could journalists fearful of their own economic security report on the insecurity of so many others? (*Freedom*, 360, 364).

The contemporary reviews of *Freedom of the Press* ranged from generally positive to largely dismissive. Among the more favorable reactions was one in the *Saturday Review* by Alexander L. Crosby, a colleague of Heywood Broun. Crosby praised the book for being groundbreaking, noting the author had dipped into his "broad background" as a newspaperman to offer an insider's view of how things really work, and the picture was far from pretty: "Mr. Seldes cites large sums spent by railroads, bankers, packers, and utility companies to buy editorial opinion. He tells what newspapers sold out, and to whom. He shows how news is suppressed, and how propaganda poisons the reader's opinion." Some readers might object, Crosby conceded, and in a follow-up review in the *New Masses*, he faulted the author for embracing the Guild rather than a true workers' press. These quibbles aside, though, a fair reading would show that Seldes's accusations "cannot be ignored."[35]

On the other side of the ledger was an assessment appearing in the December 1935 edition of the *American Mercury*. Written by Gordon Carroll, the *Mercury*'s managing editor, the review was only slightly less critical of Seldes's major premise than of its newsworthiness. Certainly, newspapers should strive to publish the truth, but exactly who is surprised when they do not? Newspapers, after all, are profit-making entities, and owners would be "foolish" not to pursue their own interests. As to the pernicious effects of this pursuit, "the sum total of harm has been negligible."[36]

Carroll also took issue with Seldes's specific indictments. There was little in the public record to support them, leading the editor to conclude that the author's real aim was not reformist but political: "There is only one conclusion to be drawn in the face of these facts: current critics of American journalism like Mr. Seldes are not so much interested in a free press as they are in a press that will preach their own Leftist doctrines." That was certainly their right in an "open journalistic market," a place where "publications of all kinds can be circulated without hindrance." At the same time, a journalistic market should operate as do all markets, with customers freely deciding what succeeds and what does not. When Seldes argues that more "radical sheets" should be better represented or circulated, Carrol wrote, he is not promoting freedom of the press but endangering it.[37]

How deeply Seldes took these reviews to heart is unclear. Certainly, in revealing the external forces acting upon the press, he had felt he was presenting underreported news. Just as certainly, he believed he had made strenuous efforts to document his case, often based on his own experiences and investigations. That his point of view slanted leftward, in favor of the working rather than the owner class, was no secret. He was, after all, a dedicated man of the left. And yet, the largely sympathetic Alexander Crosby was also correct when he complained that, at this point at least, Seldes had pinned his hopes for a freer press on a reformist not a radical proposal—on publishers freely ceding more editorial power to the men and women of the Guild. If that idea fell flat, as it eventually did, there were other options, Seldes suggested in the final pages of *Freedom of the Press*: people like him might well be forced to pursue a different course—one that realists would consider "fantastic, impractical, naive and idealistic" (*Freedom*, 363). If he was being intentionally vague, there was no mistaking his growing sense of frustration and implicit threat.

PUTTING PROFIT OVER PRINCIPLE: *LORDS OF THE PRESS* (1938)

After *Freedom of the Press*, a second book of press criticism seemed likely. Surely, Seldes had more than enough material on hand to begin, especially if the second book focused on what Alexander Crosby had termed the "capitalistic press." In mid-1936, though, history intruded when a group of Spanish military generals declared its opposition to the liberal-leaning Second Spanish Republic. By year's end, the struggle between the Loyalists and the fascist-backed Nationalists had revealed its deadly "true nature," with the Fascists willfully murdering civilians in a manner reminiscent of Hitler, Mussolini, and others, as Seldes would write in his 1953 book *Tell the Truth and Run*.[38]

Seldes and his wife Helen Larkin Seldes—they had married in 1932—were nestled in their cozy house in Woodstock, Vermont, overlooking the Green Mountains. They seemed a world apart from the Spanish Civil War taking place more than 3,500 miles away. And yet like many Americans and other Loyalist sympathizers during this period, they were not only becoming increasingly dispirited by the atrocities going on far away but convinced that what was now playing out in Spain "was a conflict of ideas involving the world," including them."[39] They resolved to bear witness to the fighting for themselves.

In late 1936, and with his war correspondent credentials in hand from the *New York Post*, Seldes and Helen flew to Paris. From there, they moved to Barcelona, Valencia, and finally Madrid, where since October Loyalist forces had fought an increasingly desperate battle to hold the capital city against a Nationalist onslaught, led by General Francisco Franco. Visiting the trenches near Madrid in early February 1937, the veteran war correspondent saw almost immediately that the Loyalists were overmatched.[40] Helen was also overwhelmed by what she witnessed at the Spanish front, and in a story filed for the *Post*, she described in quietly evocative words the battlefield as seen from a trench window: "Two yellow crocuses and a dead man suddenly catch my eye and tell the story. Spring has come to the Madrid trenches, and nothing can stop the crocuses from growing in the early spring, not even a dead man."[41]

Seldes and Helen returned home from Spain that summer. Profoundly affected by what they had seen, they vowed to continue supporting the Loyalist cause. Looking back, they were pleased that the *New York Post* and its sister newspaper, the *Philadelphia Record*, had carried so many of their Spanish dispatches. A poll indicated that many readers in both cities were sympathetic to the Loyalist cause, although Philadelphia's Catholic hierarchy certainly was not. In time, the Cardinal and other Philadelphia church leaders put pressure on the *Record*'s big advertisers, causing publisher J. David Stern to modify his editorial position. Seldes called the publisher to task, but Stern protested as he often did in such cases that he was in a bind—forced to compromise or risk going out of business. The tug between business and principle was the classic dilemma of the liberal publisher in America, as Seldes saw it.[42] His second book of press criticism would explore this conflict in far greater detail.

Lords of the Press opened at the annual meeting of the American Newspaper Publishers Association (ANPA). As always, it was a secret meeting, off-limits ironically to the press itself, and with good reason, according to Seldes:

> The publishers' meetings are secret because their actions cannot bear the light of publicity. Three hundred and sixty days in the year, the publishers speak editorially for open covenants openly arrived at, whether in international relations or in the advertising, but every April they lock the doors and make a hypocritical paradox out of their own ideals.[43]

The annual gathering of the ANPA was, in short, a chance for publishers to discuss among themselves, and only among themselves, the business side of journalism. As Seldes saw it, when their economic interests aligned with their journalistic ideals, these lords of the press were willing, even eager, to serve the public good, or at least give the appearance of doing so. But not unlike the titans of other industries, their main concern was in maintaining and advancing their economic interests. In any contest between principle and profit, the latter would almost invariably trump the former, as Seldes saw in the case of *Record* publisher J. David Stern.

ANPA's public stance on a range of issues, Seldes believed, illustrated its members' priorities. Among other things, during 1935, the third year of President Franklin Roosevelt's first term, publishers acted collectively through the ANPA to oppose the National Labor Relations Act, a law to enforce and further the rights of private sector employees; propose compulsory arbitration of labor disputes; seek a newspaper exemption from the Social Security Act, which not only helped seniors but extended unemployment insurance; and defend child labor, used and often exploited to deliver America's newspapers. The record was abysmal, Seldes thought, putting into question the right of publishers to call themselves champions of a free press and a free people (*Lords*, 19).

A look at individual publishers followed his collective indictment. His profiles included Joseph Medill Patterson, the onetime socialist founder of the *New York Daily News*, which many regarded as America's first tabloid newspaper; Arthur Hays Sulzberger, the fourth publisher of the *New York Times*; Frank Gannett, the founder of the giant holding company known today as Gannett; William Randolph Hearst, the blustery creator of a media empire that influenced millions; and James Geddes Stahlman, the publisher of the *Nashville Banner* who led the ANPA from 1930 to 1937.[44] Seldes was critical of all of them, although he acknowledged a few had at least started out with the right values.

One who had was Joseph Medill Patterson, the *Daily News* founder. Born into wealth in 1879—his maternal grandfather was Joseph Medill, one of a trio of men who midway in the last century had purchased the *Chicago Tribune*—Patterson early on was regarded by many in his Chicago social circle as a traitor to his class. In a widely reprinted 1906 "confession," from which Seldes quoted, Patterson had said, "I have an income of between ten and twenty thousand dollars a year. I spend all of it. I produce nothing—am doing no work. I . . . can keep on doing this all my life unless the present social system is changed" (*Lords*, 20–21).

Patterson was actually exaggerating for effect: Following Yale, he had worked on the *Chicago Tribune*; then served briefly in the Illinois state legislature; and then following his father's death in 1910, comanaged the family newspaper, along with his cousin Robert R. McCormick, the man for whom Seldes would eventually work. At this point, Patterson still considered himself a socialist, spelling out why in his socialist-themed novel, *A Little Brother of the Rich* (1908).

Patterson eventually decamped to New York and founded the *Daily News*, taking over full control of the paper from his cousin in 1925. (McCormick, in turn, became the sole publisher of the *Chicago Tribune*.) Patterson seemed ready finally to begin practicing the social gospel he had been preaching. And for a time, he did. Among other things, his paper chided Roosevelt's detractors for hypocrisy and supported tougher child labor laws, while Patterson himself treated his own employers better than all but a few publishers (*Lords*, 35).

And yet there was more to the story. For all his good intentions, Patterson's practice did not always measure up to his principle. Coverage of two critical beats illustrated this gap, Seldes thought. In international news, for example, *Daily News* editorials about the Spanish Civil War had often conflated the terms "Reds" and "Loyalists," thereby perpetuating the myth that all Loyalists were communists, which did not square with the facts. The paper had also risen to defend the legitimacy of foreign oil interests in Mexico, despite what Seldes's own reporting had shown him. On the domestic front, Seldes also faulted the paper's stance on economic issues. To him, it too often sided with owners over workers, as for instance during the General Motors labor disputes of the mid-1930s. Still, Seldes was not ready to give up on the former socialist: "Somewhere between his ivory tower and his soap box[,] there is still a chance that Joe Patterson will find himself" (*Lords*, 40).[45]

Seldes was far less charitable in his profiles of other publishers. There was, of course, nearly every press critic's favorite target, William Randolph Hearst, "the first of the great press lords." "It has taken forty-five years for the intelligent minority of the American people to turn against Hearst," Seldes wrote. "But the turn has come" (*Lords*, 239). But he was almost equally critical of the "Colonel," Robert R. McCormick, Patterson's cousin and the owner and publisher of the *Chicago Tribune*, one of Seldes's past employers. Despite his mostly good relations with the Colonel over the years, Seldes had little good to say about his paper: "I know of no newspaper which is so vicious and stupid in its attack on labor, no paper so consistent in its Red-baiting, and no paper in my opinion is such a great enemy of the American people" (*Lords*, 47).

On the topic of labor, for example, Seldes traced what he saw as the paper's historically anti-labor bias. In recent years, that bias was illustrated in its coverage of the notorious Memorial Day Massacre of 1937.

As workers and their supporters demonstrated against the Republic Steel Company and smaller companies, members of the Chicago Police Department had fired on and killed ten people, while wounding many others.[46] The *Tribune* claimed that the police were simply protecting life and property, Seldes pointed out. And that might have been partially true, but a subsequent Senate investigation, chaired by Robert M. La Follette Jr. of Wisconsin, relied on newsreel and other evidence to show that the reality was far more complicated and grisly. Despite this, the *Tribune* continued to editorialize about the police as heroes, while also shifting the blame for the human carnage to outside agitators. Seldes was having none of it: "The *Chicago Tribune* and the police[,] who needed a scapegoat to hide their murders, charged Reds and Communists with inspiring or leading the workmen, but this charge was proven absolutely false" (*Lords*, 51).

McCormick, like Hearst, was a larger-than-life publisher.[47] Not all publishers were, including James Geddes Stahlman, the publisher of the *Nashville Banner*. Still, as president of the ANPA during the first part of the 1930s, his power and influence outstripped his personal charisma. That, for Seldes, made him a consequential, even dangerous figure. In his profile of Stahlman, Seldes acknowledged that the Nashvillian had used his bully pulpit within the owners' group to promote the importance of press freedom, as both a good in itself and as crucial to American democracy. And yet, as he often did in *Lords of the Press*, Seldes showed how the publisher's rhetoric and practice often conflicted.

As ANPA leader, for example, Stahlman had been a vocal opponent of the American Newspaper Guild when it expanded its membership to noneditorial departments and joined the Congress of Industrial Organizations, the federation of unions founded and led by labor leader John L. Lewis. On his own Nashville turf, Stahlman had been blamed several years earlier for locking out his own typographical workers for their "pro-union tendencies" and replacing them with strikebreakers (*Lords*, 256). On editorial matters, the *Banner* was equally illiberal, as Seldes saw it. He cited, for example, that, in the fight between the private utilities and the Tennessee Valley Authority, the federally owned corporation created in 1933, Stahlman's paper came out firmly on the side of the private utilities. Even outside the newspaper industry, Stahlman had allegedly often showed his true colors. In his role as trustee of Vanderbilt University, for instance, he and even more deeply conservative members had reportedly maintained a strongly pro-segregation stance for many years.[48]

Episodes like these, Seldes argued, spoke louder than any noble-sounding rhetoric. Drawing a strict dichotomy between virtue and venality, as he often did, he blamed a litany of social ills—inequality, unfreedom of the press, worker disentrancement—on the ethical lapses of publishers, who ran their papers like businesses rather than the palladiums of liberty their mastheads proclaimed (*Lords*, 263). The remedy for this sorry state of affairs was multifaceted, and he spent the last part of his critique laying out his prescription for how to reclaim the American press from its overlords.

He offered a series of more or less "practical" suggestions. For one, he reiterated his long-standing idea that the newspaper makers should not only be permitted to unionize but to run things. He had once hoped the Guild would shoulder this mission, but it had demurred, fearful that such rhetoric actually played into the hands of its enemies (*Lords*, 383). He also called for a congressional investigation of publishers for their alleged transgressions, including their implicit biases, their manipulation by advertisers, and their open hostility in many cases to Roosevelt and his New Deal. The worst abusers, he felt, should be the targets of a public boycott. Finally, and perhaps most optimistically, he called for labor to fund its own newspapers, as Heywood Hale Broun's friend Alexander Crosby had urged several years before. In a contest with the "capitalistic press," a workers' press would level the playing field: "No editor or publisher would continue to distort and discolor the news if he was certain that his rival, a labor newspaper, would detect him in his work and expose him every day" (*Lords*, 401–2).

A book purporting to expose the dark underbelly of the newspaper industry was bound to be controversial. The more mainstream reviewers were appreciative of Seldes's project, but they faulted what they saw as his excesses. In the *Saturday Review*, for example, Herbert Brucker, a teacher at Columbia's Graduate School of Journalism who would later become president of the American Society of Newspaper Editors, recognized the book as "a competent and sincere criticism by an ex-newspaperman who knows what he is talking about." Still, Bruckner labeled it "a partisan work," written from "a pro-labor, anti-publisher, and anti-big business point of view."[49] Brucker was especially put off by Seldes's facile dichotomy between noble labor and ignoble owners. Certainly, the excesses of owners had "provided fertile ground" for the Guild and other labor organizations to take root. But the too easy assumption that owners as a class were by nature and position dishonest and unfair—and that labor had the personnel and expertise to have the controlling hand, at least editorially—struck the reviewer as "preposterous."[50]

The anonymous review in the *American Mercury* was even more critical of Seldes's alleged excesses. With a thinly veiled reference to the author's apparent communist sympathies, the reviewer noted how the unapologetically slanted book found that "all papers except *The Daily Worker* are mouthpieces of the Economic Royalists" and that the publishers' association was "nothing but a gang of crooks." The result was "a feeble and biased indictment" that sadly represented a missed opportunity, since "our ignorant and dishonest press has never been more open to legitimate attack than it is today."[51]

Left-wing press reviewers were, unsurprisingly, far more congratulatory. In fact, if they had a gripe, it was that Seldes had not gone far enough in his critique. In *The New Masses*, for instance, Morris U. Schappes, an American communist, applauded Seldes for revealing the main press lords, "usually in revolting dishabille," and for proposing strong remedial steps, in particular his idea of establishing labor-backed dailies. Schappes took Seldes to task, though, for letting going too easy on certain publishers, including his former boss David Stern.[52] The reviewer for the *Communist* was even more impatient with what he perceived as Seldes's evasions. While complimenting him for doing a "commendable job," Joseph North, a correspondent and editor on the *Daily Worker*, the party's main organ, pressed for a more thorough vetting of how a press affiliated with the working class and its allies could be published in America, "despite the power of monopoly capitalism." That Seldes failed to explore this crucial topic more fully, said North, is "the essential shortcoming of the work."[53]

Perhaps the most unequivocally positive review appeared in the *Forum*, a leading intellectual journal of the day. After praising Seldes fearlessness, the journal's reviewer commended him for his deeply researched indictments: "If only part of what he says is true, the press might be expected to come out with refutations; but . . . the larger dailies have been almost uniformly silent."[54] The alternative explanation, of course, was that Seldes's targets calculated that any rebuttals would simply generate more publicity for him. Silence may have been the right strategy. Still, if the press lords had hoped Seldes would be discouraged and simply fade away, they were mistaken. He had more he wanted to say and report.

THE *IN FACT* DECADE AND BEYOND

Seldes spent much of what remained of his long life—he died in 1995, at the age of 104—following up on themes set forth in his two main press studies. Besides several later books, his main vehicle for both commentary and reporting was *In Fact*, his no-advertisement-permitted newsletter published from 1940 to 1950.

The idea for the newsletter came from a group of friends that included Bruce Minton, a member of the American Communist Party, which may have provided seed money for the publication, allegedly without Seldes's knowledge.[55] Whatever the real case, *In Fact* served as a no-frills platform for not only underreported news but for continuing spotlight on ongoing

George Seldes, 1989, at age ninety-eight
Source: © Rick Goldsmith, 1989

press foibles. (An eventual rift between the partners over editorial direction resulted in Minton quitting and Seldes taking over as top editor.)

In Fact's first year set the agenda and tone of what was to come.
During this period, there were brief entries that outlined the selective
actions of the House Committee on Un-American Activities, under
conservative Texas Democrat Martin Dies. Others that called out Henry
Ford and other prominent Americans for being overly cozy with Hitler,
and still others that registered alarm at the growing war hysteria and il-
liberalism on campus. Some of Seldes's familiar hobby horses were also
on display, including his exasperation with American papers for letting
advertising revenues guide their news coverage. A case in point, as he
saw it, was their too-tolerant attitude toward Ford's anti-Semitism and
conspiracy theories.[56]

The newsletter's modest size was soon belied by its growing clout,
especially among working journalists. "Seldes wasn't printed by the
mainstream press any longer, so he didn't have access to the larger community," explained journalist, teacher, and media critic Ben Bagdikian in
Tell the Truth and Run, the 1996 documentary film about Seldes. "What
he did have, though, was access to a very important part of the journalistic community—journalists who knew there were flaws in the system."[57]
Many of these—more than two hundred, Seldes claimed in the film—
would regularly and secretly send him news items they believed their
own publications had passed over. At the height of its popularity, *In Fact*
had a circulation of 176,000 subscribers, rivaling both the *New Republic*
and the *Nation*. In time, subscribers began to fall away, fearful perhaps to
have their names linked during the Red Scare to a publication that made
no secret of its left-wing orientation.

Meanwhile, Seldes had continued to write books, some self-published,
others commercially released. Among these were two press-related studies: *The Facts Are: A Guide to Falsehood and Propaganda in the Press
and Radio* (1942) and *The People Don't Know: The American Press and
the Cold War* (1949). A third study, *Tell the Truth and Run: My 44 Year
Fight for a Free Press* (1953), came out three years after *In Fact* folded.
Seldes broke no new conceptual ground in these books, since his economic and class-based framework for understanding the press had been
fully set out as early as the 1930s. Still, he was applying his established

framework to new historical circumstances, including the Cold War and eventually Watergate.

The Cold War public relations effort especially troubled him. As suspicious now as before, he feared that the American government, with the willing complicity of the media, was manipulating public opinion for a hostile purpose, including, if necessary, a hot war. "In the making of war today—especially by a democracy such as ours," he wrote in the introduction to *The People Don't Know*, "the winning of public opinion, while perhaps not one of the chief objectives of the war itself, is certainly among the first, if not the very first, objective of the whole period."[58] With his typical disregard for subtlety, he outlined how efforts to win over the public were playing out, from the bending of news facts to what he called the "forces behind the war scares." He was unwilling to concede defeat, however: "We shall continue to make great progress despite the press. There is reason for impatience; but no cause for despondency."[59]

CONCLUSION

Any assessment of George Seldes's influence as a journalist and press critic must take into account his dual legacy. Unlike the patrician Walter Lippmann, Seldes was never solicited by presidents and diplomats for his advice and counsel, never invited to join establishment institutions of power, never asked to edit an influential newspaper or journal. His outsider status was in many ways a reaction to his politics, which to the end remained uncompromisingly radical. His outsider status was also a function of his tone and style—flamboyant, lacking in nuance and humor, and typically outraged, more often than not over some failing, real or imagined, of the American press. Not for him were Lippmann's philosophical musings and subtleties, which sometimes gave license to his readers to interpret him as they wished. Certainly, no reader of Seldes ever went away puzzled over where the author really stood. He was, as Liebling quipped, "as subtle as a house falling in." Finally, Seldes's outsider role was both a matter of inclination and choice. A gadfly and old-fashioned muckraker, he resisted the seductions of fame and power, lest they sidetrack him from what he regarded as his journalistic and critical mission.

At the same time, from the very start of his career, Seldes always managed to attract a fiercely loyal and devoted following, readers and fellow journalists who appreciated his pugnacious style, commended his bravery, and encouraged even his quixotic projects. Many of his longtime followers were no less admiring after his death. In the 1996 documentary about his life and work, a roster of such admirers—including fellow press critic Ben Bagdikian; Daniel Ellsberg, of Pentagon Papers fame; music critic Nat Hentoff; consumer activist Ralph Nader; and Victor Navasky, publisher emeritus of the *Nation*—look into the camera and describe what Seldes had meant not only to journalism but to their own careers. Younger journalists whose investigative work centers on, among other things, the confluence of media and democracy, have also acknowledged Seldes's influence. About one of these, Amy Goodman, someone has remarked that her work carries on "the great muckraking tradition of Upton Sinclair, George Seldes, I. F. Stone into the electronic age, creating a powerful counter to the mainstream media."[60]

Seldes's fans, both young and older, remain committed to him because they see their work in his. For them, mainstream media are still too beholden to business interests and advertising, too concentrated in the hands of a few, and too indifferent to the press's traditional democratic mission. The players in this media drama have changed, of course: Yesterday's Hearst empire is today's empire of Rupert Murdoch, the Australian media mogul whose reach and influence are international.[61] In the same way, yesterday's radio and TV are today's digital platforms, including Facebook, Google, Twitter, Instagram, and TikTok, which also transmit across national borders, affecting personal privacy, politics, and society.[62]

Were he alive today, Seldes would have undoubtedly found much to criticize in the actions of these and other media giants. At the same time, like many of his progeny, he had a hopeful heart, confident that, with the straight facts, the people were still capable of deciding how both the press and society worked best. It was at once Seldes's charm and conceit, of course, that he thought he knew precisely what these straight facts really were. Like a doctor who brooks no second opinion, he believed that through his probing and investigations he could diagnose exactly what ails the media and the body politic generally. In more than a few cases, it turns out, he was right.

NOTES

1. George Seldes, *Witness to a Century* (New York: Ballantine Books, 1987), 7–10.

2. Ibid., 11, 13.

3. Helen Fordham, "Subversive Voices: George Seldes and Mid-Twentieth Century Muckraking," *American Journalism* 33, no. 4, 424–41. https://www .tandfonline.com/doi/full/10.1080/08821127.2016.1241643.

4. See John Earl Haynes, Klehr, et al., *Spies: The Rise and Fall of the KGB in America* (New Haven: Yale University Press, 2009). The authors claim that, based on information in the spring of 1940 from the KGB New York station, Seldes was considered "a longtime fellowcountryman [communist] who is listed on a special register," 169. Seldes always denied that he was ever a member of the Communist Party.

5. George Seldes, *Lords of the Press* (New York: Julian Messner, 1938), 19.

6. *In Fact* 1, no. 12, ed., George Seldes, Internet Archive, https://archive.org /details/InFactVolume1IssueNumber12.

7. Fordham, "Subversive Voices," 434.

8. A. J. Liebling, "Reading List," in *The Wayward Pressman* (1947; repr., Westport, CT: Greenwood Press, 1972), 282.

9. Will Irwin, "The American Newspaper," *Collier's*, July 22, 1911, 58. http://progressingamerica.blogspot.com/2012/05/american-newspaper-by-will -irwin.html.

10. Seldes, *Witness*, 18.

11. See David Cannadine, *Mellon: An American Life* (New York: Vintage, 2008), 206. Applying his political muscle, Mellon pressed the Pennsylvania legislature to amend the state divorce statute: hereafter, the decision to empanel a jury for even pending cases would be left to the discretion of the court. An outraged Nora Mellon responded to her husband's hardball tactics by attacking him in the out-of-town press, including the *New York Times* and the *Philadelphia North American*. In time, the amended statute was ruled unconstitutional, although not before the Mellon divorce was adjudicated in a private hearing.

12. See Gene Roberts and Hank Klibanoff, *The Race Beat: The Press, the Civil Rights Struggle, and the Awakening of a Nation* (New York: Vintage, 2007), 44. In 1938, Sprigle won the award for his story pointing out that Supreme Court Justice Hugo Black had once been a member of the Ku Klux Klan. He had also posed as a black man in the south for a multipart series, "In the Land of Jim Crow."

13. Seldes, *Witness*, 37.

14. Ibid., 32.

15. Ibid., 41.

16. "W. W. Nolen Dies at Home in Little Hall," *The Harvard Crimson*, June 6, 1923, https://www.thecrimson.com/article/1923/6/6/w-w-nolen-dies-at-home/.

17. Seldes, *Witness*, 42.

18. Ibid., 46.

19. Ibid., 74–75.

20. Ibid., 99–100.

21. See Richard Norton Smith, *The Colonel: The Life and Legend of Robert R. McCormick*, 1880–1955 (New York: Houghton Mifflin, 1997), 279. In 1928, McCormick was asked to chair AANP's newly established Committee on Freedom of the Press.

22. Seldes, *Witness*, 140.

23. Ibid., 220.

24. See, among other historical references, "The Mexican Land and Petroleum Laws," CQ Researcher, Document Archives, 1926 https://library.cqpress.com /cqresearcher/document.php?id=cqresrre1926020800.

25. See, for example, "The Rise of Francisco Madero," in "The Mexican Revolution and the United States in the Collections of the Library of Congress," Library of Congress Digital Collections, https://www.loc.gov/exhibits/mexican -revolution-and-the-united-states/rise-of-madero.html.

26. Seldes, *Witness*, 242.

27. George Seldes, *You Can't Print That* (New York: Payson & Clarke, 1929), 327. Creative Commons, https://archive.org/details/YouCantPrintThat/page/n8.

28. George Seldes, *World Panorama* (Boston: Little, Brown, 1933), 289.

29. Seldes, *Freedom of the Press* (Indianapolis: Bobs-Merrill, 1935, x. All further references will be to this edition and cited parenthetically in the text.

30. Wikipedia, s.v. "Public Utility Holding Act of 1935," last edited May 8, 2019, https://en.wikipedia.org/wiki/Public_Utility_Holding_Company_Act _of_1935.

31. Wikipedia, s.v. "*Frankfurter Zeitung*," last edited February 21, 2019, https://en.wikipedia.org/wiki/Frankfurter_Zeitung.

32. "Jonathan Eddy, 91, Founder of a Union," *New York Times*, June 5, 1993, 28, TimesMachine, https://timesmachine.nytimes.com/timesmachine/1993/06/05 /issue.html. See also "Guide to the Newspaper Guild of New York Records Wag. 125," Tamiment Library and Robert F. Wagner Labor Archives, http://dlib.nyu .edu/findingaids/html/tamwag/wag_125/bioghist.html.

33. "Newspaper Guild Begins to Function," *New York Times*, November 16, 1933, 30, TimesMachine, https://timesmachine.nytimes.com/timesmachine /1933/11/16/issue.html.

34. Newspaper Guild of New York, Archives. "The bitter *Newark Ledger* strike of 1934–1935 proved to be a testing ground for conflicting visions of the Guild's role. While the strike settlement yielded little in the way of concrete gains for the strikers, the Guild emerged from it with an enhanced sense of national solidarity and confirmation of its ability to lead and bargain for its members."

35. Alexander Crosby, "Polishing the Brass Check," review of Freedom of the Press, by George Seldes, *Saturday Review*, September 14, 1935, 7, The Unz Review, https://www.unz.com/print/SaturdayRev-1935sep14-00007/; see also, 42. Alexander L. Crosby, "A Source Book on Corruption," review of Freedom of the Press, by George Seldes, *The New Masses*, September 17, 1935, 25, The Unz Review, https://www.unz.com/print/NewMasses-1935sep17-00025/.

36. Gordon Carroll, "The Rape of the Fourth Estate," review of *Freedom of the Press*, by George Seldes, *The American Mercury*, December 1935, 501, The Unz Review, https://www.unz.com/print/AmMercury-1935dec-00500/.

37. Ibid.

38. George Seldes, "The Call from Spain," in *The George Seldes Reader*, edited and with an introduction by Randolph T. Holhut (New York: Barricade Books, 1994), 134.

39. Ibid.

40. On March 28, 1939, Madrid was finally overtaken by Franco's forces. See, among other studies of the period, Anthony Beevor, *The Battle for Spain: The Spanish Civil War 1936–1939* (New York: Penguin, 2006).

41. Helen Larkin, *The New York Post*, n.d. (quoted in Seldes, "Call," *Reader*, 140.).

42. Seldes, "Call," *Reader*, 141.

43. Seldes, *Lords*, 4. All further references will be to this edition and cited parenthetically in the text.

44. "James Stahlman, Publisher, Dead," *New York Times*, May 2, 1976, 52. TimesMachine, https://timesmachine.nytimes.com/timesmachine/1976/05 /02/167983562.html?action=click&contentCollection=Archives&module=Lede Asset&region=ArchiveBody&pgtype=article&pageNumber=52.

45. "Joseph Medill Patterson," *Illinois Biographical Dictionary, 2008–2009*, vol. 1, ed. Caryn Hannan and Jennifer L. Herman (Hamburg, MI: State History Publications, 536–37. In fact, both Patterson and his publication drifted further to the right eventually.

46. See, for example, Michael Dennis, *The Memorial Day Massacre and the Movement for Industrial Democracy* (New York: Palgrave Macmillan, 2010).

47. One of the important biographies of McCormick is Robert Norton Smith, *The Colonel: The Life and Times of Robert R. McCormick, 1880–1955* (New York: Houghton Mifflin, 1997). Among other influences on McCormick, Smith, in his "Prologue: The Voice of America," points to the impact of his grandfather, Joseph Medill, on his character, business sense, and politics.

48. See, among other references to Stahlman's anti-integrationist stance both as publisher and member of the Vanderbilt Board of Trustees, Theo Emery, "Activist Ousted from Vanderbilt Is Back," *New York Times*, October 4, 2006, https://www.nytimes.com/2006/10/04/education/04lawson.html.

49. Herbert Brucker, "The News of the Publishers," review of *Freedom of the Press*, by George Seldes, *The Saturday Review*, November 19, 1938, 14, The Unz Review, http://www.unz.com/print/SeldesGeorge-1938/.

50. Ibid., 15.

51. "The Check List," review of *Freedom of the Press*, by George Seldes, *The American Mercury*, February 1939, The Unz Review, http://www.unz.com/print/AmMercury-1939feb-x00142/.

52. Morris U. Schappes, "The Press Versus the People," review of *Freedom of the Press*, by George Seldes, *The New Masses*, 22. The Unz Review, http://www.unz.com/print/NewMasses-1938nov29-00022/.

53. Joseph North, "That Eight Per Cent Investment—The Press," review of *Freedom of the Press*, by George Seldes, *The Communist*, April 1939, 376, 381. The Unz Review, http://www.unz.com/print/Communist-1939apr-00376/.

54. M. L. Elting, "The Book Forum," review of *Freedom of the Press*, by George Seldes, *The Book Forum*, January 1939, v. The Unz Review, http://www.unz.com/print/Forum-1939jan-x00058/.

55. Denying that he was ever a communist, Seldes described his curious experience testifying before Senator Joseph McCarthy's Senate Permanent Subcommittee on Investigations in 1953 in a chapter in his biography, *Witness to a Century*, titled, "Face to Face with Joe McCarthy," 357–61.

56. *In Fact* 1, no. 12, ed., George Seldes, 1–4. Internet Archive, https://archive.org/details/InFactVolume1IssueNumber12.

57. Rick Goldsmith, producer, director, editor, *Tell the Truth and Run: George Seldes and the American Press* (Never Tire Productions, 1996), film, 1:51, Channel Television Network, https://www.youtube.com/watch?v=j9qZ5jE_yMw.

58. George Seldes, *The People Don't Know: The American Press and the Cold War* (New York: Gaer Associates, 1949), 6.

59. Ibid., 316.

60. See Michael Parenti and Amy Goodman, speakers, "Building Independent Media: Strategies for Change," streaming and CD, October 13, 2000, Alternative Radio, https://www.alternativeradio.org/products/parm-gooa001/. The quote is attributed to the late American historian and educator Howard Zinn.

61. See, among other articles on Murdoch, Jonathan Mahler, and Jim Rutenberg, "Planet Fox," *New York Times Magazine*, April 7, 2019, 32–55, 62, 71, 73.

62. Among the many studies of Internet companies and their power, see "Digital Platforms and Concentration: Second Annual Antitrust and Competition Conference," Guy Rolnik, ed., Stigler Center for the Study of the Economy and the State, University of Chicago Booth School of Business, April 19–20, 2018, https://promarket.org/wp-content/uploads/2018/04/Digital-Platforms-and-Concentration.pdf. Also, Chris Hughes, "It's Time to Break Up Facebook," *New York Times*, Sunday Review, https://www.nytimes.com/2019/05/09/opinion/sunday/chris-hughes-facebook-zuckerberg.html.

A. J. Liebling at podium, date unknown.
Source: A. J. Liebling Collection, #4613. Division of Rare and Manuscript Collections, Cornell University Library.

Chapter Three

A. J. Liebling

Comedy of Errors

People everywhere confuse what they read about in newspapers with news.

—A. J. Liebling, *The New Yorker*, April 7, 1956

Throughout most of his relatively short life, Abbott Joseph "A. J." Liebling affected the pose of a streetwise New Yorker with a keen eye for the city's shady haunts and shadier characters. The guise served him well in his personal relations, and it served him even better as a writer: In his long-form journalism, he discovered literary gold in Gotham's lowlife culture of palookas and corner men, heels and scammers, grifters and publicity hacks.

But Liebling was not the street urchin he sometimes claimed: the first child of the former Ann Sloan and Joseph Liebling, he was born into what his biographer calls "comfortable circumstances on the Upper East Side of Manhattan on October 18, 1904."[1] His mother was a native of San Francisco whose family background and education were genteel. His father was a Jewish immigrant from Austria who arrived penniless in the United States but prospered in the wholesale fur trade and later real estate. If Abbott knew anything about the lower depths, it was partially through Joseph, "a sport and tough bird," who in his heavily accented New York English regaled his son with vivid tales of the streets.[2]

Young Abbot also learned about New York street life through another window. From an early age, he acquired a "vicarious knowledge" of the world beyond his bourgeois home from the city's newspapers, especially those in the then crowded evening field: the *New York Evening Mail, New*

York Evening Globe, New York Telegram, New York Evening World, New York Evening Journal, New York Post, and the *Evening Sun*. "I would spread them on the floor and lie down on my belly with them, or take them to bed with me, or into the bathroom," an older Liebling would write in *The Wayward Pressman,* his 1947 collection of reminiscences and press columns.[3] The city's papers had such an effect on him that he later feigned pity for those who "came up to New York and tried to compete with me."[4]

His youthful infatuation seemed to augur a career in journalism, but it was not his first choice. He dreamed of becoming a writer, perhaps a novelist. By his senior year in Far Rockaway High School—his family had moved to this largely rural seaside village in Queens in 1913—he had already published short stories in the school's literary magazine. In 1920, he entered Dartmouth, where he continued to write, contributing pieces to the college's humor magazine, *Jack O'Lantern*. His academic trajectory at this point seemed more or less set, but Liebling was something of a rebel, or at least he viewed himself that way: He flouted the school's compulsory chapel attendance and was suspended; given a second chance, he flouted the rule again and was expelled.[5]

Liebling was now at loose ends, though still interested in a writing career. Thinking newspapers might fit the bill, he enrolled in the School of Journalism at Columbia University, now the Columbia University Graduate School of Journalism. Looking back on the experience, he claimed to have learned nothing. He managed, though, to graduate and land a job as a copyreader on the sports desk of the *New York Times*. The briefly held position—he later complained his editor fired him for inserting a fictitious referee's name into basketball copy—was the start of his journalistic career, one that unfolded on a series of newspapers. In 1935, he left daily journalism for good and began contributing features to the *New Yorker,* edited by the already legendary Harold Ross. In 1939, Ross sent him to Paris to cover the European war, an assignment that, off and on, would last until late 1944.

He had been a working reporter by this point for the past twenty years, someone who could, as he would famously boast, "write better than anyone who could write faster, and faster than anyone who could write better."[6] He had also become a discerning observer of the American press. Back in New York after his war assignment, he began to read newspapers regularly again, everything from foreign news reports to theater and music criticism. What he read often exasperated him, especially news of overseas, which as a former war correspondent he knew well.

Perhaps the American press itself was a promising beat, he thought. Reaching out to Wallace Shawn, the magazine's managing editor and future top editor, he proposed reprising "The Wayward Press" department, initiated in 1927 by humorist Robert Benchley. The proposal made it up the masthead to Ross, who gave Liebling the green light.[7] In May 1945, Liebling wrote his first column. With a few interruptions over the next twenty years, some eighty more columns followed, many of which were collected during his lifetime in three books: besides 1947's *The Wayward Pressman*, there were *Mink and Red Herring: The Wayward Pressman's Casebook* (1949) and *The Press* (1961).

Liebling made little effort in his columns to disguise his biases. He was not only suspicions of publishers who put profits above all else but believed that newspaper consolidation was not only pernicious but inevitable. "American cities with competing newspapers will soon be as rare as those with two telephone systems," he wrote in "Do You Belong in Journalism?," a May 14, 1960, column later reprinted in *The Press*.[8] Liberal, prolabor, and a longtime member of the American Newspaper Guild, Liebling was clearly a critic with a political point of view, one who felt, in his more reflective moments, the press was "the weak slat under the bed of democracy."[9]

Yet unlike his older contemporary George Seldes, he was not fiercely wedded to an ideology.[10] For him, journalistic errors of fact, judgment, technique, and style were less evidence of "a deliberate and universal conspiracy," as he had said of Seldes in *The Wayward Pressman*, than occasions for ridicule and mockery.[11] He took an impish pleasure in unearthing, reporting, and correcting such errors, making sure by means of a witty and irreverent style that his readers not only shared in the fun but in the hope for a better press and thus a better democracy.

FROM NEW YORK TO PROVIDENCE

Liebling's swift departure from the *Times* endeared him to his older colleagues, who mistook his youthful irresponsibility for pluck and audacity. But Liebling himself was disconsolate, convinced of his worthlessness.

He was eager to restart his career, and in the process perhaps minimize the shock to his parents, who at this point knew nothing of his dismissal. Desperate, he got in touch with a former Columbia classmate who was working in Rhode Island as the city editor of the *Providence News*, owned by the Providence Journal Company. There was nothing for Liebling on the paper, but there was on the *Evening Bulletin*, owned by the same company. He then broke the news to his parents, who were puzzled why he or anyone would trade a job on the *Times* for one in Rhode Island. Undeterred, in mid-March 1926, he boarded a train to Providence, ready a few days later to begin his job as general assignment reporter on the staff of the *Bulletin*.[12]

What Liebling's new paper lacked in cachet, it made up in opportunity. Finally, he was a real reporter, and in a port city that had a substantial population, was the county seat and state capital, and served as the site of the United States District Court. He handled his early assignments well, including a prohibition case at the Federal Building that convinced his superiors that he was not only a good writer but had "a humorous touch." Before long, they transferred him from the *Bulletin* to the second shift on the company's morning paper, the *Journal*, "where" as he later said, "there was more space for the leisurely deployment of my talent." From this point on, he "oozed prose over every aspect of Rhode Island Life," including stories about lost schooners, colliding trains, diplomatic banquets, horse shows, and the establishment of Rhode Island's State Boxing Commission.[13]

He was not covering earthshaking events, he knew, although he felt he was turning out good copy and in the process enjoying himself. It was a situation that might well have continued for a time, but one day, after he had been in Providence for only a few months, his father made a proposal: a period of study abroad, all expenses paid. Liebling was elated, and if anything, worried his father might change his mind:[14] His plan was to study medieval French at the Sorbonne. His editors tried to get him to stay, a sign of their regard, but he was determined to go abroad. Still, there would be a job waiting for him when he returned, and he had a secret sense he would return, if not to Providence than somewhere else with a good paper. The journalistic "taint" had clearly infected him.[15]

PROVIDENCE REDUX AND FAREWELL

In fall 1927, Liebling returned from abroad to America, his father now less willing and less financially able to stake his overseas study. A job in New York was an outside chance, but a spot again on the *Providence Journal* seemed a better prospect. This time around, he was greeted with a somewhat better salary and the chance to work on a variety of stories. One of the biggest of these was an investigative piece on the Rhode Island State Hospital for Mental Diseases, in Howard, now known as the Eleanor Slater Hospital.[16] The series, as it turned out, was a blockbuster: it not only broke news, led to a state-level inquiry into the administration of state hospitals, and caused several commissioners to resign, but it also vividly illustrated for the young reporter how money influenced both politics and policy.[17]

In September 1930, Liebling's second stint on the *Journal* came to an end, almost exactly three years after it had begun. He had left of his own accord, furious that a fellow reporter and friend had been let go on the flimsiest of pretexts, something that would not have occurred, he believed, had there been at the time an American Newspaper Guild. His bold gesture of solidarity was not all it seemed, however. For one thing, he acknowledged he had far more freedom to act than his married colleagues with families to support. Of greater consequence perhaps was that he had also grown weary of his job. Eager to return to New York, he hoped to land a position on the *New York World*, a real writer's paper, he thought, with a roster of writing talent bigger than all of the other New York papers combined.

BACK WHERE HE CAME FROM

Liebling went to extravagant lengths to attract the attention of *World* city editor Jim Barrett.[18] But this was just a year after the stock market crash, and neither the *World* nor any other New York newspaper, it seemed, was hiring. He had some freelance ideas, though, and in short order he was offered a $75-dollar-a-week account as an advance against future stories. He continued to want a salaried spot on the *World*—to become a full-fledged *World* man—but he was nevertheless content for now to at least be a regular contributor.

The arrangement lasted until the following year. At this point, Joseph Pulitzer's three male heirs went to court to sell their father's paper to the *New York Telegram*, part of the Scripps-Howard chain. The new owners promptly closed the *World*, fired its staff, and launched the newly combined *New York World-Telegram*. Liebling was heartbroken at the loss of the *World*, but he needed a job. In March 1931, he visited the *World-Telegram's* offices south of Washington Market, on the West Side, and applied for and landed a reporter's staff position at his previous weekly salary. For the next four years, roughly, he wrote an estimated three hundred and fifty signed features, along with scores of unsigned pieces.[19] The hefty output taught him nothing new about writing, he later complained.[20] Still, he came to regard some of the pieces well enough to include them in his first collection of published pieces, *Back Where I Came From* (1938).[21]

Liebling may have felt creatively stalled on the *Evening-Telegram*, but he also considered himself underpaid. Since his hire, his salary had been cut twice, along with the salaries of other reporters. On March 22, 1935, the now married Liebling made a final pitch for a pay boost. Denied, he found what turned out to be an interim position with Hearst's King Features Syndicate. Meanwhile, he was in negotiations with the *New Yorker*, where like his friend, the brilliant reporter Joseph Mitchell, he had been a contributing writer while on staff at the *World-Telegram*. The magazine invited him to join the staff, and he accepted. (Three years later, the magazine also extended an invitation to Mitchell.) His career as a newspaperman, begun ten years earlier on the sports copy desk of the *Times*, had officially come to an end.[22]

FROM MAGAZINE WRITER TO WAR CORRESPONDENT

The switch to magazine writing eventually proved congenial. "I had opportunities to work on better news stories as a member of the *New Yorker* staff than I had ever had on a daily," Liebling later explained.[23] His first year was a struggle, however. Looking back, he attributed his early problems to the new journalistic format: as a newspaper reporter, he had become adept at the short-feature method, brief, punchy profiles and vignettes tailored to both the newspaper's limited space and its readers' shorter attention spans. That method was not always well suited to a magazine famous for its longer-form pieces.

But Liebling also struggled early on with shorter pieces, including his front-of-the-book contributions to "Talk of the Town." His copyeditor during this period, William Shawn, thought the problem lay in the clash between Liebling's idiosyncratic style, a mix of high and low diction, and the more genteel house style.[24] Whatever the case, Liebling soon adapted to his new journalistic home, while doing his best to enliven its traditional style. If in time he succeeded, his influence is apparent in such pieces as "Broadway Storekeeper," a profile of the owner of an all-night tobacco store; "Tummler," a portrait of a fast-talking, horse-racing tipster and nightclub entrepreneur; and "The Man in the Corner," a profile of Morris "Whitey" Bimstein, the much-in-demand trainer and "cut man" for Jack Dempsey and other famous boxing champions.[25]

Meanwhile, World War II had begun in Europe. In 1939, and with Liebling's wife now under private treatment in a psychiatric hospital in Maryland, Harold Ross dispatched him to France to write "Letter from Paris." The following year, after the fall of France, he returned to New York, rented a room in the home of a friend, and continued on staff at the magazine. In 1941 and then in 1942, Ross sent him back to Europe, first to Great Britain and then to North Africa, where the battle for control of the vital Suez Canal had been raging since 1940. Once again, he returned home, and once again, in summer 1943, Ross sent him abroad, this time to cover Great Britain and the preparations for D-Day. After the Allies landed at Normandy, he continued to follow Allied combatants as they pushed from Paris to the Rhine. By the campaign's end in March 1945, Liebling was finally back in New York to stay. Readers who had been following his war coverage in the pages of the *New Yorker* could now also read a collection of his dispatches, published in book form the year before by Doubleday, Doran, under the title, *The Road Back to Paris* (1939).[26]

WAYWARD PRESS CRITIC, 1945–1953

On home soil, Liebling resumed his early habit of reading the daily newspapers. His interests, as catholic now as then, included foreign

Liebling Operating on Newspaper Corpse.
Source: A. J. Liebling Collection, #4613. Division of Rare and Manuscript Collections, Cornell University Library.

news, domestic news, sporting news, editorials, op-eds, and drama and music criticism. He was no longer the novice reader he once was, though; he was rather a veteran journalist who both knew his craft and many of the events of the day. "After a few months at home," he recalled with his typical comic exaggeration, "I began to react to some of the things I read. Some of my reactions resembled severe attacks of the mental hives or prickly heat. Occasionally they verged on what the psychiatrists call the disturbed and assaultive."[27]

He was especially distressed by the quality and accuracy of the foreign news he read. Professionalism in journalism mattered, he believed, not only for working reporters but for press services, news syndicates, and above all publishers. Their all-too-frequent professional lapses were infuriating, offering the ideal rationale for reprising a favorite magazine department: the "The Wayward Press," inaugurated by humorist Robert Benchley on December 24, 1927, under the pseudonym "Guy Fawkes," the English conspirator.[28] Both Shawn and Ross agreed, and Liebling wrote his first column, "The A.P Surrender," on May 19, 1945. More than sixty additional columns—about three-quarters of his entire output—would follow from 1945 to 1953.

In many ways, his first column established a template for his future ones over this eight-year period. The background of the piece was historic—the German surrender, on May 7, 1945, at Reims, France, the site of the Supreme Headquarters Allied Expeditionary Force (SHAEF), under the command of General Dwight D. Eisenhower. But Liebling's focus was on what he regarded as another sort of capitulation, this one involving some of America's largest news organizations, led by the Associated Press (AP). To control news coverage, SHAEF public relations had tightly restricted access to the signing ceremony. Beyond a small group of foreign reporters, the brigadier general in charge of the event had limited the American presence to just three reporters—one from the United Press, one from Hearst's International News Service, and one from the AP.

The small band of correspondents was under another restriction as well, which members learned about en route by air from Paris to Reims: For the "privilege" of covering the meeting, they were forbidden to report any news until explicitly told to do so. Such restrictions had not been uncommon in the European Theatre of Operations, where commanders routinely imposed gag orders and news blackouts to keep war plans secret. But this order was unusual—one, because no lives were at stake, and two, because of the ceremonial nature of the event. Nevertheless, the journalists acquiesced and continued on to Reims to attend the signing.

Then, something strange happened. After the ceremony but before reboarding the return flight to Paris, the AP's man on the scene, one Edward Kennedy, heard a curious tidbit from the general chaperoning the group: at Eisenhower's request, reporters at command headquarters had already been granted permission to release news of the signing event. Given this, the traveling reporters would be wise to have their dispatches ready for the SHAEF censor once they landed in Paris. And yet once on the ground, Kennedy and his colleagues discovered their gag order was still in effect, despite sketchy news of the Reims ceremony having already been broadcast on radio. Feeling duped, Kennedy commandeered an Army telephone with a direct line to London, put in a call to a colleague at the AP London bureau, and read his prepared story. He then braced for the inevitable fallout.

"The AP Surrender" appeared some ten days later in the *New Yorker*. In the column, Liebling leveled a range of criticisms. First, he scolded SHAEF for first imposing such an absurdly low cap on the number of American press representatives. Journalistic access was always key, he knew, and the Reims signing was "one of the most memorable scenes in the history of man." Second, he raised doubts about the overall legitimacy of the high command's quid pro quo. Employing his customary comic slyness in such matters, he questioned "whether a promise extorted as this one was, in an airplane several thousand feet up, has any moral force is a question for theologians." He reserved his sternest rebuke, though, for the news organizations, and especially the AP. In the past as now, they had been willing to accept arbitrary and at times stupid official rules. He saw this sort of collective subservience as an illustration of "Liebling's Law"—the tendency of smart people to participate in their own abuse. Such self-imposed punishment was a difficult habit to break, he knew, which is why Edward Kennedy was so brave for breaking it[29]—and why he deserved to be defended against his critics, who believed he had reneged on a trust.

One of those critics, as it turned out, was Kennedy's own employer, the AP. Initially, the press service had not seem bothered by the hubbub, and it distributed its employees' scoop widely to its member papers. After the State and War Departments objected, though, the AP backtracked, apologized, and eventually pressured Kennedy into resigning. In his column, Liebling pointed to the rank hypocrisy of not only the AP but of other news outlets that had run the story in one edition and then criticized its release in a subsequent edition. Kennedy had done nothing to risk Allied lives, Liebling believed. And, in fact, if there had been any rationale for SHAEF's initial news blackout, it was not to save lives but to give Russian dictator Joseph Stalin enough time to host his own signing ceremony in Berlin a few days later, a charge now generally regarded as true.[30]

"The AP Surrender" telescoped some of what Liebling had in store for future columns. Here on full display was his sly humor—his ability to use wit and the put-down to skewer stupidity and hypocrisy on all sides. Here, too, was evidence of his tendency to view press owners as unprincipled, putting their corporate interests ahead of the public interest. And finally, here was a preview of some of his pet subjects, including the official impulse to restrict the press and the press's complicity in its own mishandling. With the war now ended and matters closer to home of greater reader interest, Liebling trained his wit and focus on a range of other topics.

In "Preliminary Bout" (November 1, 1947), for example, he focused on the demonstrable pro-owner default of so many papers. The strike at the center of the column was a relatively minor one—a dispute at the former Jamaica Racetrack in New York between the union representing grooms and exercise riders and owners and trainers. That the communist *Daily Worker* had unequivocally backed the strikers was no surprise, of course. More indicative of the coverage, though, was the reporting and commentary of Joseph Palmer Hill, a sports columnist and racing expert on the *Herald Tribune*. Palmer had praised the owners and trainers for their fierce independence, specifically their willingness to pick up stakes and move to another racing venue if pushed to negotiate with the strikers. The commentary struck Liebling as high-handed: knowing the industry's unsavory public reputation, Palmer had blithely assumed that most people would rally to support the higher-ups' refusal to negotiate. He was wrong, Liebling insisted, since "to some people [the owners and trainers] seemed objectionable even though they were only in the industry of racing horses"[31]

But there was more to the story than mere high-handed reporting. In the clash between haves and have-nots, the Jamaica Racetrack strike suggested a broader national movement, which pitted owners against workers in what some regarded as the Red Scare. Clearly, the Jamaica conflict did not rise to this level. Nor did it occasion anything like the HUAC (House on Un-American Activities Committee) hearings soon to take place. Still, in his seriocomic way of squeezing big drama out of seemingly small events, Liebling persisted in the notion that, upon looking back, some "future Edward Gibbons" would discern a link, however tenuous: "To the historian's eye they may seem of a piece, and equally symptomatic of the unrest of our times" (*Mink,* 57).

As this unrest intensified, Liebling devoted more of "The Wayward Press" to not only labor issues but to the hunt for communists and communist sympathizers. The gist of this series was his belief, occasionally strained, that the hunt was often a case of much ado about very little. And so in mid-1949, and now married to his second wife, Harriet Lucille Hill, he turned his attention to coverage of perhaps the biggest Red Scare story of the era: the first Alger Hiss trial, begun May 31, 1949.[32]

Hiss had been accused by Whittaker Chambers of lying during their joint HUAC appearance a little more than a year earlier, and he, Hiss, was now on trial for perjury before US District Judge Samuel H. Kaufman, of the Southern District of New York. In "Spotlight on the Jury" (July 23, 1949), which appeared about two weeks after a divided jury failed to convict the defendant, Liebling considered how the press had performed. Certainly, the first trial had produced some very good reporting. One of the best pieces was by a writer for the *Herald Tribune* who had provided an impartial account of jury stumbling blocks, including a debate over a key piece of prosecutorial evidence—a typewriter once owned by the Hisses.[33]

But other coverage struck him as less impartial. Almost immediately after the acquittal, for instance, the *World-Telegram* and the *Journal-American*, owned by Scripps-Howard and Hearst respectively, had each devoted eight-column headlines to the accusation by then California Congressman Richard Nixon that Judge Kaufman's conduct during the proceedings had indicated a clear anti-prosecution bias. Other newspapers soon began echoing a similar theme, including the *Herald Tribune*, which Liebling accused of repeating the same story and calling it news, as the Scripps-Howard papers were prone to do. The likely effect of this practice, he feared, was "to intimidate any judge who in the future presides over a similar trial, or a retrial of the Hiss case" (*Press*, 810, 817–18).

Liebling confessed to a second fear as well. In covering the Hiss trial, the New York press had played up the attacks of the pro-conviction jurors on their pro-acquittal colleagues. In one instance, the names and addresses of two of the four pro-acquittal jurors had been published, resulting in anonymous threats and intimidation. The attacks had made for sensational headlines and stories, of course. But Liebling was concerned that, like the coverage of Judge Kaufman's alleged bias, the press's treatment of juror feuds would also reduce the chances of a fair second trial.

When that trial was scheduled, Hiss's lawyers pressed for a change of venue, requesting that the new trial be heard in Vermont. This was all to the good, Liebling noted in a later postscript to his column, since Vermonters tended not to read New York papers and any Green Mountain

State jurors would "own shotguns" and thus be less susceptible to intimidation (*Press,* 819–20). The request was denied by the US Circuit Court of Appeals, however, and Hiss was tried in the same New York courtroom as before, albeit before a different judge. As Liebling had predicted, the second trial ended in Hiss's conviction on two counts of perjury, for which he ended up serving somewhat under four years in federal prison. Both Hiss's actual guilt and the effect of public opinion remains a topic of intense debate even today.[34] Less controversial is what the trial did to accelerate the careers of two of the period's prominent anti-communists—Richard Nixon, who went from the House to the Senate in 1950, and Wisconsin Senator Joseph McCarthy, who announced shortly after the trial in a now famous speech that there were currently hundreds of Communists in the State Department.

But not all of Liebling's columns during this period throbbed with outrage over big events. A writer as much as he was a reporter, he also cared deeply for words and their proper use. Their misuse was a personal hobbyhorse, especially when perpetrated by members of his own profession. Indeed, he believed the act "should be punished as severely as the misappropriation of funds."[35] In "Antepenultimatum" (September 7, 1946), for instance, he accused the press of being profligate in its use of the word "ultimatum," which in headlines usually succeeded in arousing reader alarm but often overstated or misstated the actual status of events.[36]

Other verbal sins became the focus of later columns. In "The Scribes of Destiny" (September 28, 1946), for example, he needled entertainment-minded sports writers for spinning typically overwrought morality tales, even when there was nothing especially substantial or entertaining to write about: "Upon small, coiled springs of fact, he [the sports writer] builds up a great padded mattress of words."[37] In "Probe Use Hit in Press Flay; Reds' Button Attack Bared" (September 6, 1947), he demonstrated what he saw as the dyspeptic temper of the times by listing instances of headline writers' penchant for words that expressed physical violence—hit, fight, poke, probe, flay, attack, slug, and the like (*Mink,* 29). And in "Horsefeathers Swathed in Mink" (November 22, 1947), he surveyed the ways in which even so-called liberal newspapers employed various verbal shorthands for the idea of the "Undeserving Poor," including the reference to "the Lady in Mink" for a woman receiving welfare payments (*Mink,* 76).

Liebling concluded the first eight years of "The Wayward Press" with a four-column retrospective on New York's newspaper history. The series, titled "Of Yesteryear," roughly coincided with the span of years between the inauguration of Franklin Roosevelt on March 4, 1933, and the inauguration of Dwight D. Eisenhower, some twenty years later, on January 20, 1953.

First to be considered was the *World-Telegram*, which he had joined in the early 1930s. While he remembered learning little about writing during his brief tenure on the paper, he nevertheless recalled that the recently merged publication had covered the Depression with a certain sympathy for the poor and out of work. Post-merger, it had even retained the liberal activist and commentator Heywood Broun, who had once been fired by the *New York World* for "disloyalty."[38] Under Scripps-Howard management, however, the *World-Telegram* (and later the *World-Telegram and Sun*) eventually moved steadily to the right. In time, readers who had become accustomed to the commentary of Broun and others voted with their feet, switching their allegiance to what was then at least the more liberal *Post*.[39]

Other New York papers also came under Liebling's microscope. One was the *Journal-American*, the result of a 1937 merger of Hearst's *American* and *Evening Journal*. As Liebling saw it, the paper had not significantly changed its business model over the span of its existence. Then as now, its editors and publisher seemed intent on isolating their readers from the news rather than informing them about it. In fact, readers of the *Journal-American* were invited into a cocoon, "a self-contained world which has little relevance to the one outside but which has its own constants—gossip, xenophobia, the movies, and a continual Byzantine-palace struggle for precedence among by-liners."[40]

There were two papers that Liebling believed had actually modified over the years: the *New York Times* and the *New York Herald Tribune*. In 1933, at the start of the Roosevelt administration, the *Times* was bigger than its morning rival in almost all ways—more staff, pages, stories, news, and circulation. At this point, the *Times* was generally counted a Democratic paper, one that had supported Roosevelt with reservations against the incumbent Herbert Hoover, while the *Herald Tribune* was a vehicle of mainstream Republicanism. Up for grabs was the large swath of centrist readers—"the large mass of political skeptics," as Liebling called them. The *Times* hoped to win them over by the sheer scope of its news coverage, while the *Herald Tribune* was counting on its lighter-hearted, much more whimsical style.[41]

Much had changed on the papers over the next twenty years. If the *Tribune* had lost the circulation war—bleeding about six thousand readers during this period, while the *Times* had gained almost six times that number—it had nevertheless developed into a world-class newspaper, rivaling the *Times*. Jettisoning its signature tone, it had hired superb writers and columnists (Walter Lippmann, Dorothy Thompson, and Red Smith, among others) and won multiple Pulitzer Prizes, all the while stubbornly maintaining its conservative political tilt. Meanwhile, the *Times* had held fast to its traditionally sober tone, but it had shifted rightward politically, supporting "the Republican candidate in three of the last four Presidential elections—Willkie in 1940, Dewey in 1948, and Eisenhower in 1952."[42] The shift did not surprise Liebling—the *Times*, after all, was a singular member of the establishment press—but neither did it sit well with him.

WAYWARD PRESS CRITIC, 1954–1963

By the early 1950s, Liebling had resumed writing boxing pieces for the *New Yorker* and other magazines, which would eventually be collected in one of his most famous books, *The Sweet Science* (1956). He also wrote two other books—*Chicago: The Second City* (1952) and *The Honest Rainmaker: The Life and Times of Colonel John R. Stingo* (1953)—and contributed a variety of other articles to the *New Yorker*, including profiles, travelogues, true-crime reports, comments, book reviews, and even the occasional short story. For the five-year period from 1954 to 1959, however, he took something of an extended holiday from "The Wayward Press," contributing just one column each year in 1954, 1955, and 1956, and nothing thereafter until 1960. If the critical impulse struck him during this hiatus, it was usually because some press blunder or person had irked him, or a combination of both.

In "The Tonsorial Election" (November 20, 1954), for instance, he took out after, among other figures, Westbrook Pegler, the syndicated newspaper columnist on Hearst's *Journal American*. A staunch Republican who had made his name as an opponent of the New Deal and labor unions and a fierce defender of Joseph McCarthy, Pegler had cynically applauded the Democrats' narrow success in gaining control of congress in the recent off-year election (by a hair, as it were) because he was fed up with his party and with Eisenhower in particular. Their sins? Eisenhower had come out against McCarthy, albeit obliquely, and the GOP had been corrupted by a Fabian Socialism that promoted aid programs to the "scratchy, half-civilized parasites" of the world. Pegler's dire, death-of-the-Republic pronouncement, wrote Liebling, was only the latest in his series of "national obituaries," including one issued in 1950 after Truman and the Democratic party had also managed to maintain control of Congress. This time around, though, the conservative commentator seemed to be making the best of a bad situation and adjusting "to life in the cemetery of the Republic."[43]

By 1960—and at this point married to his third wife, the short story writer and novelist Jean Stafford—Liebling was once again regularly contributing columns to "The Wayward Press." From that year until nearly his death in late 1963, at age fifty-nine, he wrote on a variety of topics, including coverage of the U-2 spy-plane incident, editorial endorsements during the Kennedy-Nixon presidential race, newspaper consolidation, and the New York newspaper strike.

For coverage of the U-2 spy-plane incident and the Kennedy-Nixon-race, two of the biggest events of the day, Liebling gave the press varying reviews. The former event took place during the final year of the Eisenhower administration. On May 1, 1960, the Soviets downed a US spy plane that had intruded over their airspace. Initially, US officials had assumed that both the high-flying U-2 plane and its pilot, Francis Gary Powers, were lost. On this basis, they falsely declared that, at the time of its downing, the plane had been conducting weather reconnaissance for the National Aeronautics and Space Administration (NASA). The cover-up appeared to be working, until, that is, the Soviets, led by Premier Nikita Khrushchev, revealed that both the pilot and parts of what was clearly a spy plane were in their possession.[44]

In "The Coast Recedes" (May 21, 1960), Liebling ridiculed some early press accounts for their credulousness. It was yet another instance, he believed, of the press's habit of "coasting"—that is, taking the US government at its word without further probing. Soviet news of the pilot and plane altered that stance, though, and soon the New York papers began doing their jobs and sifting through competing US claims and disinformation. Even the *Wall Street Journal*, a paper safely shielded from the "imputation of liberalism," Liebling wrote, had acquitted itself admirably in arguing that both the provocative act itself and the US dissembling afterward had dramatically weakened claims of American exceptionalism. Collectively, the papers' response was "not . . . a bad performance," though he exempted from his appraisal the city's two "impossible morning tabloids," the Hearst-owned *Journal American* and *Daily Mirror*.[45]

The press's coverage of the 1960 presidential election was more of a black eye. His central complaint, outlined in a column titled "The Big Decision" (October 29, 1960), was that the nation's one-party GOP papers, some 80 percent by his reckoning, including those in the Scripps-Howard chain, the Hearst papers, and the late Joseph Patterson's *New York Daily News*, were perpetuating what amounted to editorial fraud. In public, partisan newspapers pretended to withhold their endorsements until the last minute. In fact, their support of Republican candidates, in this instance the incumbent Richard M. Nixon, was typically a foregone conclusion (*Press*, 710). That 80 percent of the press consistently adopted a position at odds with 50 percent of the people was, Liebling thought, unhealthy for newspapers in any election year. The situation was especially harmful, though, for newspapers in *this* election year, when the industry was "meeting its greatest challenge as the medium through which the public gets its political information" (*Press*, 713).

That challenge was coming, of course, from television, which in total aired four debates between Nixon and his telegenic Democratic challenger, Massachusetts Senator John F. Kennedy. Kennedy's edge seemed most in evidence during the first debate, seen by an estimated 70 million people. Nixon took steps to improve both his appearance and performance in subsequent meetings, seen by somewhat fewer viewers, but many Americans had already made up their minds.[46] Though largely indifferent to television, Liebling recognized its power and the precedent the Kennedy-Nixon debates had set. From this point on, candidates could address the public directly rather than having their views run through the same partisan press filters. The only hope of regaining "public confidence," he cautioned, was for newspapers to become less predictable—"to work up some difference of opinion among themselves" (*Press*, 714).

In a somewhat earlier column, "Do You Belong in Journalism?" (May 14, 1960), Liebling offered one of his frankest assessments to date of the dangers posed by newspaper mergers and consolidation. The theme of the column was occasioned by the recent annual convention, in New York, of the American Newspaper Publishers Association. At past ANPA meetings, the publishers had pretended that either the phenomenon was not taking place or it signaled a healthy economic competition, assuring the survival of the fittest. At this year's meeting, however, there was not only an acknowledgment of the trend but an attempt by the group's outgoing president to explain the economic rationale undergirding it, namely the owners' desire to increase their operating efficiencies "through joint production plants" (*Press*, 705). Liebling regarded this explanation as so much publisher-speak, obfuscating as much as it made clear: if consolidation enhanced surviving newspapers' efficiencies—while also of course reducing their competition for advertising dollars—it also further limited news coverage. This last effect sent shudders up Liebling's reporter's spine.

By now, even papers in large cities like Chicago, Los Angeles, Philadelphia, and New York had been overtaken by the merger wave. In New York, for example, what had been a feast of riches in his youth was now down to just seven general-circulation dailies. By comparison, though, smaller cities and towns had been affected the most, with predictable consequences, as he saw it: "A city with one newspaper or with a morning and evening newspaper under one ownership is like a man with one eye, and often the eye is glass" (*Press*, 704–5.) And while it was encouraging that some monopoly owners were good journalistic stewards, it was nevertheless "not right that a citizen's access to news should be completely aleatory, depending on the character of the monopoly publisher in the city where he happens to live" (*Press*, 704–5, 707).

Liebling's final press columns were centered, in whole or part, on the New York newspaper strike, which ran for nearly four months, from December 8, 1962, to March 31, 1963. The precipitating event had been a simple wage dispute between the American Newspaper Guild and the *Daily News*. That dispute had now broadened to other papers and other issues, including the proposed automation of printing presses, which the New York Typographical Union had opposed. In "Offers and Demands" (January 26,

1963), the self-proclaimed lifelong "wage slave" offered a tepid endorsement of the union position. He also saw merit, though, in the conclusion, put forward by a judicial review panel, that any settlement would almost certainly require each of the disputing parties to yield ground.

There was another thing about the labor stoppage that troubled Liebling. Early on, publishers of some of the striking papers had put out a "replacement" publication, known as the New York *Standard*. It was a makeshift operation, to be sure, with a scratch staff pulled together from the non-striking members of existing staffs. The result was a paper with a modest news hole and all but a few of its tabloid pages filled with advertisements. Despite this, copies of the paper had been "gobbled up with gratitude by readers who had been reduced to a diet of out-of-town newspapers, supplemented by specialized organs like the *Wall Street Journal* and the *Journal of Commerce*," explained Liebling. The response struck him as ominous, a harbinger perhaps of a nightmarish time when the city's other dailies had collapsed and what remained were ad-filled tabloids masquerading as real newspapers.[47]

Two weeks after the New York City strike ended, Liebling's final press column appeared. In "Step by Step with Mr. Raskin" (April 13, 1963), Liebling took his usual delight in poking fun at newspapers' self-dealing, including their predictable post-strike "mass of how-glad-you-must-be-to-see-me-again-prose."[48] He was pleasantly surprised, though by a post-strike story in the *Times*. It presented readers, through detailed and expert reporting, an illuminating overview of the event. The reporter was A. H. Raskin, who covered labor issues at the paper and would soon go on to become the assistant editor of its editorial page. His report, some twenty-thousand words, not only provided a "tick-tock" of events—a detailed chronology of how things had unfolded—but an analysis of why such a widespread strike had occurred in the first place. It was that rare instance, Liebling felt, of the press willing to write about itself.

The strike's actual roots, Raskin wrote, went back to 1950, when the New York Newspaper Guild conducted a walkout against the *World-Telegram*. For seventy-three days, the Guild of reporters, copy editors, and other editorial workers had forced the paper to suspend publication, largely because other unions variously representing printers, pressmen, and other mechanical employees refused to cross their picket line. The new solidarity led to a Guild victory, but the city's publishers responded by forming a "united front" against future strikes. The upshot, as Ruskin explained, was "a bargaining system . . . under which a contract negotiated with one union fixed a pattern for all the unions and a strike called against one paper generated an employer-enforced blackout of all papers."[49] It was precisely this system that had given rise to the recent 114-day strike and city-wide news blackout.

Raskin's reporting, Liebling believed, had resisted the easy temptation to impute an unfair bargaining advantage to either labor or management. Refusing the role of PR agent for either party, the reporter had called it as he saw it, apparently with the blessing of his managing editor and even more remarkably his publisher, for which "the *Times* earns the highest marks."[50] The Ruskin piece had provided, in fact, "new evidence of what newspapers at their best are for—turning a first-class reporter lose on a story, giving him ample time to develop it, and then printing what he brings in." For all this, said Liebling, "I doff my bowler."[51]

These were his final words as a press critic.

CONCLUSION

The contemporary reader searching for a grand theme in Liebling's press criticism is bound to be disappointed. Certainly, he was politically liberal in both his sympathies and in many of his targets, including publishers, newspaper concentration, Red hunting, government censorship, infotainment, and the like. And there is at least some truth in a modern commentator's charge that Liebling's liberal bent caused him to underreport the Cold War and become too cozy with Hiss to be objective.[52]

Still, even those skeptical of Liebling because of the alleged taint of politics are forced to acknowledge that he could, when sufficiently motivated, also lampoon liberal shibboleths and publications. His willingness to take on the home team was of a piece, in fact, with his refusal to be doctrinaire, to become the kind of ideologue he had accused his fellow press critic George Seldes of being. It seems fair to say that Liebling's politics, such as they were, rarely interfered with the task at hand, which was to examine closely not only what reporters and editors reported but how they went about doing their jobs.[53]

This dual focus goes a long way to explaining why so much of his press criticism remains vital today, even after so many of the key issues and personalities have long since faded from memory. When Liebling ridicules the big news organizations for acquiescing to government terms and evasions at the end of World War II, we are reminded of similar journalistic missteps in the run-up to more recent wars. When he faults some of the papers of his day for their pretense of evenhandedness, we are compelled to think of contemporary news sources that purport to be "fair and balanced" but end up repeatedly championing the same side. And when he lampoons his colleagues' many abuses of language, we find it easy to cite similar examples today of voguish, clichéd, or imprecise journalistic usage.

Liebling's lasting appeal also has much to do with his unique stylistic zest and comic sensibility. Writing in delightfully digressive prose and a curious mélange of high and low diction—which incorporated at once Latin and French phrases, familiar and obscure historical allusions, and a New York–accented street patois—he brought the issues, newspapers, and personalities of his day to vivid, memorable life. Along the way, he coined a series of what have been called Lieblingisms—"Freedom of the press is guaranteed only to those who own one," "The press is the weak slat under the bed of democracy," "The function of the press in society is to inform, but its role in society is to make money." All these and others have served as epigrams for more than a few contemporary press critiques and essays.[54]

Finally, we continue to be drawn to Liebling today for the sheer delight he took in his own profession. It was one, of course, that often gave short shrift to self-reflection, as he often complained. In a review of a history of the *New York Daily News*, for example, he was clearheaded about the obstacles, noting with characteristic wit, "when a man writes a book about a newspaper where he is still employed, there are likely to be serious omissions."[55] It was also a profession that often reacted badly to criticism, especially if it came from within its own ranks, which Liebling also knew first hand.[56]

At the same time, because he loved newspapers and newspaper people, he took special pleasure in assigning them his stamp of approval if he thought they had acted courageously or done well. A. H. Raskin's indepth look at the city's newspaper strike for the *Times* was one example, but there were many others: Edward Kennedy's courage at the end of World War II, the sportswriters' sympathetic reporting of the racing world's lowest-paid workers, the *Herald Tribune*'s balanced coverage of the first Hiss trial, the press's refusal to accept the government line during the U-2 incident, and so on.

These, for Liebling, were instances of the press at its finest. At such rare but notable moments, it had showed itself to be not a feeble institution unable to serve democracy but the essential foundation for a free government of informed and engaged citizens.

NOTES

1. Raymond Sokolov, *Wayward Reporter: The Life of A. J. Liebling* (New York: Harper & Row, 1980), 13.

2. Ibid., 14–15. Liebling's interest in the less pampered side of life is reflected in such books as *Back Where I Came From* (1938), *The Telephone Booth Indian* (1942), and *The Sweet Science* (1956).

3. A. J. Liebling, *The Wayward Pressman* (1947; repr., Westport, CT: Greenwood Press, 1973), 16.

4. *Wayward Reporter*, quoted in, 18.

5. *Wayward Pressman*, 26

6. *Wayward Reporter*, quoted in, 9.

7. *Wayward Pressman*, 116.

8. A. J. Liebling, *The Press*, in *Liebling: The Sweet Science and Other Writings*, ed. Pete Hamill (New York: The Library of America, 2009), 702. All further references will be to this edition and cited parenthetically in the text.

9. Ibid., 742.

10. See, for example, Pete Hamill, interview by Rich Kelly, The Library of America e-Newsletter, March 2009, https://loa-shared.s3.amazonaws.com/static/pdf/Hamill_Interview_on_Liebling.pdf.

11. *Wayward Pressman*, 282.

12. Ibid., 54.

13. Ibid., 60.

14. To ensure his father did not change his mind, Liebling concocted a story about an "inappropriate" woman whom he was thinking of proposing to. *Wayward*, 62–63.

15. Ibid., 63.

16. See "Eleanor Slater Hospital," State of Rhode Island, Dept. of Behavioral Healthcare, Developmental Disabilities and Hospitals," accessed September 17, 2019, http://www.bhddh.ri.gov/esh/.

17. *Wayward Pressman,* 75–76.

18. In a chapter in *The Wayward Pressman* titled "My Name in Big Letters," Liebling described how he had attempted to attract the attention of Barrett with a sign reading "Hire Joe Liebling" (84–91).

19. *Wayward Reporter*, 86.

20. *Wayward Pressman*, 103.

21. See A. J. Liebling, *Back Where I Come From* (1938; repr., San Francisco: Greenpoint Press, 1990).

22. *Wayward Pressman*, 104, 110.

23. Ibid., 115.

24. *Wayward Reporter*, 104.

25. These pieces were collected in both *Back Where I Came From* and *The Telephone Booth Indian* (1942; repr., New York: Broadway Books, 2004).

26. See A. J. Liebling, *The Road Back to Paris* (1944; repr., New York: Modern Library, 1997).

27. *Wayward Pressman*, 117.

28. See Guy Fawkes (Robert Benchley), "The Wayward Press," *The New Yorker,* December 24, 1927, 23–24, *The New Yorker* Archives, http://archives.newyorker.com/?i=1927-12-24#folio=022.

29. *Wayward Pressman,* 118–119, 126.

30. Ibid., 118–120. Nearly seven decades later, the AP formally apologized for firing Edward Kennedy, who died in an automobile accident in 1963. See "AP Apologizes for Firing Reporter over World War II Surrender Scoop," Associated Press, *Telegram.com*, May 4, 2012, https://www.telegram.com/article/20120504/NEWS/120509725.

31. A. J. Liebling, *Mink and Red Herring* (1949; repr., Westport, CT: Greenwood Press, 1972), 60. All further references will be to this edition and cited parenthetically in the text.

32. In July, Liebling had gone to Reno, Nevada, in order to obtain a divorce from his first wife, Ann McGinn, whose psychiatric problems had continued throughout their marriage. His second wife was Harriet Lucille Hille, a former model.

33. According to prosecutors, the Woodstock Model 5, at one time owned by the Hisses, as the machine used by Priscilla Hiss, Alger's wife, to type manuscript pages intended for the Soviet Union. The pages became known as the "Baltimore Documents."

34. Among the many books and studies that grapple with the Hiss question and especially the role of media in keeping it alive, see Susan Jacoby, *Alger Hiss and the Battle for History* (New Haven: Yale University Press, 2009).

35. *Wayward Pressman*, 190.

36. Ibid., 191.

37. Ibid., 197.

38. According to Liebling, the trouble for Broun on the *World* started when he wrote an article for the *Nation* critical of the *World.* See A. J. Liebling, "The Wayward Press," *The New Yorker*, November 7, 1953, 107, *The New Yorker* Archives, http://archives.newyorker.com/?i=1953-11-07#folio=106.

39. Ibid., 110. The *New York Post* was bought by conservative Australian publisher Rupert Murdoch in November 1976.

40. A. J. Liebling, "The Wayward Press," *The New Yorker*, November 14, 1953, 89, *The New Yorker* Archives, http://archives.newyorker.com/?i=1953-11-14#folio=088.

41. A. J. Liebling, "The Wayward Press," *The New Yorker*, November 21, 1953, 197, *The New Yorker* Archives, http://archives.newyorker.com/?i=1953-11-21#folio=196.

42. Ibid.

43. A. J. Liebling, "The Wayward Press," *The New Yorker*, November 20, 1954, 184, *The New Yorker* Archives, http://archives.newyorker.com/?i=1954-11-20#folio=184.

44. "U-2 Spy Incident," History.com, updated August 21, 2018, https://www.history.com/topics/cold-war/u2-spy-incident.

45. A. J. Liebling, "The Wayward Press," *The New Yorker*, May 21, 1960, 129–30, *The New Yorker* Archives, http://archives.newyorker.com/?i=1960-05-21#folio=128.

46. See, for example, James N. Druckman, "The Power of Television Images: The First Kennedy-Nixon Debate Revisited," *The Journal of Politics*, vol. 65, no 2, 559–71, JSTOR, https://www.jstor.org/stable/10.1111/1468-2508.t01-1-00015?seq=1#page_scan_tab_contents.

47. A. J. Liebling, "The Wayward Press," *The New Yorker*, January 26, 1963, 110, *The New Yorker* Archives, http://archives.newyorker.com/?i=1963-01-26#folio=110.

48. A. J. Liebling, "The Wayward Press," *The New Yorker*, April 13, 1963, 144, *The New Yorker* Archives, http://archives.newyorker.com/?i=1963-04-13#folio=144.

49. Ibid.

50. Ibid.

51. Ibid., 152.

52. Jack Shafer, "The Church of Liebling," *Slate*, August 25, 2004, https://slate.com/news-and-politics/2004/08/worshipping-at-the-church-of-liebling.html.

53. Hamill, interview, 5.

54. Shafer, "Church."

55. A. J. Liebling, "On Looking into Chapman's *News*," *Columbia Journalism Review*, Fall 1961, *Columbia Journalism Review* Archives, https://archives.cjr.org/fiftieth_anniversary/on_looking_into_chapmans_news.php.

56. After he wrote "The Scribes of Destiny," for example, Liebling felt the "smoldering wrath" of his colleagues who had assembled in the office of Harry Markson, the press agent of the Twentieth Century Sporting Club (*Wayward Pressman*, 196).

Ben H. Bagdikian, on the *Washington Post* in the early 1970s
Source: Clark University

Chapter Four

Ben H. Bagdikian

Media for the People

Never forget that your obligation is to the people. It is not, at heart, to those who pay you, or to your editor, or to your sources, or to your friends, or to the advancement of your career. It is to the public.

—Ben Bagdikian, to his Berkeley journalism students

Ben Bagdikian was neither an American by birth nor a journalist by design. Born in Marash, southeastern Turkey, on January 30, 1920, during the second phase of what is now known as "the Armenian genocide," Ben-hur Haig Bagdikian came to America as a child under harrowing circumstances.[1] Once here, he was raised by his father and stepmother outside of Boston, eventually enrolling as a premed student in nearby Clark University. Despite his immigrant status and seeming indifference to journalism, he not only went on to play a key role in some of the most important American journalistic events of the second half of the twentieth century; he also became one of his generation's most important and outspoken media critics. His most famous book on the press, *The Media Monopoly* (1983), was released in seven editions over the years, the last a completely revised and updated edition published under the reinvigorated title, *The New Media Monopoly* (2004). It has become a classroom staple.

Bagdikian's career in journalism began by happenstance on the *Springfield Morning Union*. For six months, from the summer of 1941 until the Japanese attack on Pearl Harbor, he covered local news on the paper.[2] After a four-year stint in the US Army Air Forces and a brief turn on an aviation magazine, he returned to civilian life and, in 1947, joined the *Providence Journal*, the same paper on which Liebling had worked two decades earlier. He would remain on the paper for the next fourteen years, working as a reporter, Washington bureau chief, and foreign correspondent. In 1961, he turned to freelance writing, over the next several years contributing to the *Saturday Evening Post* and other publications.

Then, in 1970, he accepted an offer to become the assistant managing editor for national news at the *Washington Post*, where he and legendary executive editor Ben Bradlee helped to guide the paper through the tumultuous days of the Pentagon Papers. While still holding his editor's title, Bagdikian was appointed the *Post*'s first ombudsman, a role that eventually brought him into conflict with not only with the mercurial Bradlee but with publisher Katherine Graham. In August 1972, Bagdikian quit the *Post*, contributed for the next several years to the *Columbia Journalism Review* and other journals and magazines, and finally took up a friend's suggestion to join the faculty at the UC Berkeley Graduate School of Journalism, from which he retired as professor and dean emeritus in 1990.[3]

During his lifetime, Bagdikian wrote scores of articles on the press, along with two books of media criticism in addition to *The Media Monopoly*: *The Information Machines: The Impact on Men and the Media* (1971), based on his research at the Rand Corporation, a California-based nonprofit think tank, and *The Effete Conspiracy: And Other Crimes by the Press* (1972), a collection of his articles. But it is *The Media Monopoly*, a book that lays outs his view of the faults and promises of the media in American society, for which he will be best remembered. Candid, obsessively researched, and morally driven by the same impulse that drove his involvement in the Pentagon Papers and other journalistic forays, the study puts forth an argument that still speaks to the corrosive effects on democracy when what is read, seen, and heard by the many is controlled by the few.

A JOURNALIST BY CHANCE

Ben-hur was only eleven days old when his mother, father, and four sisters were suddenly uprooted from their Marash home. Fearful of being slaughtered by the advancing Turkish National Forces, the family, including a pair of servants, fled into the snow-covered Caucasus Mountains, enduring terrible hardships along the way. At one point, it was feared the newborn had succumbed to the freezing temperatures. But all eventually made it over the mountains, first to a French-controlled railroad station, and ultimately to Constantinople, now Istanbul, where family members, minus the servants, boarded a boat for New York.[4]

In the city, the family stayed with friends for a short time and then traveled north to Boston, a city with a substantial Armenian Congregationalist population. Ben-hur's parents—the former Dudeh "Daisy" Uvezian and Aram Toros "Theodore" Bagdikian, a onetime chemistry teacher—had hoped to settle in the Boston area and pursue a new life with their children among friends. Shortly after landing in America, though, Daisy had been diagnosed with tuberculosis. Over the next several years, she would require near-constant hospitalization, but her illness eventually proved fatal, as it often did in those days. Ben-hur was just three years old when his mother died, and a year later his father remarried. Theodore's new wife was also Armenian, but an especially difficult childhood had hardened her character. To Ben-hur's sisters, their stepmother was their biological mother's "opposite" in almost every way.[5]

The reconstituted Bagdikian family made their home in Stoneham, Massachusetts, about ten miles north of downtown Boston. In time, two more children, both boys, were born into the crowded household, which Theodore supported by working as a minister at several Congregationalist churches in the Boston area. (He had been ordained after taking courses at Harvard Theological Seminary.) Stoneham for the most part was a Yankee redoubt. By the time he was old enough to notice, Ben-hur felt that he and his family, and indeed the few other Armenian families in town, were regarded as "foreigners," although he still managed to make good friends. Despite being a "a pretty lazy student," in high school, he did well enough to hope against hope for a Harvard scholarship. In 1937, though, he accepted a first-year scholarship from Clark University, in Worcester, where his family had moved after his father became the pastor of the local Armenian church. Living at home, Ben Bagdikian, as he was now known, walked four miles each day to campus and back.[6]

His plan was to become a doctor, a decision partially inspired by his mother's illness and the pulmonary books his father had collected in his library. While his premed focus was on chemistry and lab courses, though, he also enrolled in one history and one English course. In the latter, he caught the attention of the starch-collared Professor Ames, who foresaw a different future for the premed student. "You could be a good writer," said Ames. Bagdikian politely thanked his teacher but reiterated his goal.

Still, in the area of extracurricular activities, Bagdikian soon made a couple of surprising choices for an aspiring doctor. For one, he joined the staff of the college newspaper, the *Clark News*, rising in time to become its editor and, in a controversial move, changing its name to "*The Scarlet*."[7] During this period, he also became the campus stringer for the local newspaper, the *Worcester Gazette*. Working at ten cents a word, he reported on the comings and goings of prominent students, faculty, and visiting faculty, making sure to pad his copy by inserting whenever possible the full middle names, degrees, and academic histories of his subjects. As his graduation approached, Bagdikian seemed to be having second thoughts about his chosen field. Not only had he skipped applying to Harvard Medical School, but he had also failed to consider any of the second-tier schools that might have actually admitted him.[8] His actions were partially a sign of professional ambivalence, not uncommon then as now in graduating undergraduate students. But his actions also indicated something more, namely that his real interest was increasingly trending elsewhere, to the idea of being a writer.

The change of heart would not obviate the need, of course, to make a living following graduation. And after four years at Clark, his one marketable skill, as he saw it, was chemistry. In Springfield the day after receiving his diploma, he entered the offices of Monsanto Laboratory, certain he was a shoo-in for a job as a chemist's lab assistant. His interview was delayed, though, and in the interim he wandered about the town, by chance spotting a building sign reading "Springfield Morning Union," at the time one of several local papers. Bagdikian later recalled what happened next: "So without thinking about it I walked in, [and] said, 'Do you need a reporter?' They said 'Yes,' and I never went back [for my Monsanto interview]."[9] Bagdikian's career in journalism had been officially launched.

THE RIGHT KIND OF PAPER

His months-long tenure covering local news on the *Morning Union* proved to be something of a training school, thanks to a demanding city editor who taught him his first "lessons in journalism."[10] After the

Japanese bombed Pearl Harbor on December 7, 1941, however, the not-yet-nationalized American citizen enlisted, serving as a navigator in the U.S. Army Air Forces, the forerunner of today's U.S. Air Force. Both his training and service were largely confined to the American South. In early August 1945, though, he was reassigned to Mather Field, in California, in anticipation of a predawn flight via Honolulu to Okinawa Island, the site not quite two months earlier of a fierce battle between the Allies and Japanese military forces. He and his fellow airmen had already been briefed about their air-sea rescue mission, but that mission never took place. New devices—so-called atomic bombs—had been dropped over the Japanese cities of Hiroshima and Nagasaki. "With the two cities wiped out, the Japanese were suing for peace," Bagdikian would later recall in his memoir, *Double Vision.*[11]

His thoughts now turned to the future. His wife and one-year-old baby were back East—shortly after enlisting, he had married Elizabeth "Betty" Ogasapian, originally from Worcester—and the *Springfield Morning Union* had already sent a letter saying that his old job was available for the asking. He still saw his future as a newspaperman, but his experience had taught him "the kind of paper made a difference."[12] Refusing the job offer, he mustered out of the service, returned East to New York, took what he might well have regarded as a transitional job as assistant editor of a new air travel magazine, and started house hunting. His plan was to relocate his wife and child, now living in Providence, Rhode Island, to New York. His experience on the aviation magazine eventually soured, though, and he quit. He then joined his family in Providence, where the *Providence Journal* just happened to be looking for a labor reporter. "Well, I've covered labor but not as a specialty," Bagdikian told his interviewers, who were nevertheless sufficiently impressed by the returning veteran to extend a job offer.[13]

The *Providence Journal* turned out to be the right kind of paper, at least mostly.[14] Working for both the morning and evening editions, he covered not only labor-related stories but others as well. Soon, he became the paper's go-to reporter for certain special series, those multi-part reports on a single subject. One of his earliest was a critical analysis of the major news magazines of the period, including *Time* and *Newsweek*, which he found placed a greater premium on entertainment than straight news coverage. He was just as interested in the less glamorous police-court beat, in large part because it offered him a window on "that part of the population that you usually don't see," which is to say the subterranean world of people arrested for loitering, public drunkenness, petty thievery, prostitution, and the like.[15]

There were other journalistic adventures on the *Journal* as well. In 1953, he was part of a combined morning-evening team that won the Pulitzer Prize for Local Reporting. Pooling its work and on-the-ground sources, the team tracked in nearly real time a group of bank robbers as it was being pursued by the police through several states. "By our final edition of the afternoon, they had been caught," Bagdikian remembered years later, "and we covered every single place they had been and what happened."[16] In 1955, he reported on the unintended consequences of President Truman's executive order mandating loyalty oaths for federal employees, a step seen by some scholars today as an effort in part to quell GOP allegations of Democratic squishiness on communism.[17] And in 1957, after returning from a yearlong stint in Europe, during which he served as the paper's foreign correspondent, he wrote a series with *Journal* reporter James Rhea, a Black American, about the state of race relations in the South in the wake of the Supreme Court order to deseg-regate public schools.[18]

In 1961, his *Journal* bosses invited Bagdikian to head up the paper's Washington Bureau. The new post was a nice addition to his lengthening résumé, although as bureau chief he oversaw only two reporters. Still, with the Kennedy administration newly arrived on the scene, it was an exciting time to be in Washington. Besides, he had already covered the presidential campaign for the paper, doing his best to confirm rumors that Kennedy suffered from chronic back pain so severe that it could interrupt or even jeopardize his presidency. Bagdikian had not been able to confirm the rumor, but now, after the election, there was another rumor circulating around town about the photogenic and famously married young president: in the noontime White House on many days, he was being visited by a series of young and somewhat older women. The press corps was well aware of the rumor—as were many other Washington insiders. And yet, as Bagdikian later recalled, not much reporting energy was expended on "the President's private life if the President didn't want it." The silence of the largely male press corps on such matters reflected the norms of the day, of course. But even if some enterprising reporters had directed their time and energy to uncovering the truth behind the rumor, they would have had a hard time getting their story published in a mainstream news outlet. "Publishers probably would hesitate to print them, except for very hostile publishers," Bagdikian would later point out.[19]

ADVOCATE FOR SOCIAL JUSTICE

His tenure as the *Journal*'s Washington bureau chief was relatively short-lived. By the end of 1961, he had been awarded a John Simon Guggenheim Fellowship, which for the next year offered him income sufficient to exit daily journalism and expand an article on poverty he had written earlier for the *Saturday Evening Post*. The book that resulted, *In the Midst of Plenty: The Poor in America* (1964), was in many ways a companion to Michael Harrington's influential work, *The Other America: Poverty in America* (1962).[20] Like this earlier study, Bagdikian's book was an examination, both scholarly and reportorial, of the "invisible" poor who had been left behind during the nation's postwar economic boom. "Most of the poor are caught up in a vast convulsion in the human landscape of the United States," he wrote in the opening chapter, "a change that reflects brilliant prosperity with deep shadows of persisting poverty."[21] In contrast to Harrington, though, Bagdikian did not consider himself a socialist or, for that matter, a "radical" of any kind. He "was not so much a radical as an advocate for social justice," as he later described, a reporter with a liberal bent whose self-described job was to "make people feel what it's like to be in the disadvantaged part of the society."[22] Meanwhile, Bagdikian had also launched what turned out to be a successful if relatively short-lived free-lance writing career. On the advice of a friend, he signed a contract with the *Saturday Evening Post*, which would soon switch from a weekly to a biweekly general interest magazine.[23] Bagdikian appreciated the reporting freedom and time the *Post* granted to him. A self-described "bottom-up" reporter, he was especially keen to know how policies adopted at the top of society affected those at the lower ranks. He wanted, in short, to place himself in the company of, and tell stories about, "the population affected," such as southern blacks now migrating on trains and buses to the north.[24]

He now also contributed to other publications, including the recently established *Columbia Journalism Review*, for which he wrote a regular

column, "Letter from Washington," and a series of media-oriented features. In "The Gentle Suppression" (Spring 1965), for example, he bemoaned the censoring of news likely to offend the public, such as protests
by George Lincoln Rockwell and the American Nazi Party. In a latter
Journalism Review (Spring 1967), he voiced his concern over news operations more and more becoming the "appendages to conventional businesses," a topic he would revisit later in his career. Besides the *Journalism
Review*, he also wrote for the *New York Times Magazine*, at this point
offering more of a subject-oriented summary of the past week's news than
original long-form journalism; the *New Republic*; the *Nation*; *Esquire*;
and *Harper's Magazine*. For the March 1967 issue of *Esquire*, for example, he listed the ills currently besetting the American press, including
its seeming indifference to its growing "monopoly status," a subject he
would also return to later in his career. A selection of his media-oriented
pieces was collected in his 1972 book, *The Effete Conspiracy: And Other
Crimes by the Press.*[25]

THE NEW "REALITY" MACHINES

In 1969, Bagdikian moved with his wife and youngest son (his older son
was now employed in Washington) to Pacific Palisades, in California. The
move west at the invitation of another friend, who had invited Bagdikian
to become a researcher at the Rand Corporation, headquartered in nearby
Santa Monica. Established in 1948 by Douglas Aircraft Company to provide research and analysis to the US armed forces, the think tank over the
years had broadened its mission to include a wide array of clients and research projects.[26] As a result, Rand had recruited a staff of highly regarded
technical analysts and scientists, including several Nobel Prize winners. It
was comparatively light on "generalists," however, and Bagdikian's appointment was a small step in righting that imbalance.

His appointment made sense in another way too: he already had a project in mind when he set out for the West Coast. His research would focus
in part on the technologies, the "information machines," as he called them,
that were likely to "change the way the next generation receives it news."[27]
Some of these technologies—microphotographs, the television, radio—
were already well-established by the time he began his work. Others—like

the facsimile machine, the integrated circuit, microprocessors, and other electronic components of computers we now take for granted—were either relatively new or still on the near horizon. Working partially on the cutting edge, he knew his technological projections would require a degree of speculation, as well as a healthy dose of humility.

His research would focus, though, not only on the new technology itself, as interesting as that was, but on how it was likely to reshape information delivery, including news delivery. How would news be reported in the future? Who would do the reporting? What kind of news and other information would people read, see, and hear? The answers to these questions would depend, Bagdikian strongly suspected, on the eventual ownership, organization, and deployment of the new technologies. In the United States at least, that future seemed more predictable than in other countries, since news here was already a rather firmly planted commercial institution that needed to turn a profit to survive.

In *The Information Machines: Their Impact on Men and the Media* (1971), the book that resulted from his Rand research, Bagdikian described this likely future in more detail. His main argument was that the existing corporate news structure would employ the new technologies not in the service of a better informed and enlightened public but to deliver the kind of news designed to turn steadier and bigger profits. As he saw it, the norm would become quicker, slicker, glossier news, on the one hand, and what he called "parlor entertainment" in the case of television, on the other hand. Moreover, by efficiently consolidating and controlling the "instruments of communication," corporate news and entertainment interests would more and more harness the ability to define "reality itself."[28]

His cautionary message was similar, of course, to one that George Seldes and A. J. Liebling had delivered in a less technologically advanced age. And one that media critic Neil Postman, among others, would put forth in the future. For now, though, it was Ben Bagdikian who defined most clearly what the newer information technologies held in store for public opinion and democracy, as then FCC head Nicholas Johnson commented in a complimentary review of the just-published book in the *New York Times*.[29] A little over a decade later, Bagdikian would expand on the thesis of *The Information Machines* in his most famous book, *The Media Monopoly*.

THE *POST* AND THE PENTAGON PAPERS

As his two-year tenure at Rand was ending, Bagdikian received a call from Katharine Graham, the owner and publisher of the *Washington Post*, inviting him to lunch at the Beverly Hilton, the legendary LA hotel. The other guest that day would be *Post* company official Paul Ignatius, a former secretary of the navy and like Bagdikian the son of Armenian parents who immigrated to the United States. Both Graham and Ignatius knew the journalist and author by reputation. And each had also read his commentary on their paper in the *Columbia Journalism Review*. The upshot of that commentary was simple: as good as it was, the *Post* could be made better.

Was Bagdikian up for the challenge of making it better? Graham and Ignatius were eager to find out, and so, as it happened, was the paper's executive editor, Ben Bradlee, who saw the paper competing head-to-head with all comers, especially the *New York Times*. The specific job the *Post* higher-ups had in mind for Bagdikian was assistant managing editor for national news, the most important position on the masthead below editor and the position that the former person in it had allegedly mishandled by demoralizing his staff. Bagdikian liked being a reporter, but he was eager to take up the challenge that Graham, Ignatius, and Bradlee had laid down for him, as long as he could name his own deputy assistant managing editor. His condition was agreed to, and, in early 1970, he and his family moved back to the nation's capital. He was ready to assist the paper's rise into the major leagues.[30]

The job proved more difficult than he had anticipated, in part because of what some staffers termed the "snake pit"-like atmosphere of the *Post*'s newsroom. Aided by his handpicked assistant, though, he managed to restore morale and a semblance of calm. And not a minute too soon, as it turned out. Before long, not only the new assistant managing editor but the entire *Post* staff would be at the crucial center of a high-stakes drama, one that would go a long way to securing the recognition its owner and top editors sought.

The *Post*'s decision to publish a series of articles based on the "Pentagon Papers" is generally known, thanks in many ways to the collection of articles, books, movies, and TV dramas depicting the episode.[31] The bare-bones narrative of that episode is not complicated: in 1967, then Secretary of Defense Robert McNamara tasked analysts at the Rand Corporation to put together a secret history of the Vietnam War from 1945 to 1967. Among those analysts was Daniel Ellsberg, a brilliant if intense economist and former Pentagon special assistant whom Bagdikian had come to know while at Rand. What Ellsberg learned in the course of his research convinced him that Vietnam was not a civil war but a war of foreign aggression, first French-led and then American-led. His research led him to the further belief that continued American involvement was both futile and wrong.

By fall 1969, the analyst had become an activist. Using a rented copy machine while still in California and assisted by a colleague, Ellsberg began reproducing several sets of the nearly 7,500-page secret report. After this, he resigned from Rand, headed east, and started a position at MIT's Center for International Studies, in Cambridge. Here, he attempted to share his photocopied materials not only with select scholars but with leading congressional opponents of the war, in the hopes they would use their senatorial immunity to read portions of the document into the congressional record on the Senate floor. When that tactic seemed to stall, Ellsberg contacted Neil Sheehan, the well-respected Pentagon reporter of the *New York Times*. On June 13, 1971, Sheehan wrote the first of what was supposed to be a nine-part series on the secret cache of documents.[32]

The Nixon administration reacted. Making a dash to federal court in New York, it won an order temporarily restraining the *Times* from publishing any further excerpts of the Pentagon Papers or commentaries about it. With the *Times* now under a gag order, Ellsberg turned to his old friend Ben Bagdikian, who not only shared the former analyst's anti-war views but was high enough on the *Post*'s masthead to be influential. A series of elaborate cloak and dagger maneuvers followed, inspired by Ellsberg's growing paranoia, and Bagdikian eventually came into possession of the documents, which he warily handed over to his bosses.[33]

The hand-over caused as much consternation as delight on the *Post*. Eager to protect corporate interests while sensitive third-party negotiations were going on, the parent company's lawyers argued for a middle ground: why not make a symbolic statement in the paper and then battle "the right to publish through the courts"? they proposed. Bagdikian was having none of it. "No . . . the way to assert the right to publish is to publish, he responded to one of the lead lawyers."[34] Publisher Graham would have the final say, of course, and in the end, she sided with her editors. And while the *Post* soon faced its own Nixon gag order, this time in an appeal joined by both the *Times* and *Post*, the US Supreme Court ruled 6–3 that the government's "prior restraint" was an unconstitutional violation of the first amendment right to a free press.[35]

The high court decision permitted both papers to resume publishing. For the *Post*, though, it meant something more: it confirmed for ownership and top management that, with no mean courage, they had asserted their right to publish and that right had prevailed. The episode had marked the start of a new era at the paper, as Bradlee would later recall in his memoir: "After the Pentagon Papers, there would be no decision too difficult for us to overcome together."[36] Up ahead, certainly, there was still a difficult period of labor-management tension at the *Post*, which Bagdikian knew well.[37] But Bradlee's evaluation was not wrong. In 1972, the *Post* lost the Pulitzer Prize for Public Service to the *Times*, but the following year it won the prize for its investigation of the Watergate scandal, which like the Pentagon Papers went on to become the stuff of legend.[38]

EXPOSING THE MEDIA MONOPOLY

By this point, Bagdikian had left the *Washington Post*. (He had also divorced Elizabeth and married fellow journalist Betty Medsger.) His departure from the *Post* was perhaps inevitable after he was appointed to the new role of newspaper ombudsman, a job he had championed for years before joining the paper. In many ways, the position (held simultaneously with his editor's title) was perfectly suited to his critical temperament. But what Bagdikian saw as problems—the status of Black employees in the newsroom, ownership's attitude toward unionization, the advantage that larger papers like the *Post* held over smaller papers—were not seen the same way by Graham or higher management. After less than a year, Bagdikian was as unhappy with his bosses as they were with him. They reached a mutual decision, each side "feeling that it was time for me to leave."[39]

He was suddenly without a full-time job, although not without opportunities. There was, for one, his freelance work, including his recent appointment as national correspondent for the *Columbia Journalism Review*. There was also his seat on the board of trustees of Clark University, a seat he had held since 1967, and his new position as project director of the "Newspaper Survival Study," sponsored by the Markle Foundation, a private nonprofit focused on examining "the potential for information technology to address previously intractable public problems."[40] Much of the research on a book about the American prison system had also been completed by this point. The book was inspired by one of his *Post* series, and he was now ready to head back to California, accompanied by his new wife, to begin writing it up.[41] Once out west again, he also planned to follow up on a friend's introduction to the dean of the Berkeley Graduate School of Journalism, part of the University of California. The introduction resulted in an invitation to teach a summer course, "Mass Media in America," and then to join the journalism faculty.[42]

In the early 1980s, he began work on his most important book of media criticism, *The Media Monopoly*, which would establish him as one of the era's most famous and controversial press commentators. A seminal idea for the study was Bagdikian's observation, later recalled, that many of the "best papers were being bought up by the chains and then getting cheaper and cheaper in content"—that is, delivering less news and more ads.[43] His fears of consolidation square with the historical data: in 1900, independent owners, or publishers operating a single newspaper, controlled 90 percent of daily newspaper circulation. By the early 1980s, when Bagdikian began his research, that percentage had dipped to approximately 25 percent, with a corresponding rise in the percentage of daily circulation now under the control of publishers with two or more dailies.[44]

The consolidation trend was also reflected over time within individual markets. In the 1920s, for example, there were five hundred US cities that had two or more daily newspapers, each competing for local advertising revenue. During the Great Depression, when so many advertisers folded, this competition became even fiercer, driving many smaller papers out of business and leaving many of the surviving ones to be acquired by group publishers. As a result, by the early 1980s, the number of metropolitan areas with two or more papers had declined sharply, to roughly thirty cities. The Gannett Company during this period was among the biggest consolidators, completing "60 daily newspaper transactions between 1945 and 1980." In *The Media Monopoly*, Bagdikian devoted a whole chapter to the chain and what he derided as its self-mythologizing, including its tendency to promise local papers independence while actually requiring acquired papers to toe the corporate line.

Another powerhouse at this point was Knight Newspapers. In 1974, the chain merged with Ridder Publications, so that by 1978 the combined Knight-Ridder company was the largest newspaper group in the United States before being overtaken by Gannett.[45]

Bagdikian focused much of his attention on newspaper consolidation, a subject he had followed over the years and knew well. He could not ignore, though, what he regarded as similar market trends affecting the broadcast media, specifically radio and television. Certainly, consolidation in this industry had been less freewheeling to date than in the newspaper industry, thanks in large part to a series of policies and rules laid down over the years by the Federal Communications Commission (FCC), the independent government agency overseeing radio, television, and related media. As part of its efforts in the 1940s to promote media pluralism, for instance, the FCC had adopted rules that limited the number of local radio or television stations a single broadcasting company could own. (By the 1980s, that number had risen to seven.) Over time, the agency had also adopted other rules, including one limiting cross-ownership of local radio and television stations, one limiting cross-ownership of newspapers and television, and one capping the number of national broadcast networks a single company could own.[46]

Despite these regulatory efforts, Bagdikian saw that much of the contemporary broadcast audience was monopolized by relatively few media corporations, the result of strategic purchases in the largest and most viewer-rich local markets. In television at the national level, moreover, three networks—ABC, CBS, and NBC—dominated the American viewing audience. (Cable TV's subscription model was also steadily gaining market share during this period.) Radio presented a similar picture. Along with perhaps seven additional companies, including Gannett, the TV giants of the period also held sway over more than "half the audience for AM and FM commercial radio."[47]

The upshot of this trend toward newspaper and broadcast concentration—to say nothing of consolidation in the magazine and book publishing industries—had been to place much of what Americans read, saw, and heard into fewer and fewer hands. How many hands? As of the time of his book, Bagdikian concluded that just fifty giant corporations controlled "the majority of all major American media" (*Monopoly*, xv). Such control was clearly not, he believed, in the American spirit, as historian Richard Hofstadter had made clear some two decades earlier in his essay and subsequent book, *The Paranoid Style in American Politics*.[48] In specific terms, America's media monopoly had jeopardized the free and open flow of information and ideas, the sine qua non of a pluralistic democracy. It had also, through its reliance on mass advertising to turn an ever-bigger profit, shaped the form and content of the nation's news and entertainment (*Monopoly*, xviii). In his book, Bagdikian set out to explore each of these topics.

MONOPOLY AND PLURALISM

In a series of chapters collectively titled "The Private Ministry of Information," he focused on issue one, the current political situation. The echo here to the Soviet Union's propaganda agency was clearly intentional: through it, Bagdikian wanted to suggest an analogy between authoritarian and corporate control of information: "If the same control over public ideas is exercised by a private entrepreneur, the effect of a corporate line is not so different from that of a party line" (*Monopoly*, 37). This raised the following question: did America in the early 1980s actually have a *private* ministry of information? Bagdikian feared it was very much trending in that direction.

He offered several recent examples, drawn from a variety of media industries, to make his case. One involved a proposed book on the snakebitten Ford Pinto by then forty-year-old investigative journalist Mark Dowie, the author of a 1977 piece for *Mother Jones* titled "Pinto Madness."[49] In that article, Dowie had laid out the dangers posed by the design of the subcompact's fuel tanks, which were prone to catching fire in rear-end collisions and rollovers, despite some preproduction tinkering in 1971. In 1973, following a number of fire-related deaths, the Ford Motor Company was forced to weigh the legal, financial, and societal costs of doing nothing compared with the cost of issuing a recall and fixing the Pinto's design flaws, a step it finally undertook in 1978. Perhaps unfairly, Dowie's article had played up the mercenary motive at the heart of the company's cost-benefit analysis. Now, in his book, he intended to expand on this theme, citing historical examples of similar corporate decision making. His proposed title, "Corporate Murder," was not intended to be subtle.[50]

The project had aroused the interest of New York–based publisher Simon & Schuster and one of its star editors, Nan Talese, the wife of well-known literary journalist, Gay Talese. The editor thought the book was important and would sell well, but she seemed concerned when Dowie mentioned his proposed title: was Gulf + Western one of the corporations mentioned in the book? she asked. Her question was not an idle one, since only a few years before the American conglomerate had acquired the publishing house that now employed her. When Dowie assured her that his manuscript did not mention Gulf + Western, Talese seemed relieved, assuring him in turn that the title would pass muster with her corporate bosses.

She was wrong: among other things, Simon & Schuster president Richard Snyder thought the proposed book gave all corporations, and not just the ones profiled, a black eye. For Bagdikian, the moral of the episode was clear: "If Simon & Schuster had been an independent book company, as it once was, Talese would not have asked an author the question she asked Dowie. It is also possible that Dowie's manuscript would now be available to the public, which, as of 1982, it was not" (*Monopoly*, 32).[51]

Most corporate interference was not this blunt, Bagdikian acknowledged. In fact, it was often the case that wary employees learned to police themselves, thereby obviating the need for higher-ups to intrude. If such employees were hesitant to fess up to their self-censorship, that was certainly understandable, although that reluctance tended to mask the degree to which certain information did *not* get written, or broadcast, or published. Nevertheless, it was still possible, Bagdikian believed, to shed light on the secret suppression of news. Among other things, he cited a contemporary survey by the American Society of Newspaper Editors that found that "33 percent of all editors working for newspaper chains said they would not feel free to run a news story that was damaging to their parent firm" (*Monopoly*, 32). That such omissions would go unnoticed by most Americans was hardly surprising. Like the Holmesian dog that did not bark, underreported or suppressed news rarely was missed unless someone called attention to it.

MONOPOLY AND THE ADVERTISING EFFECT

Media consolidation had also led to mass advertising, and that in turn had tended to dictate both the form and the content of what the public read, heard, and saw. For readers, the consequences of this relationship were manifold, Bagdikian believed. One especially pernicious effect was that, as mass advertising and mass media became cozier, the latter had become more attuned to advertiser needs than to audience needs. And because advertisers' primary need was to create a "buying mood" in as big an audience as possible, fluff, not hard news had become the order of the day. As Bagdikian saw it, the former editor of the *London Sunday Times*, Harold Evans, had had it right when he quipped that the challenge of American newspapers "is not to stay in business—it is to stay in journalism" (*Monopoly*, 139).

The challenge was not limited to newspapers. America's magazines were similarly attuned to their commercial advertisers and had been for a time, since magazines had preceded newspapers as the platforms of choice for national advertisers. In fact, for many years legacy publications like *Collier*'s, the *Saturday Evening Post, Munsey's Magazine, Mc-Clure's,* and *Liberty Magazine* were the only national ad media around. Magazines offered other advantages for mass advertisers too: they were graphically more appealing than newspapers, and after 1900 the largest of them were printed in four-color; they were subscription-based, offering a more or less stable readership; and, unlike newspapers, they "remained in households for extended exposure," as Bagdikian noted (133). Later, large corporate-owned magazines—including Hearst's *Life*, started in 1936, and *Look*, begun the following year by Cowles Media—permitted big advertisers even wider circulations, sometimes in the many millions.[52]

As magazine advertising expanded, so too did the pressure on editors and publishers to keep advertiser priorities top of mind. The accommodations were seemingly minor at first, Bagdikian noted. Ads that had once been exiled to the "back of the book" so as not to distract from the editorial content, for example, were soon intermingled with the pages of content toward the front. Eventually, some of these ads ran opposite the opening pages of major articles. From here, it was just a small step for editors to select "articles not only on the basis of expected interest for readers but for their influence on advertisements" (*Monopoly*, 140). As in the case of newspapers, softer features offered better support for fantasy-based ads than did more serious articles. The final step in this evolution, at least for the time, was the development of so-called special-interest magazines—publications aimed at a specific audience (mothers, hunters, audiophiles, coin collectors, auto enthusiasts, doctors) and sold to advertisers trying to target that audience. Even such special-interest or trade magazines, of course, had to pay some attention to their readers, since subscribers also contributed to the parent company's bottom line, albeit far less so than did advertisers. In the main, though, it was advertisers' needs that prevailed.

In contrast to the subscription model of magazines and newspapers, the broadcast industry of the time seemed to offer its content free of charge. The "free lunch" idea was a myth, however, as Bagdikian took pains to show. On the one hand, TV and radio broadcasters bombarded their consumers with all manner of pricey advertisements, the cost of which was "added to the cost of the products [and services] advertised." On the other hand, because the larger radio and TV outlets were mass media, they could charge their advertisers mass advertising rates, which not only made the commercial broadcast industry uniquely profitable but placed enormous power in the hands of their advertisers. If anything, these radio and TV advertisers wielded that power even more bluntly than they did when advertising in magazines and newspapers (*Monopoly*, 150).

In the case of radio, the advertising juggernaut developed gradually. Initially, as Bagdikian pointed out, "[t]he most popular stations were noncommercial, operated by universities, states, municipalities, and school districts" (*Monopoly*, 140). Less popular commercial stations were run, meanwhile, by a private cartel named the "Radio Corporation of America" (RCA), the members of which would share variously in both manufacturing radios and other equipment and stimulating their sales on member stations. It was a neat arrangement, and even the noncommercial stations at the time played an unwitting role in it, since their popular programs also served to boost radio sales. Eventually, though, the commercial owners came to see how much additional revenue could be generated by selling their airtime to advertisers. No longer willing now to split audience share with their noncommercial counterparts, these for-profit stations exercised their collective legal and lobbying clout to squeeze the educational and other broadcasters to the lower radio-dial frequencies, thereby diminishing their audiences. "By the 1930s, radio made all its money from advertising and created its programs to support advertising," observed Bagdikian (*Monopoly*, 141–42).

Examples are easy to come up with. They included the many programs that carried their sponsors names in their very titles: "The A&P Gypsies" (1924–1936), "Camel Caravan" (1933–1954), "The Bing Crosby

Show for Chesterfield" (1949–1952). There were also myriad radio programs—"The Adventures of Sherlock Holmes" (1930–1935), "The Air Adventures of Jimmie Allen" (1933–1937), and "Five Star Theater" (1932–1933)—that hid their single sponsors.[53] The producers of such shows quickly learned what lines they could and could not cross with advertisers, although at times the drama in the studio and back offices rivaled what was happening on the air. One of many movies centered around such drama was the post–World War II satire starring Clark Gable, Deborah Kerr, and Sydney Greenstreet, *The Hucksters* (1947).[54]

Television also had its so-called golden age. According to Bagdikian, it was the time after World War II when "whole programs were produced and controlled by single advertisers" (*Monopoly*, 142). As with radio, many of these early shows offered popular content targeted to a mainstream audience. But some of the most celebrated shows—"Kraft Television Theater," "Philco Television Playhouse," and "Westinghouse Studio One"—produced original, live dramas by such well-respected authors as Paddy Chayefsky, Horton Foote, Ben Hecht, Rod Serling, and Gore Vidal. The single-sponsor model had its financial drawbacks, though, and producers and networks soon discovered they could generate more money per TV-hour from multiple sponsors instead of just one. And so out went single-sponsorship and in came the "spot ads," commercials of whatever duration paid for by the various sponsors of the same program. The switch also had an effect on content, Bagdikian believed: In place of "emotionally involving" programs by authors like Chayefsky, networks now favored programs that put viewers in a lighthearted mood that both left them receptive to sponsor messages and encouraged buying (*Monopoly*, 143). And as single-sponsor shows were being shown the exit, shows aimed at a popular audience brought in to replace them included "The Adventures of Ozzie and Harriet" (1952–1966), "Bonanza" (1959–1973), "Dragnet" (1952–1970), "Gunsmoke" (1955–1975), "I Love Lucy" (1951–1957), "Leave It To Beaver" (1957–1963), "Make Room for Daddy" (1953–1964), "The Many Loves of Dobie Gillis" (1959–1963), and "Rawhide" (1959–1965).[55]

MASS ADVERTISING'S PRO-BUSINESS LINE

In many ways, of course, Bagdikian's critique of the corrosive effects of commercialism was not new. Critics since the nineteenth century had been hurling similar charges. Of even more concern to him, though, was that monopoly media in America had become so focused on profits and the strategies to augment them that they had turned conservative, eager to preserve the status quo. As a result, on the one hand, "pro-corporate ideas" had been permitted to infiltrate news and entertainment. On the other hand, and perhaps posing the greater danger, any systematic criticism of "contemporary enterprise" had become vanishingly rare, "almost as complete [a taboo] . . . in the United States as criticism of communism is explicitly forbidden in the Soviet Union" (*Monopoly*, 157).

Bagdikian offered several case studies to illustrate his point. These ranged from Procter & Gamble's insistence that its sponsored television programs portray business people positively, or at least in ways that framed "villains" as outliers; to the early directives of companies like Brown & Williamson, the manufacturer of such well-known cigarette brands as Kool, Lucky Strike, Pall Mall, and Tareyton that their products not "be used as a prop to depict an undesirable character"; to the tacit understanding between special-interest magazine publishers and their advertisers that the latter's interests would be treated sympathetically.[56] In the case of cigarette manufacturers, for example, Bagdikian saw that the injunctions had gone well beyond depicting cigarettes in a bad light. There were also the very real threats against media that too aggressively pursued the link between smoking and cancer. As a result, coverage tended to be cautious, consistently offering the industry the chance to tell its side of the story (*Monopoly*, 172). Even the august *New York Times* was not immune to such pressure, Bagdikian claimed. And neither some fifteen years after the publication of *The Media Monopoly* was CBS News, which delayed its full interview with a Brown & Williamson whistleblower until it was shamed into doing so.[57]

REFORMING THE SYSTEM

The current media system needed to be reformed, Bagdikian argued in a final chapter. It needed to be made more responsive to the expressed needs of the people, not by eliminating private ownership, since this was not the core problem, nor by ensuring that such ownership was less consolidated. And in this new atmosphere, a greater pluralism would flourish, as smaller entrepreneurs and entities entered market and introduced "fresh personalities and perspectives" (*Monopoly*, 230).

This was an idealistic scenario, certainly, fraught with practical problems. One of the biggest obstacles, as he saw it, was the inherent paradox of any media reform, namely the very sources the public counted on for information were the least reliable when their own power was at stake. "In the past," he argued, "media corporations have not treated issues that hurt them with fairness and fullness," an observation that A. J. Liebling had made earlier (*Monopoly*, 231). And even if this formidable hurdle could somehow be overcome, the reforms enacted during one administration tended to be modified or rescinded altogether if an administration with a different outlook succeeded it.

Still, Bagdikian did not despair. He set out a series of possible reforms, some geared specifically to the media, others addressing more general societal inequities. Among the former category, he was in favor, for example, of capping the number of newspapers a single chain or entrepreneur could legally acquire. Once that cap was hit, the potential buyer would be banned from acquiring "existing newspapers but would be free to *create* new ones," thereby reducing consolidation while preserving constitutional principles enshrined in the First Amendment (*Monopoly*, 229). In the case of magazines and book publishers, he offered a roughly similar formula, although with qualifications that addressed the unique circumstances of each industry. And for the broadcasting industry, he proposed further restrictions on those who wished to enter local markets; on cross-ownership of different media platforms; and on corporate control of what in the early 1980s he termed "new media," including cable satellite, pay television, computer-connected television screens, and the like. Beyond these fixes, he also hoped to see levied a progressive tax on advertising; a lower postal-rate structure for non-ad-dependent publications; a greater staff input in the election of editors, producers, and directors; and finally, a fuller disclosure of big media's major outside financial interests.

Media reform also required, he believed, "a reordering of economic power" generally (*Monopoly,* 233). A small "d" democrat to his bones, he was not calling for a Marxist-style revolution but rather a public debate, informed by "smaller voices at the margins of power," that addressed how to bring economic disparities more into line. Among other things, he championed stronger antitrust laws; higher corporate tax policies, which in the 1980s had been set at 46 percent; and restrictions on large, single-entity campaign contributions. As with the media reforms he set out, he knew that such broader changes would not be enacted easily, given the tendency of those in power to try to hold on to it. Still, he maintained a Jamesian optimism in the "civic genius of the people" to fashion a better, more equitable society and media (*Monopoly*, 239).

THE MEDIA CRITIC AND HIS CRITICS

The Media Monopoly was initially turned down by fourteen publishers, including Simon & Schuster. Eventually, it was accepted by Beacon Press, founded in 1845 by the American Unitarian Association, of which Bagdikian was a member. After the book's 1983 release, some mainstream reviewers were appreciative of its scope and boldness but critical of its methodology and major conclusions. Other, more progressive reviewers found a lot to like in what the author had concluded.

Writing in the *New York Times*, American political scientist Andrew Hacker presented a fair summary of *Monopoly's* major findings before looking skeptically at what the reviewer took to be its underlying thesis: "the United States has become a corporate state, with its own 'Private Ministry of Information and Culture.'" If that is the case, he contended, the author has provided insufficient "elaboration and documentation" to support it. Among other things, he faulted Bagdikian's claim that the public wants and deserves more serious news but has been victimized by being methodically "deprived of data on how the system works." For Hacker, an alternative and more "realistic explanation of this finding might be that when confronted by a pollster with a clipboard people say they want weightier fare. In practice, they are apt to turn the page or flip the dial if a news analysis gets unduly complicated."[58]

Hacker was equally skeptical of another Bagdikian claim: the corporate media's outsized effect on public attitudes and values. Such attitudes and values were also shaped by "a nation's character and culture," he argued. And so, if the masses in America seemed to prefer entertainment over information, recreation over citizenship, it had as much to do with free choice, an embedded cultural value, as it had to do with being "seduced by television and glossy magazines." Still, the developments that Bagdikian had decried could not be readily dismissed, Hacker noted. America's commercialism, its addiction to mass entertainment, the loss of local community identity, these and other trends were all too real in the modern world. At the same time, they were also aspects of a broader, more encompassing social phenomenon, one the author had failed to identify, much less pose an alternative to.[59]

In the *Christian Science Monitor*, the book editor, Bruce Mandel, also cited flaws in Bagdikian's study, including its allegedly polemical tone, occasional factual inaccuracies, and reliance on outdated evidence. On the question of tone, for example, he noted, "[Bagdikian] sometimes exaggerates the consequences of interlocking corporate directorates and the penetration of corporate policy into day-to-day editorial decisions." Still, Mandel believed that Bagdikian had done his homework, resulting in a book that deserved the public's attention. For one, he liked its "groundbreaking" examination of how the nation's media had shifted its attention "further away from the needs of the individual and closer to big business." He also gave Bagdikian credit for shedding light on a major national paradox—why at a time of unprecedented access to information so many US voters "feel ill-informed and apathetic about their choices in the democratic process." Mandel applauded the author for tracing this paradox to a series of material changes in both media and politics, including a loss of local newspapers, the corrosive effect of advertising on media form and content, the amount of big money sloshing through the electoral system, and so forth.[60]

Perhaps Bagdikian's most appreciative reviewer at the time was Ralph Nader, the consumer advocate and fellow corporate critic. Nader began his review by noting the comparatively tepid journalistic response to such a "penetrating, specific, and reflective" book. He was not surprised, though, since clearly the author had taken on subjects that often cut too close to the media bone for comfort. Consider the issue of media consolidation and its effects, he said. If anything, Bagdikian's "examples of suppression and censorship barely scratch the surface of media's largest untold story." Certainly, such suppression and censorship are often the subject of wry humor among professionals in private, but they rarely acknowledge it publicly, in part because, as Bagdikian had noted, it is so often self-inflicted. ("The signals are so clear from on high that there is no need to engage in regular pummeling.") Here Nader cited his own experience with suppression, instances when his own freelance journalism proved unpalatable to one corporate publication or another.[61]

Nader was equally appreciative of Bagdikian's second major topic—his examination of mass advertising and its destabilizing effects on media. This second part of the book, Nader said, is likely to prove the most controversial, since it pulls back the curtain on how even supposedly skeptical editors have been enlisted by giant media "to deliver a certain type of audience or readership . . . to its advertisers." As in the case of self-censorship, of course, no self-respecting journalist would readily admit as much, at least not in public. Nevertheless, as Bagdikian had pointed out and Nader confirmed, writers, editors, and producers who managed to survive in commercial media soon learned the long-standing lesson—he who pays the piper calls the tune.[62]

A NEWER MEDIA MONOPOLY

Despite its share of negative reviews, *The Media Monopoly* sold well. In time, six subsequent editions appeared, each offering minor updates by the author to reflect the changing media landscape. By 2004, though, Bagdikian's editors at Beacon Press believed enough had changed over the subsequent years to warrant the publication of a significantly revised book, with seven new chapters. *The New Media Monopoly* looked over this new landscape: the rise of the Internet and digital media generally, the introduction of new players on the media scene, the further concentration of media into fewer and fewer hands. Now, in 2004, just five behemoths controlled much of what the public read, heard, and saw: Time Warner, Disney, Rupert Murdoch's News Corp, Viacom, and the German multinational conglomerate Bertelsmann. So concentrated had Big Media become, in fact, that, as Bagdikian joked early in the book, its all-male, all-white, and allegedly more conservative leadership would probably "fit in a generous phone booth."[63]

But what had not changed in the intervening years—what in fact had become more pronounced—was the effect that such consolidation and its drive for more and more ad revenue had on America's democratic system. In an opening chapter titled "Common Media for An Uncommon Nation," for instance, he bemoaned the continuing reliance of an increasingly diverse country on an increasingly narrow, homogenized group of profit-seeking multimedia news and entertainment providers. This reliance was dangerous not because these providers were would-be authoritarians, at least not in the typical mold. Rather, the real danger lay in ceding control of vital sources of information about one's country and identity to others, some of whom were from other countries. Compounding the problem was that the small clique of media giants only occasionally competed on content, which at the least might have presented a diverse American population with a wider menu of sources and perspectives. More often, this clubby group of giants behaved "like any close-knit hierarchy," discovering ways to work together to expand a collective power that had become "a major force in shaping contemporary American life" (*New Monopoly*, 4).

Some critics had hoped the Internet would prove a corrective to all this. And clearly, it had succeeded in offering users a wider variety of news and entertainment platforms and more diverse sources of information. Bagdikian acknowledged as much, adding that the Internet's apparent lack of a "centralized control," a single entity "deciding what shall be disseminated to the general public," was a clearly positive development. And yet, writing in the early 2000s, he also sensed a prospective reality that has more or less come to pass with the rise of Google, Facebook, Amazon, Netflix, Bloomberg LP, Twitter, and other Internet giants: like other mediums of news and entertainment, and perhaps more so, the Internet is also subject to consolidation, placing what many read, see, and hear in the hands of a relative few (*New Monopoly*, 56).

Digital media have also proven, of course, just as dependent on advertising, albeit of a different kind. Disrupting the traditional ad model, in particular the one that fueled newspaper growth until recently, digital media have found innovative and often unseen ways of targeting electronic ads to consumers. In *The New Media Monopoly*, Bagdikian the old newspaper hand was clearly on unfamiliar and shaky territory when he surveyed the new digital approach to advertising. Still, he noted gamely that e-mail spam had now overshadowed the mass of junk mail delivered daily to Americans by the US Postal Service.

He was on firmer ground when he surveyed the new advertising methods employed by traditional media. Here, too, he saw, practitioners were increasingly relying on modern technology to more precisely target their messages to consumers. One of these newer technologies was data mapping, the process of linking a data field from one source to the data field of another. Employing this process, a retail advertiser might combine, for instance, customer, product, and sales data to create a richly detailed potential buyer profile, thereby tailoring its ad messages more precisely.[64] The big advertisers had also become more adept at, and indeed insistent on, managing the "context" of their ads, whether in the pages of a newspaper or magazine or during a broadcast. "An ad for a sable fur coat next to an article on world starvation is not the most effective association for making a sale," Bagdikian noted dryly (*New Monopoly*, 230–31).

He was convinced, as before, that real reform required a variety of actions. Certainly, regulators and lawmakers had a role to play. Once again, in an effort to break up the most threatening monopolies, he called for antitrust action by the US Department of Justice. He also pushed for several new actions: For one, he urged the repeal or total revision of the 1996 Telecommunications Act, which he believed had gone too far in relaxing many of the earlier restrictions placed on broadcast media.[65] He also called for a reinstatement of the Fairness Doctrine, introduced in 1949 and rescinded in 1987, which had required FCC-licensed broadcasters both to air topics of public interest in a balanced way.[66] And he pushed for a louder public voice when a TV or radio station's license came up for renewal.

As before, he knew that such reforms challenged vested interests and would therefore not be enacted easily. Still, he remained hopeful, buoyed by developments that, if not promising specific changes, suggested countervailing forces were nevertheless at work. Among other things, he took heart in the rise of media reform organizations, in the growing number of academic book publishers, and in the "digital commons" movement—that multi-party effort to keep the ownership and distribution of informational sources and technology in communal rather than private hands.[67]

THE CRITICS WEIGH IN A SECOND TIME

The updated book garnered fewer reviews than the original, and several of those that did appear faulted the author for clinging to a thesis that was no longer newsworthy. (The book had long since become assigned reading in college journalism and media courses.) His discussion of "new media," in particular the Internet, was also ridiculed by some as superficial at best and at worst ill-informed.[68]

One reviewer, however, took the revised book's publication as the chance to question Bagdikian's consistent idea of a closely guarded cartel deciding "what most citizens learn." In an August 2004 column titled "The Media Monotony," then *Slate* press critic Jack Shafer, a self-described libertarian, said the claim was overstated because "the Big Five determines what the majority learns only in those places where the newsstand sells only the *New York Post* and *Time* and where TV receivers have been doctored to accept signals only from CNN, ABC, and the Fox News Channel—which is to say nowhere." Conspicuously not under Big Five control—a list that included the top national newspapers, which actually had more to do with setting the national agenda—are many influential news organizations "and scores of local TV stations." Not only has Big Media not gotten bigger over the past decade, but "much of the best-known merger activity has been like rearranging the industry furniture," said Shafer, who was quoting the author of a January 2004 *Reason* magazine cover story, "Domination Fantasies."[69]

If the financially risky dance of acquisitions and divestitures had any bright spot, Shafer said, it was the arrival of Murdoch's News Corp, which against all odds had established itself as a fourth TV network: "You don't have to like Fox News Channel to acknowledge that . . . [Murdoch has] added ideological diversity to TV news and talk shows." And was not such diversity the very point of "competition and the dynamism of markets"? Shafer thought it very much was: "I'm sure my testament that, for all the news media's faults, its quality and variety have never been better sounds Panglossian to Bagdikian. But I challenge him to name a time in America's history when the news media did a better job than it does today."[70] No record exists that Bagdikian ever accepted the challenge.

Asked six years before his death whether he still collected information about the media, he answered yes but then quickly added that another edition of his most famous book was unlikely. The international media scene, he acknowledged, had simply become too difficult to decipher.[71]

CONCLUSION

At the end of what he was reluctant to call his memoir, Bagdikian reflected on his career in journalism: "And when from time to time, some student asks if I were choosing my life work all over again, would I be a reporter, I always answer without hesitation, 'You bet I would.'"[72] His response was, clearly, a modest one, since during his long and productive life he was much more than simply a reporter, although it was the job that grounded everything else he did.

Following his death in 2016, at ninety-six, both the mainstream and progressive media paid homage to his varied career. His former paper, the *Washington Post*, referred to him as "an influential educator, author, and media critic" and recalled his key role in the *Post*'s publication of the Pentagon Papers, including his secret mission to deliver the cache of documents "to the home of then-editor Benjamin C. Bradlee."[73] The *New York Times*, a paper that during his lifetime he had variously ridiculed and applauded, said he "became a celebrated voice of conscience for his profession," although adding that in the current era of seemingly limitless news and entertainment choices "some observers contend that the Orwellian perils envisioned by Mr. Bagdikian have receded or become moot."[74] And the Associated Press, which ran an obituary carried by papers all over the country, including the *Providence Journal*, one of Bagdikian's first employers, noted the "adventurous" life he had led, both before escaping from Turkey to the United States and during his "five-decade career in journalism."[75]

It was in the progressive media, however, where Bagdikian's life and work were most warmly remembered. Writing in the *Nation*, for instance, John Nichols, the magazine's then national affairs correspondent and himself a media critic, praised the "award-winning" journalist's work for not simply documenting "the steadily increasing control of communications by a handful of conglomerates" but for making clear "the danger that was inherent in allowing the dominance of the discourse by a handful of wealthy and self-interested corporations." His own media criticism, Nichols said, had been built on a foundation laid down by *The Media Monopoly*, and, in a direct reference to the *Times* review, he labeled as "fabulists" those "who imagine that a new age of click- and rating-driven communications somehow provides Americans with a range of digital and cable TV options that will avert 'the Orwellian perils envisioned by Mr.

Bagdikian.'"[76] The *Daily Kos*, an internet forum focused on center-left politics, said Bagdikian was "a journalism giant who first alerted the nation to the dangers of concentrated ownership of the media more than 30 years ago."[77] And in a personal remembrance in *Mother Jones*, the magazine's former deputy editor, Maria Streshinsky, recalled her own family's lively, chat-filled evenings with the Bagdikians; his embrace of aspiring journalists like her; the *Mother Jones* fellowship created in his name in 1980; and his belief that the true aim of journalism was not simply to report the "factual realities" but to make more likely "true democracy and genuine social justice."[78]

Public-interest journalism was clearly not everyone's ideal, not least because it placed journalists in the role of social justice crusaders. Nevertheless, starting from his fundamental premise that a journalist's obligation was above all else "to the people," Bagdikian championed, and practiced, a form of his profession that was unapologetically civic-minded, much like those predecessors he admired most, including George Seldes. If the media was structured in ways that impeded the public from understanding the society in which it lived, then the media had failed to do its job and needed to be reformed. At another time and place, Bagdikian might well have raised a similar critique of some government-run news and entertainment bureaucracy, as his frequent references to Soviet-style information control make clear. His own mission, though, was mostly confined to his adopted country, the ideals and promise of which he continued to believe in throughout his life with an immigrant's unique zeal.

Those whom he influenced through his articles, books, teaching, and fellowship will almost certainly be inspired to carry out his work, although the nature of that work will of necessity change in the years ahead. The "curse of bigness," to use a contemporary reworking of a phrase made famous in the early twentieth century by Justice Louis Brandeis, may still be upon us, but what worried Bagdikian in 1983, and even what drew his attention more than two decades later in 2006, is different today, as Internet giants compete for control with more traditional media companies.[79] And the "curse," if that is what it is, will inevitably be different tomorrow, as other new media emerge. Some will dismiss the threat as overblown, alarmist, even Orwellian. Despite this, there is likely to be at this future date, as there is now, a cadre of journalists and critics who follow in the tradition of Bagdikian and insist that an essential element of our democracy is in jeopardy.

NOTES

1. There is a shelf of scholarly books and memoirs centering on the Armenian genocide. Among the former are Taner Akçam, *The Young Turk's Crime against Humanity: The Armenian Genocide and Ethnic Cleansing in the Ottoman Empire* (Princeton: Princeton University Press, 2012). Well-reviewed memoirs of the Armenian genocide include Fethiye Çetin, *My Grandmother: A Memoir*, trans. Ureen Freely (Brooklyn: Verso Books, 2008) and Aram Haigaz, *Four Years in the Mountains of Kurdistan: An Armenian's Boy's Memoir of Survival*, trans. Iris Haigaz Chekenian (Bronxville, NY: Maiden Lane Press, 2015).

2. Ben Bagdikian, journalist, media critic, professor, and dean emeritus, UC Berkeley's Graduate School of Journalism, interview by Lisa Rubens, May 18 to August 3, 2010, Regional Oral History Office, The Bancroft Library, University of California, Berkeley, 2011, 23–24, https://digitalassets.lib.berkeley.edu/roho/ucb/text/bagdikian_ben.pdf.

3. William Drummond, "In Memoriam," Ben H. Bagdikian, Professor of Journalism, Emeritus, UC Berkeley, 1920–2016, Academic Senate, University of California, 2018, https://senate.universityofcalifornia.edu/in-memoriam/files/ben-bagdikian.html.

4. Rubens, interview, 1–6; also, Ben Bagdikian, *Double Vision: Reflections on My Heritage, Life, and Profession* (Boston: Beacon Press, 1995), 67–94.

5. Rubens, interview, 9; See also, Bagdikian, "My Mother," *Double Vision*, 95–107.

6. Ibid., 16–19.

7. Ibid., 19–21. Bagdikian was not pleased by the generic-sounding "news" in the paper's title, which he thought echoed too many other college newspapers. His new name for the paper, "*The Scarlet*," has persisted to the present day, although at the time Bagdikian was forced to explain that the new "scarlet" title was a nod to the school's colors, not to the Soviet flag.

8. Ibid., 19.

9. Ibid., 22.

10. Ibid., 24.

11. Bagdikian, *Double Vision*, 174.

12. Ibid., 176.

13. Rubens, interview, 38.

14. Bagdikian was troubled by the paper's consistently antiunion editorial stance and its resistance to organizing by staff, including efforts by Bagdikian himself. See Bagdikian, *Double Vision*, "I Discover I Have a Union Problem," 193–208.

15. Rubens, interview, 38–39.

16. Ibid., 41; See also the Pulitzer Prizes, "1953 Pulitzer Prizes Journalism," Local Reporting, Editorial Staff of the *Providence (RI) Journal and Evening Bulletin*, https://www.pulitzer.org/prize-winners-by-year/1953.

17. See, for example, David McCullough, *Truman* (New York: Simon & Schuster, 1992), 551–53; also, Paul S. Boyer, Clifford E. Clark, et al., *The Enduring Vision: A History of the American People*, 8th ed. (Boston: Wadsworth, 2014), 817.

18. See Bagdikian, *Double Vision*, 51–56.

19. Rubens, interview, 59; See also Mimi Alford, *Once upon a Secret: My Affair with John F. Kennedy and Its Aftermath* (New York: Random House, 2008) and Robert Dallek, *An Unfinished Life: John F. Kennedy, 1917–1963* (Boston: Little, Crown, 2003), 152–54.

20. Ben H. Bagdikian, *In the Midst of Plenty: The Poor in America* (Boston: Beacon Press, 1964); Michael Harrington, *The Other America: Poverty in the United States,* 3rd ed. (New York: Macmillan, 1963).

21. Bagdikian, *Midst of Plenty*, 8.

22. Rubens, interview, 112. For Harrington's socialist background and involvement, see Maurice Isserman, *The Other American: The Untold Story of Michael Harrington* (New York: Public Affairs, 2000).

23. Beginning in 1964, the *Saturday Evening Post* changed to a biweekly publication; see *The Saturday Evening Post* Issue Archive, 1964, https://www.saturdayeveningpost.com/issues/page/3/?issue-year=1964.

24. Rubens, interview, 60.

25. Ibid., 67; Ben H. Bagdikian, *The Effete Conspiracy and Other Crimes by the Press* (New York: Harper & Row, 1972), 3–17, 40–46, 59–68.

26. See "A Brief History of Rand," Rand Corporation, https://www.rand.org/about/history/a-brief-history-of-rand.html.

27. Ben H. Bagdikian, *The Information Machines: Their Impact on Men and the Media* (New York: Harper & Row, 1971), xi.

28. Ibid., xii–xiii.

29. Nicholas Johnson, "Further Communications about Communications," *New York Times*, March 21, 1971, https://www.nytimes.com/1971/03/21/archives/the-information-machines-their-impact-on-men-and-the-media-by-ben-h.html.

30. Rubens, interview, 88.

31. In addition to Bagdikian's *Double Vision,* among the many books that include descriptions of the Pentagon Papers episode are Katherine Graham, *Personal History* (New York: Knopf, 1997) and Ben Bradlee, *A Good Life*: *Newspapering and Other Adventures* (New York: Simon & Schuster, 1995). The best-known movie about the event is *The Post*, with Meryl Streep and Tom

Hanks, 2017, directed by Steven Spielberg, 20th Century Studios, Prime Video, 2018, Streaming.

32. Bagdikian, *Double Vision*, 9–10. About two weeks after Sheehan's report appeared, a Democratic senator, Mike Gravel of Alaska, convened the press and read portions of the Pentagon Papers into the Congressional Record.

33. Bagdikian, *Double Vision*, 12–18.

34. Ibid., 18.

35. For the federal court decision, see *New York Times Co. v. United States*, 403 U.S. (713), 1971, The Supreme Court, Justia, https://supreme.justia.com /cases/federal/us/403/713/#tab-opinion-1949387.

36. Bradlee, *A Good Life*, 314.

37. See Rubens, interview, 111.

38. The Pulitzer Prizes, "1972 Pulitzer Prizes Journalism," Public Service, *Washington Post*, https://www.pulitzer.org/prize-winners-by-year/1973.

39. Rubens, interview, 116.

40. Markle Foundation, "About Markle," https://www.markle.org/.

41. See Ben H. Bagdikian, *Caged: Eight Prisoners and Their Keepers* (New York: Harper & Row, 1976).

42. Rubens, interview, 138–43.

43. Ibid., 145.

44. "History of Ownership Consolidation," Research Reports, 3/31/17, Dirks, Van Essen, Murray, & April, http://dirksvanessen.com/articles/view/223/history -of-ownership-consolidation-/.

45. Ibid.

46. In time, the Telecommunications Act of 1996 would overhaul many of these long-standing rules. See Dana A. Scherer, "The FCC's Rules and Policies Regarding Media Ownership, Attribution, and Ownership Diversity," December 16, 2016, Reports, Congressional Research Service, https://www.everycrsreport .com/reports/R43936.html.

47. Ben H. Bagdikian, *The Media Monopoly* (Boston: Beacon Press, 1983), 15. All further references will be to this edition and cited parenthetically in the text.

48. See Richard Hofstadter, *The Paranoid Style in American Politics*, with a new foreword by Sean Wilentz (1952; repr., New York: Vintage, 2008), 196.

49. Mark Dowie, "Pinto Madness," *Mother Jones*, September/October, 1977, https://www.motherjones.com/politics/1977/09/pinto-madness/.

50. Ford challenged what it regarded as Dowie's sensational tone and numbers. See, for example, United Press International, "Report on Ford Pinto Deaths Called False by Ford," *New York Times*, August 30, 1977, https://www.nytimes .com/1977/08/30/archives/report-on-pinto-deaths-is-called-false-by-ford.html.

51. Other books did make it into print, however, a few of which questioned Dowie's underlying argument of deliberate corporate malfeasance. See, for example *The Ford Pinto Case: A Study in Applied Ethics, Business, and Technology*, eds., Douglas Birsch and John H. Fielder (Albany: State University of New York Press, 1994), and Mark Rossow, *Was the Ford Pinto a "Death Trap?"* 2015, Kindle Edition.

52. See, for example, Erika Doss, *Looking at* Life *Magazine* (Washington, DC: Smithsonian, 2001); also, David Plotz, "The Greatest Magazine Ever Published," *Slate*, December 23, 2013, https://slate.com/human-interest/2013/12/life-magazine-1945-why-it-was-the-greatest-magazine-ever-published.html.

53. For books on the "Golden Age" of radio, see, for example, Gerald Nachman, *Raised on Radio* (New York: Pantheon, 1998); John Dunning, *On the Air: The Encyclopedia of Old-Time Radio* (New York: Oxford, 1998); and Erik Barnouw, *A Tower in Babel: A History of Broadcast in the United States to 1933*, vol. 1 (New York: Oxford, 1966).

54. See Clark Gable, Deborah Kerr, and Sydney Greenstreet, *The Hucksters*, 1947, directed by Jack Conway, MGM, Prime Video, Streaming.

55. Among the many books on the early days of television are Rick Marshall, *The Golden Age of Television* (New York: Bookthrift, 1988); Max Wilk, *The Golden Age of Television: Notes from Survivors* (New York: Delacorte, 1976); and Albert Abramson, *The History of Early Television, 1942 to 2000* (Jefferson, NC: McFarland, 2003).

56. Quoted in Bagdikian, *Monopoly*, 160.

57. See Marie Brenner, "The Man Who Knew Too Much," *Vanity Fair*, May 1996, Archive, https://archive.vanityfair.com/article/1996/5/the-man-who-knew-too-much. The article was the basis, three years later, for a film about the episode: see Al Pacino and Russel Crowe, *The Insider*, 1999, directed by Michael Mann, Touchstone Pictures (Disney), Prime Video, Streaming.

58. Andrew Hacker, "Our Ministry of Information," review of *The Media Monopoly*, by Ben H. Bagdikian, *New York Times*, June 26, 1983, https://www.nytimes.com/1983/06/26/books/our-ministry-of-information.html.

59. Ibid.

60. Bruce Mandel, "Dangers of Media Concentration," review of *The Media Monopoly*, by Ben H. Bagdikian, *Christian Science Monitor*, August 10, 1983, https://www.csmonitor.com/1983/0810/081003.html.

61. Ralph Nader, "'Media Monopoly' Explores Press Self-Censorship," review of *The Media Monopoly*, by Ben H. Bagdikian, *The San Bernardino County Sun*, June 26, 1983, 80, Newspapers.com, https://www.newspapers.com/image/64232242/?terms=media%2Bmonopoly%2Bexplores%2Bpress%2Bself-censorship%2B%2B%2Bnader.

62. Ibid.

63. Ben H. Bagdikian, *The New Media Monopoly* (Boston: Beacon Press, 2004), 27. All further references will be to this edition and cited parenthetically in the text.

64. See, for example, "What Is Data Mapping," Informatica, 2022, https://www.informatica.com/resources/articles/data-mapping.html#:~:text=Data%20 mapping%20is%20the%20process,%2C%20for%20example%2C%20with%20 identities.

65. "Telecommunications Act of 1996," Federal Communications Commission, last modified June 20, 2013, https://www.fcc.gov/general/telecommunica tions-act-1996.

66. *The First Amendment Encyclopedia*, "Fairness Doctrine," by Audrey Perry, last modified May 2017 by John R. Vile, https://www.mtsu.edu/first -amendment/article/955/fairness-doctrine.

67. Wikipedia, "Digital Commons (Economics)," last modified March 13, 2020, https://en.wikipedia.org/wiki/Digital_commons_(economics).

68. See, among other reviews, Derek Hrynyshyn, "The Mainstreaming of the Media Critque," review of *The New Media Monopoly*, by Ben Bagdikian; *The News about the News: American Journalism in Peril*, by Leonard Downie Jr., and Robert G. Kaiser; *The Problem of the Media: US Communications in the Twenty-First Century*, by Robert McChesney; and *The No-Nonsense Guide to the Global Media*, by Peter Steven, *Canadian Journal of Communication*, vol. 30, no. 4 (2005), *CJC-Online*, https://www.cjc-online.ca/index.php/journal/article /view/1581/1736.

69. Jack Shafer, "The Media Monotony," *Slate*, August 4, 2004, https:// slate.com/news-and-politics/2004/08/the-media-monotony.html; see also Ben Compaine, "Domination Fantasies," *Reason*, January 2004, https://reason.com /2004/01/01/domination-fantasies-2/.

70. Ibid.

71. Rubens, interview, 185.

72. Bagdikian, *Double Vision*, 241.

73. Matt Shudel, "Ben H. Bagdikian, Journalist with Key Role in Pentagon Papers Case, Dies at 96," *Washington Post*, https://www.washingtonpost.com /local/obituaries/ben-h-bagdikian-media-critic-and-journalist-with-key-role -in-pentagon-papers-case-dies-at-96/2016/03/11/9515bb8c-e7bb-11e5-bc08 -3e03a5b41910_story.html.

74. Robert D. McFadden, "Ben H. Bagdikian, Reporter of Broad Range and Conscience, Dies at 96," *New York Times*, March 11, 2016, https://www.nytimes .com/2016/03/12/business/media/ben-h-bagdikian-reporter-of-broad-range-and -conscience-dies-at-96.html.

75. Robert Jablon, "Renowned Media Commentator Ben Bagdikian Dies at 96," Associated Press, March 12, 2016, https://apnews.com/859604124b554d97 89d65f274415a46b.

76. John Nichols, "Ben Bagdikian Knew That Journalism Must Serve the People—Not the Powerful," *Nation*, March 14, 2006, https://www.thenation .com/article/archive/ben-bagdikian-knew-that-journalism-must-serve-the-people -not-the-powerful/.

77. Meteor Blades, "Open Thread for Night Owls: Ben Bagdikian, Who Warned Us of Media Monopolization, Died Friday at 96," *Daily Kos*, March 14, 2006, https://www.dailykos.com/stories/2016/3/14/1501283/-Open-thread -for-night-owls-Ben-Bagidikian-who-warned-us-of-media-monopolization-died -Friday-at-96.

78. Maria Streshinsky, "Is Basic Social Justice Really a Matter of Personal Opinion?" remembrance of journalist and friend Ben Bagdikian, *Mother Jones*, March 15, 2016, https://www.motherjones.com/media/2016/03/ben-bagdikian -tribute/.

79. See, for example, Tim Wu, *The Curse of Bigness: Antitrust in the New Gilded Age* (New York: Columbia Global Reports, 2018); also, Jennifer Szalai, "A Look at Competition in Business Urges Us to Think Small," review of *The Curse of Bigness*, by Tim Wu, *New York Times*, December 12, 2018, https://www.ny times.com/2018/12/12/books/review-curse-of-bigness-antitrust-law-tim-wu.html.

Reed John Irvine, founder, Accuracy in Media.
Source: Courtesy of Don Irvine.

Chapter Five

Reed Irvine

The Advocate

Like the steady dripping of water that wears away granite, our criticism has had an effect.

—Reed Irvine, preface to *Media Mischief and Misdeeds*, 1984

To his admirers, Reed Irvine did more than almost anyone to inject the charge of liberal media bias into the American mainstream. Irvine was actually building on the earlier work of others, but his influence was nevertheless significant, despite never having spent a day in his life as a full-time working journalist.

In 1969, the bespectacled former Federal Reserve official founded a media watchdog group with the vaguely ominous-sounding acronym of "AIM," short for Accuracy in Media. It was a shoestring operation at first, run out of the basement of his Washington, DC, home. He had few illusions about the David and Goliath struggle ahead of him: "How do you go about taking on such powerful media giants as ABC, CBS, NBC, the *New York Times* and the *Washington Post* with nothing but $200 [from a good friend] and a typewriter in your basement that you can bang away at only on nights and weekends?"[1] But he believed his cause was just, and so armed with just his typewriter and his own righteousness, the Utah-born Mormon proceeded headlong into battle.

Almost immediately, the fight proved more difficult than he had anticipated. Additional armaments were clearly required. In 1972, he began his own newsletter, the *AIM Report*, which eventually gained a circulation of more than thirty thousand subscribers. In 1975, AIM started purchasing small amounts of stock in the major media companies, thereby permitting

Irvine and his colleagues to raise impertinent questions at annual share-holder meetings. In 1976, he launched a syndicated newspaper column, "Accuracy in Media," which was picked up by about a hundred mostly smaller-circulation papers around the country. A daily radio commentary followed a few years later; in 1981, AIM began a speaker's bureau, de-livering five hundred talks by 1983. And in 1985, it started a companion organization, Accuracy in Academia, which focused on alleged political bias in higher education.[2]

Irvine's interests over the years tracked closely with the news. He fo-cused on media coverage of Vietnam in the late 1960s and early 1970s, on the Nixon presidency and those that followed during the next three decades, and on the start of the Iraq War in the early 2000s. Among his favorite targets were CBS anchorman Walter Cronkite and his replace-ment, Dan Rather. (In the 1980s, AIM launched its "Can Dan" campaign.) In 2002, Irvine retired as AIM chairman, succeeded by his son, Don, who had been executive secretary of its board and a longtime financial and operational overseer.[3]

During his lifetime, Reed Irvine also wrote or coauthored four books, which were essentially collections of his various columns and other public communications. In addition to *Media Mischief and Misdeeds* (1984), they included *Profiles of Deception: How the News Media Are Deceiving the American People* (1990); *The News Manipulators: Why You Can't Trust the News* (1993); and *Why You Can't Trust the News* (2003). As their titles indicate, Irvine's books, like his activism generally, were directed to an audience that, he believed, was being ill-served by the left-leaning "Big Media." Despite a personal civility and generosity, he was relentless in exposing what he saw as liberal bias in those who reported, edited, and produced the news. And his self-appointed mission was not simply to cor-rect the record but to offer a compelling counternarrative to it.

A SHOESTRING OPERATION

Reed John Irvine was born on September 29, 1922, to Edna May and William J. Irvine in Salt Lake City, Utah. Public details of his upbringing are sketchy, although he was raised by his mother and father in a Mor-mon household. At nineteen, he graduated with a bachelor's degree in economics from the University of Utah. Following graduation, and with the United States now fighting in World War II, he enlisted in the navy, was selected to participate in an intensive Japanese-language program, and emerged with a Marine Corps commission as an interpreter-translator. As an intelligence officer, he participated in campaigns in Saipan, Tinian, and Okinawa. From 1945 to 1948, he was part of the Allied occupation of Japan, under the direction of General Douglas MacArthur. During this period, he met and married Japanese native Kay Araki, a Nagasaki atomic bomb survivor. At the end of his military service, Reed returned to the states with Kay and won a Fulbright scholarship.[4]

The grant enabled him to study at Oxford, from which he earned a BLitt degree in economics in 1951. That same year, he joined the Federal Reserve Board, in Washington, DC, working as an economist in the Far East section of the Division of International Finance. Over the next twenty-six years, his solidifying views on central planning and foreign aid followed a strict conservative line. As his admirers described on a website following his death in 2004, "He lectured and wrote extensively about free market economics, advocating sound monetary and fiscal politics . . . and encouraging private enterprise and investment as the best policies for developing countries."[5]

Irvine's Washington activities also included memberships in several groups, some organized, others less so. Among the former were University Professors for Academic Order, founded in 1970 at the height of student protests over the Vietnam War; the Council for National Policy, started in 1981 as a forum for conservative Christians; and the National Conservative Campaign Fund, begun in 1999 as a political action committee.[6] After 1966, Reed also hosted several luncheon groups around Washington. These included the International Economists Club, which brought together other professionals in the field of international finance, and a gathering that gave itself the curious label of the "Arthur G. McDowell Luncheon Group." Named in honor of a deceased union leader and former socialist who in 1951 had formed the Council Against Communist Aggression, to which Reed also belonged, the lunch assembly comprised friends and other professionals who shared their namesake's committed anti-communism.[7]

It was probably at a McDowell luncheon, sometime in 1969, that Irvine hatched the idea for AIM. Recent years by any measure had been tumultuous, with continuing urban uprisings and escalating Vietnam War protests.[8] Irvine and his fellow conservatives attributed much of the civil unrest to errors and distortion in the media, and in particular television news. In the case of Vietnam, for instance, they believed that TV had slanted its coverage with an unsubtle anti-war message, thereby inflaming opposition to both the fighting and US South Asian policy generally. AIM would keep tabs on such coverage, as well as on the myriad other sins allegedly committed by the mainstream press.

Irvine knew enough about conservative history to know he was not the first right-wing press scold. One of the pioneering efforts in this direction was the newsweekly *Human Events*, begun in 1945. Conceived as an organ of the right-tilting isolationists, the newsweekly was the brainchild of a pair of veteran journalists, Felix Morley and Frank Hanighen, and a wealthy onetime New Deal Democrat named Henry Regnery. The later partner served as the publication's treasurer, and in time he would go on to start a book company that released a pair of seminal works in the developing conservative movement: William F. Buckley's *God and Man at Yale* (1951) and Russell Kirk's *The Conservative Mind* (1953).[9]

The founders of *Human Events* were clearly eager to correct a public record that they regarded as incomplete or, worse, distorted. They saw themselves as more than mere fact checkers, however. Their larger mission was to tell the conservative story, in hopes of not simply leveling the playing field but for once perhaps tilting it in their direction.[10] In time, they attracted like-minded followers and publications, including Buckley's news and opinion magazine, *National Review*, started in 1955.[11] Other conservatives also followed the lead of *Human Events*. In the wake, for example, of Barry Goldwater's lopsided loss to President Lyndon Johnson—a loss many supporters blamed on unfounded and sensational press coverage—two right-tilting media watchdogs emerged.[12] One was the Committee to Combat Bias in the Media, begun by disgruntled Goldwaterites. The other was Irvine's Accuracy in Media.

Irvine's first impulse was to enlist a well-respected journalistic professional to head up his media group. His first choice was Arthur Krock, the three-time Pulitzer Prize winner and retired Washington bureau chief of the *New York Times*. But Krock demurred, citing a potential conflict of interest with his former employer. For Irvine, the refusal was revelatory: "The reporters, editors and broadcasters could not be expected to criticize each other without pulling their punches," he wrote in the preface to his first book, *Media Mischief and Misdeeds*." For this reason, he decided that AIM should be run not by the professionals but "by the consumers of the journalistic product," which initially meant just him.[13]

VIETNAM: THE DISINFORMATION WAR
ON THE HOME FRONT

The primary focus of AIM in its early days was on the Vietnam War and its stateside representation, especially on television. Irvine blamed this representation for much of the current social unrest: the 1968 Democratic Convention in Chicago, which had devolved into anarchy; the growing violence on American campuses; and the American public's increasing skepticism about the progress and very wisdom of the war, especially after 1968's Tet offensive, the series of surprise attacks by the joint forces of Vietnam against strategic military and civilian targets in South Vietnam. For Irvine, these and other signs of the times were directly related to what citizens saw and heard nightly on their TV sets and read about in their morning newspapers. "The key role played by the media is one of the most important lessons of the Vietnam experience," he recalled in 1984. "This was the first war fought by the U.S. in which propaganda, disinformation and incompetent and irresponsible journalism proved to be more decisive than guns."[14]

As part of his one-man AIM show, Irvine registered his frustration with the war coverage, among other issues, through a series of letters to the editor, op-eds, and direct communications with publishers and network executives. He was hopeful, as he later remembered, that his "accurate and well-documented" criticisms would prick guilty consciences and thereby correct the record. When that failed to happen, his initial optimism soured, and he decided to take his case directly to whatever public he could muster through a newsletter, the *AIM Report*, and eventually his weekly newspaper column. Once again, he realized, he was engaged in a terribly lopsided battle.[15]

Irvine's full critique of Vietnam War coverage would have to wait until nearly two decades after America's involvement had ended. The occasion was a thirteen-part series on the war broadcast on PBS in late

1983. Produced by public television's WGBH-TV in Boston, and based on a companion book titled *Vietnam: A Television History* by journalist Stanley Karnow, the series charted the long arc of the war: its roots in the mid-1940s and early 1950s, America's escalating involvement in the mid-1960s, the pivotal Tet offensive, life on the "home front," and finally the Nixon cease-fire and its aftermath. The documentary was widely viewed and generally regarded as fair and balanced, although many commentators on the right and some veterans groups viewed it as slanted.[16] Irvine saw a chance to set the record straight. With funding from supporters, including a $30,000 grant from the National Endowment for the Humanities, then chaired by Reagan appointee William Bennett, Irvine produced a two-part documentary film titled *Television's Vietnam* (1985), narrated by Democrat-turned-conservative celebrity spokesman and gun-rights advocate Charlton Heston.[17]

The documentary was initially rejected by PBS and then accepted, possibly under White House pressure. To make its case that Vietnam was a noble cause, and that the nation's will to win was sapped by media coverage in general and TV reporting in particular, it trained its sights on several key episodes of the war, including the Tet offensive. Regarding that pivotal campaign, the film argued that, despite the major media's portrayal, the multiphase incursion was actually a defeat for the Vietcong and their North Vietnamese sponsors, which suffered heavy casualties.[18]

The film also alleged misleading coverage of other pivotal battles. One was the Battle of Khe Sanh, the earlier fight that is now widely seen as part of the North Vietnamese military's strategy to divert US troops from the main targets of the Tet offensive.[19] In defending their Khe Sanh combat base, US forces were in fact outmanned, eventually staging what American commanders claimed was a strategic withdrawal. After that, some in the press had perhaps too casually compared the US withdrawal at Khe Sanh with the French withdrawal at Dien Bien Phu in 1954. Suffering what was clearly a humiliating defeat there at the hands of the Vietminh, the precursors of the Vietcong, the French soon after took steps to extricate themselves from the region. But Khe Sanh was no Dien Bien Phu, the AIM documentary argued, and suggestions to the contrary were part and parcel of the media's distorted war reporting. The film also criticized journalists for exaggerating the Vietcong's breach of the US Embassy in Saigon and for underreporting the Vietcong's massacre in Huê', where as many as six thousand civilians and prisoners of war may have been killed.[20]

AIM's documentary—like other right-leaning critiques of Vietnam War coverage—scored some valid points and fumbled others, as several media scholars have suggested. Certainly, media coverage of the war had become in time more negative, more prone to question the war's course and very rationale. But, as these scholars have pointed out, that negative coverage tracked closely with a more general fraying in the initial war consensus, especially among elites. In this view, establishment media of the time was not simply waging their own anti-war crusade but rather reflecting a discernable shift in establishment opinion. Certainly, the media was also amplifying and consolidating this shift, just as they had when the establishment view of the war was more unified. But this was markedly different, commentators argued, from being part of a nefarious conspiracy to undermine America and its interests, as many right-wing pundits charged.[21] Nevertheless, in large part due to Irvine and AIM, this indictment of establishment media would persist, informing conservative critiques of not only later documentaries but also of books, memoirs, movies, and conferences on the Vietnam experience.[22]

BAD PRESS BEHAVIOR: TWO ALLEGATIONS

In 1984, Regnery Gateway, Henry Regnery's reorganized publishing company, released Irvine's first book, *Media Mischief and Misdeeds*, a collection of his weekly syndicated columns from the previous year. In those columns, he had skewered the press for its handling of some of 1983's most-discussed news stories, including General William Westmoreland's ongoing libel suit against CBS; the fall of Secretary of the Interior James Watt; the slander suit against CBS and anchor Dan Rather; US support efforts in Nicaragua and El Salvador; the Soviet Union's downing of Korean Airlines Flight 007; and ABC's nuclear Armageddon film, *The Day After*. As in his critiques of Vietnam War coverage, Irvine was ever on the alert for what he viewed as "the tilt to the left . . . of the reporters, editors, and the producers of TV news programs."[23] And the more he examined this seemingly fertile field, the more he found to raise his ire.

Allegation One: Westmoreland

Irvine devoted some half-dozen columns exclusively or partially to the Westmoreland lawsuit. The commander from 1964 to 1968 of US forces in Vietnam, Westmoreland sued CBS for accusations leveled against him in the documentary *The Uncounted Enemy: A Vietnam Deception*, which aired on January 23, 1982. The television report, hosted by *60 Minutes* correspondent Mike Wallace, charged the commanding general and his top military officers with conspiring to misrepresent enemy troop strength. Their purpose, the documentary claimed, was to paint a rosier-than-warranted picture of the war's progress in the year leading up to the Tet offensive.[24]

Westmoreland came in for special criticism. Based on interviews with several of his intelligence officers, as well as with a former CIA analyst, producers claimed the commanding general had exerted pressure on those below him, leaning on them to in effect cook the books. Under aggressive on-camera questioning by Wallace, Westmoreland seemed to further damage his case, appearing ill-prepared and confused. Once the broadcast aired, though, he vigorously contested its thesis in a news conference, despite his legal advisers' continuing doubts that a suit against the network could succeed.[25]

They had a change of heart a few months later, however, when *TV Guide* published an article criticizing CBS for violating its own journalistic norms. Among other things, the article accused the network of failing to prove the conspiracy charge, not including enough rebuttal witnesses and not identifying the CIA analyst as a paid consultant.[26] In response, CBS appointed Burton Benjamin, a senior executive producer, to investigate the criticisms. Benjamin arrived at a mixed judgment: while the premise of the CBS report could not be dismissed out of hand, the report's execution "was seriously flawed."[27] In September 1982, Westmoreland filed a $120 million libel suit against the network and the team responsible for the documentary.[28]

Irvine soon began criticizing both CBS's response to the libel suit and its handling of the "Benjamin Report," as it came to be known. In a column titled "Paranoia Hits CBS News" (February 11, 1983), he chided then news president Van Gordon Sauter for a speech in which he said the Westmoreland affair was becoming "a rallying point for people who seek to use it as an instrument for damaging the image, spirit and aggressiveness of the news media" (quoted in *Misdeeds*, 28). One of those people, as it happened, was Irvine, whose group had been from the first vocally critical of the conclusions reached by *The Uncounted Enemy*. As the AIM chairman saw it, Sauter should have known better than to level such a charge, since his division's own internal inquiry had laid out "the unethical, dishonest conduct involved in making that documentary" (*Misdeeds*, 29). If that inquiry was now under lock and key, making it impossible for Irvine or other outsiders to read it, it was not to protect the privacy of those who had participated in it but to contain the damage (*Misdeeds*, 30). Other columns followed, each casting doubt on the network's good faith.

Finally, in a June 24 column titled "CBS at Last Enforces Its Rules," Irvine took note of what he regarded as the network's belated suspension of George Crile, the producer of *The Uncounted Enemy*. To the critic's dismay, Crile had not been suspended over his alleged journalistic lapses but over "a petty technical violation" that had surfaced. (Crile had apparently taped an interview with former Secretary of Defense Robert McNamara without prior notification, as CBS rules required.) "He has been lowered over the side, ever so gently, with full pay, perhaps in the hope that he will not blab to the press that he was only doing what many others have been doing at CBS for many years," Irvine wrote (*Misdeeds*, 94–95).[29] As for the Westmoreland suit, on February 17, 1985, the former commanding general and CBS reached a nonmonetary settlement, followed by a joint statement that confirmed that no further legal action was necessary because "their respective positions had been effectively placed before the public for consideration."[30] Meanwhile, Irvine had also made clear his views on the whole affair.

Allegation Two: Korea Airlines Flight 007

Irvine also wrote multiple columns on another of the big stories of 1983, the downing of Korean Airlines Flight 007. This tragic event took place on September 1, when a South Korean passenger jet originating from New York City strayed into Soviet airspace and was shot down by air-to-air missiles near Sakhalin Island, killing all 269 passengers on board, including US Representative Larry McDonald (GA-D). The incident, among the most tense during the Cold War, provoked recriminations on both sides. For its part, the United States immediately condemned the attack as, in the words of then President Reagan, "an act of barbarism."[31] The official view of things continued, even after US intelligence data indicated the Soviets had most likely mistaken the passenger jet for a reconnaissance plane.[32] Soviet reaction was equally recriminatory. Initially denying responsibility for the incident until presented with radio communications to the contrary, Soviet officials abruptly shifted ground, arguing that the Korean passenger jet had been on a US spy mission, although internal Soviet intelligence questioned that theory as early as November 28, 1983.[33]

As a long-standing cold warrior, Irvine was in no mood either to dispute the intentional nature of the incident or encourage press attempts to probe the official US line. In a column published about a week after initial reports, he labeled the downing a "deliberate murder" and argued the time was long overdue to "pariahtize" the Soviet Union. Laying out a list of earlier "communist atrocities"—from the building of the Berlin Wall to the invasion of Afghanistan—he marveled at how adept the Soviet propaganda machine had been in inducing a collective, worldwide amnesia. The same would happen with the Flight 007 massacre, he worried, "unless the civilized world decides that the time has come to turn the tables on the communists" and treat them as the outcasts they have become. Fed up with all the happy talk about better US-Soviet understanding, he called on the American media to make clear that "the Soviets are ruled by cruel, ruthless men who don't share our Judeo-Christian values" (*Misdeeds*, 130–32).

Meanwhile, the press was still trying to discern what actually happened over Sakhalin Island. Both the *New York Times* and the *Washington Post*, for example, had been proceeding cautiously, reporting official US explanations but not necessarily endorsing them. On September 3, though, the *Washington Post* took a step further, raising the possibility of an alternative explanation for the disaster. In a report of a congressional briefing, the paper quoted unnamed officials who explained that, at some point before it was shot down, the Korean passenger jet had "crossed paths" with an Air Force RC-135 reconnaissance plane. The temporary proximity of the two aircraft may well have led to some initial Soviet "confusion." Still, the Soviet fighter pilots should have been able after a time to distinguish between a passenger and a reconnaissance jet. Besides, noted the officials, when the incident finally took place, the Air Force reconnaissance plane was as much as one thousand miles away, over international waters.[34]

In effect, the *Washington Post* was reporting a well-sourced story, including all the necessary caveats. It was also a story that, after US experts concluded the Soviet air attack was probably a case of mistaken identity, other newspapers would soon repeat [35] But Irvine was impatient with the *Post*'s early reporting. In a September 16 column titled "The 'Knock-America' Media," he accused some "skeptical journalists" of having "developed an attitude of mistrusting anything that is said by the U.S. government" (*Misdeeds*, 133). A corollary to this attitude, he wrote, was one that then White House spokesman Larry Speakes had identified: the habit of reporters to "search for some Soviet mistake that would apologize for them or mitigate their responsibility." In contrast, Irving's own instinct told him to trust President Reagan, who in his address to the nation had debunked the misidentification theory by insisting that the reconnaissance plane had been on the ground in Alaska "an hour before the jetliner was shot down" (*Misdeeds*, 135).[36]

Irvine continued to cast doubt on the skeptics and their motives. Finally, in an October 14, 1983, column, he took issue with the reconnaissance plane theory put forth by a pair of former RC-135 crewmen. In their article, the former crewmen had disputed President Reagan's explanation of events, arguing that on that September evening, the RC-135 might well have returned to Alaska, as the president had claimed, but another reconnaissance plane would have immediately taken its place in the air, keeping alive the theory of a Soviet mistake. Irvine was still not convinced: Around-the-clock deployments may have been the order of the day during Vietnam, when the former crewmen had done their tour of duty, but not necessarily today. "There was ample reason to question the outdated experience of . . . [the crewmen] and check their doubt-casting claims," Irvine complained. "Unfortunately that was not done. The readers and the nation were badly served" (*Misdeeds*, 147).

SLANTED COVERAGE: THE IRAN-CONTRA AFFAIR

Media Mischief and Misdeeds was not widely distributed in bookstores and received few press reviews, despite Irvine's attempts to promote it in TV appearances and elsewhere. In an August 8, 1984, interview on the public service network C-SPAN, for example, he offered his collections of the previous year's columns free to viewers who signed up for a twelve-month subscription to *Media Monitor*, AIM's newsletter. He promised those who did receive the free book would find it "very informative and provocative" and still "very timely."[37]

By this point, though, Irvine and AIM had turned their attention to more contemporary events, albeit with a similar focus on the distortions of the liberal media. One of these events was the "Iran-Contra Affair," as it came to be known. In late 1985, senior Reagan administration officials put together a secret arms sale to the Islamic Republic of Iran, part of the proceeds of which were diverted to the US-backed right-wing rebels in Nicaragua, who were engaged in a civil war with the ruling far-left Sandinista National Liberation Front (FSLN). Led by Lieutenant Colonel Oliver North, a National Security Council member, these senior officials had ample reason for maintaining secrecy: not only was the current government of Iran under a strict arms embargo, but congressional lawmakers had cut off any additional unauthorized aid to the Contras. Further complicating matters was the administration effort to use the arms sale as a quid pro quo with the Iranians. Specifically, it hoped to leverage their assistance in freeing seven American hostages being held in Lebanon by Hezbollah, a paramilitary group affiliated with the Islamic Republic. Evidence uncovered at the time suggested that Reagan was aware of the potential hostage deal, although he may have been in the dark about the North-engineered diversion of funds to the Contras.[38]

Media coverage of Iran-Contra was intense. Beginning in late 1986, for example, the *New York Times* ran detailed reports with titles such as "The Iran Affair: A Presidency Damaged" and "Helping the Contras," while the *Washington Post* added stories of its own with titles like "Who Got the Iran Contra Money?" and "The Lid on the Iran-Contra Story."[39] Irvine and AIM found many of these reports slanted against the administration and the Nicaraguan "freedom fighters," fueling his suspicion those who wrote and edited them were closeted Sandinista sympathizers.

Looking back, AIM's then director of media analysis, Cliff Kincaid, a former columnist on *Human Events* who had joined Irvine in 1978, recalled the "liberal media" coverage, and in particular the reporting of Ben Bradlee's *Washington Post*. It was, charged Kincaid, another high time for Bradlee, who had supposedly admitted employing "various Watergate reporting techniques . . . to finger Reagan . . . and bring him and his administration down."[40] If that had really been Bradlee's intent, it did not work: After a dramatic drop in popularity, Reagan's approval rating eventually recovered, remaining strong today.[41] As for North, he was dismissed from the National Security Council, stood trial, and was found guilty of a variety of federal crimes. But the charges against him were later dropped on appeal after a prosecution witness's testimony was shown to be tainted.

As the 1980s and the Reagan administration drew to an end, both Irvine and his AIM colleagues were feeling a reinvigorated sense of purpose. What had started as a one-person, basement operation had developed over the past two decades into an increasingly influential voice in media scrutiny and conservative politics. Membership in AIM had risen impressively—by the mid-1980s, it was already at forty thousand and growing—and over the years the group had won the support of several major funders of right-wing causes. These included the Carthage Foundation and the Sarah Scaife Foundation, both part of a still larger group then directed by Richard Mellon Scaife, the banking, oil, and aluminum billionaire who died in 2014.[42] With such backing, a loyal following, and an expanding staff, Irvine was unsettling what he regarded as the liberal media establishment. He even succeeded in getting under the skin of the notoriously hard-driving Ben Bradlee, who in a personal letter called the AIM chairman "a miserable, carping, retromingent vigilante" whom he "was sick of wasting his time" communicating with." Irvine was reported to have kept the letter displayed prominently on his conference room wall.[43]

PROMOTING DECEPTION, SOWING DISTRUST

In the early 1990s and the first years of the George H. W. Bush administration, Irvine self-published two additional collections of his columns and other communications: *Profiles of Deception: How The News Media Are Deceiving the American People* (1990), with his AIM colleague Cliff Kincaid; and *The News Manipulators: Why You Can't Trust The News* (1993), with Kincaid and also Joseph C. Goulden, a former political reporter who had taken over as AIM's director of media analysis. Like

Irvine's earlier solo effort, the newest books had a clear purpose: to document the many ways in which the left-leaning news media had deceived
the American people through factual error, distortion, and the thinly
veiled biases of its frontline workers.

Profiles of Deception

The columns and radio broadcast transcripts included here—it is not
always clear which is which—cover events both before and during the
Bush administration. In several of the collected items, Irvine and Kincaid
come to the defense of Bush team members, including Vice President Dan
Quayle, and also of Bush himself.

In "Media Fire Guns at Bush" (May 18, 1988), for example, they defended then candidate Bush against accusations that had been kept alive
by his opponent, Massachusetts Governor Michael Dukakis, and printed
ten days earlier in front-page stories in the *Washington Post* and the *New
York Times*.[44] In those stories, reporters had written that, as CIA director and then vice president, Bush maintained relations with Panamanian
General Manuel Noriega, despite existing intelligence that showed him
to be a drug smuggler. Irvine and Kincaid claimed that "both papers
missed their target": In the *Post*'s case, because it had run its story while
acknowledging that nothing in the "available record" established that
Bush had the facts linking Noriega to drugs; and in the *Times*'s case,
because it had excluded a statement from the former Panamanian ambassador that would have cast doubt on the Noriega allegation.[45] Once
again, Irvine and Kincaid believed, the left-leaning establishment press
had manipulated coverage to deceive the public—in this instance, to
advance Dukakis over Bush.

In their rush to indict, though, the AIM authors may have themselves
missed the mark: while the *Post*'s May 8 story had in fact acknowledged
deficiencies in the "available record," it nevertheless went on to distinguish between available and top-secret intelligence: As a key official,
Bush would have been privy to top-secret intelligence and that very likely
did contain information about Noriega, as a former National Security
Council aide quoted by the *Post* made clear.[46] As for their critique of the
Times story, Irvine and Kincaid were being equally selective: To be sure,

two days after that story ran the former ambassador to Panama reiterated his claim at a news conference that he could not have briefed Bush on Noriega's drug dealing early on because "evidence of those activities" were not yet in hand. Nevertheless, asked at that same news conference whether he "was drawing a distinction between evidence of drug trafficking and allegations of drug trafficking," the ambassador replied "no further comment" through his spokesperson (*Profiles*, 95–96).[47]

After candidate Bush became President Bush, Irvine and Kincaid also rallied to his defense. In "CBS Goes after Bush" (June 23, 1989), for example, they cited studies from two media watchdog groups—like AIM, conservative leaning—that found that, in the first one hundred days of the administration, CBS had aired more negative coverage of the president than either ABC or NBC. While the authors of one of the studies had qualified their findings, noting that such coverage did not necessarily suggest liberal bias at the network, Irvine and Kincaid were not convinced: "The network [CBS] is populated by Democrats." As partial evidence, they pointed to both a network executive and an editor who had worked for well-known Democrats. The AIM authors also pointed to *CBS Evening News* anchor Dan Rather, who "is known to have a prejudice against Bush, if not Republicans in general" (*Profiles*, 3).

Rather had long been among their favorite media targets. In "Dan Rather Misfires in Afghanistan" (August 13, 1987), for example, they criticized him for what they regarded as misstatements in a CBS documentary on the Soviet-Afghan war, begun in late 1979. Among other things, they cast doubt on his suggestion that the Soviets might have invaded the country to create a buffer state between them and fundamentalist Iran. Such speculation of a "defensive move" on the part of the communists, Irvine and Kincaid wrote, seriously mischaracterized the Soviets' strategic designs in the Middle East and the Persian Gulf. Even more misleading, they believed, was Rather's idea that the US decision to supply rocket launchers and other arms to the Afghan guerrillas had probably escalated the war. "An honest observer might say that the anti-aircraft missiles were a necessary and proper response to overwhelming Soviet airpower," wrote the authors (*Profiles*, 157–58).

Rather and CBS may have been among the author's favorite broadcast targets, but they were certainly not the only ones. Irvine and Kincaid criticized ABC, for instance, for giving airtime to an Oregon businessman who claimed to have been directed to fly arms to the Nicaraguan Contras by an aide to then Vice President Bush. They also faulted NBC for what they said were two distorted and highly manipulated reports—one on Reagan's conservative Supreme Court nominee Robert Bork and another that allegedly promoted teenage homosexuality. The Public Broadcasting System did not escape their notice, either. They went after PBS for various documentaries and other broadcasts that, among other alleged infractions, misstated the historical record on Vietnam's My Lai massacre in order to "blacken America," condemned "the use of covert action by the US intelligence agencies," and presented in an overly sympathetic light Castro's putative successes in Cuba (*Profiles*, 14, 41).

They also saw villains on the print side of the news. The *Washington Post*'s Bob Woodward, for example, raised their ire for what they regarded as an inadequately sourced report on former Senator John Tower, whose nomination as Reagan's secretary of defense was later derailed by allegations of problems in his personal life.[48] Irvine and Kincaid also took the *Times* editorial board to task for a December 15, 1989, editorial that, they claimed, understated social progress in as yet racially divided South Africa. And a pair of *Newsweek* reporters drew their attention for supposedly insinuating that the *Dartmouth Review*, the school's conservative newspaper, was anti-Semitic.[49] The AIM authors were clearly writing in a target-rich environment.

THE NEWS MANIPULATORS

That environment was no less rich three years later, judging at least from Irvine's next book, *The News Manipulators*. In it, he and his two coauthors examined a range of media stories, but three in particular claimed most of their attention: the Bush-Clinton campaign, the environment, and homosexuality in America.

On the Bush-Clinton contest, the authors spelled out their essential thesis in their book's preface: "A continuing pro-Democratic bias was manifested during the 1992 presidential campaign by the media's reluctance to pursue the 'character issue.'"[50] By this anodyne-seeming phrase, they were actually referring to the storm of charges that had swirled around the candidate, led by allegations of his sexual infidelity over the years. In "Who is Lying? Does It Matter ?" (January 31, 1992), for example, they took issue with the media's coverage to date of the Gennifer Flowers claim of having had a multiyear affair with then Arkansas governor Clinton. In contrast to the circus-like reporting on Anita Hill's sexual allegations against Supreme Court nominee Clarence Thomas, they argued, the coverage of the alleged Clinton-Flowers affair had been tentative and overly cautious, a sure sign a double standard was at work. In another Clinton-related piece, "Hiding Candidate Clinton's 'Bimbos'" (August 7, 1992), they continued to point an accusatory finger at the media's timidity. After calling attention to a *Washington Post* story about Clinton campaign efforts to discredit his former paramours, the authors questioned why other major media had largely given the revelation a pass. Again, they suspected a conspiracy of silence: It was one thing, after all, to tread carefully when reporting on the confessions themselves, but quite another to pass over a story about possible witness intimidation (*Manipulators*, 123–25).

Irvine and his coauthors also took aim at the press for its apparently alarmist environmental reporting. As in the case of Clinton's philandering, there was no shortage of press villains to accuse. The authors faulted ABC, for instance, for what they regarded as its alarmist claims of pesticide dangers to children. CNN drew their ire for a segment on whether cellular phones caused brain cancer, while the *Washington Post* came in for criticism for its "uncritical" story on the EPA's efforts to ban asbestos and CBS's *60 Minutes* for a story on the dangers posed by amalgam dental fillings. They were also especially critical of NBC for giving a platform to "radical" environmentalist Paul Ehrlich, who had dared to warn about overpopulation and its effects on natural resources (*Manipulators*, 167, 280).

In a piece titled "Earth Day 1990: Truth, or Media Pollution" (January 5, 1990), the authors neatly summed up their skepticism of most environmental reporting:

What alarms us about the forthcoming Earth Day [April 22] is that the media seem on the verge of one of their periodic take-no-prisoners assaults on truth and reason. The pastoral visionaries who dominate the ecological movement are long on condemnation of modern society—and short on suggestions as [to] how man can live in comfort if he is forced to abandon such amenities as electrical power and heat.

That most media of the day focused on efforts to identify alternative sources of electrical power and heat, rather than the abandonment of these "amenities," seemed beside the point. Even such reporting would have seemed skewed to the trio of AIM critics—another instance, in fact, of media pointing an accusing finger at "the traditional ecological bugaboos of business, nuclear energy and the auto" (*Manipulators*, 290).

The third focus of attention in *The News Manipulators* was the media's coverage of gays, both in regular society and the military. In "What TV Did Not Show about Homosexual Parade" (April 27, 1993), for instance, Irvine and his fellow authors were seemingly sympathetic to the press because of the "unique challenge" it faced in reporting on the Washington, DC, event. Full reporting was out of the question, they observed, since "much of what happened on the public streets of the nation's capital was too obscene and disgusting to display on national television, or to describe full in family newspapers." A month later, they were back in full attack mode, especially against the *New York Times* for its hiring of openly gay reporters to cover the movement for gay rights. In hiring reporters with a clear personal bias, Irving and company argued, the paper had thereby ensured that that movement would appear in subsequent coverage "more mainstream than it really is" (*Manipulators*, 9, 28).

They regarded such journalism as irresponsible, especially at a time when the incidence of AIDS infections was still rising: "Maybe we're asking too much, but perhaps it occurred to the editors of this once-great newspaper that several of the characters mentioned in these stories were either dying or dead. And that is why the homosexual lifestyle must not be promoted, especially to children."[51] They were equally insistent that the media not promote the admission of gays into the military. Thus far, the press had presented a "one-sided" view of the issue, proceeding from the faulty assumption that gays "are victims of American society" and thus "deserve compensation from the government in the form of special rights to serve in the military and other sectors of society" (*Manipulators*, 9–10,

16). A more balanced view of the matter, they believed, would not take these putative rights for granted.[52]

THE VINCE FOSTER AFFAIR

The election in 1992 of Democrat Bill Clinton put Irvine and his organization on high alert. If the press had slanted its coverage during the campaign, it would almost certainly repeat itself now that Clinton occupied the White House. AIM's mission—never more critical, its leadership believed—was to ensure that the American public continued to learn the whole truth about someone who had already revealed his character. There turned out to be, as Irvine and his AIM colleagues saw it, no shortage of controversies and scandals to draw their attention. Using columns, newsletters, TV appearances, radio broadcasts, forums, and conferences, they examined how the media had handled or more likely mishandled, among other things, Whitewater, the allegation of a Clinton-engineered illegal loan linked to an Arkansas land deal; Travelgate, the flap arising over the firing of seven members of the White House Travel Office; and, most famously, Monica Lewinsky, the White House intern whose sexual affair with the president would lead to his impeachment. Over time, though, perhaps no Clinton controversy was more closely linked with Irvine and his group than an event that had occurred in midsummer 1993—the sudden death of Deputy Counsel to the President Vincent W. Foster.

Vince Foster, as he was known, was a childhood friend of Bill Clinton and a colleague of Hillary Rodham Clinton at the Rose Law Firm, in Little Rock, Arkansas. (Foster had been responsible for recruiting her to the firm as its first female associate, and she eventually became its first female partner.) Following Bill Clinton's presidential election, he joined the transition team. In early 1993, he was appointed deputy counsel, working under White House Counsel Bernard Nussbaum. Among his first duties, Foster was tasked with vetting prospective administration appointees, an assignment he found difficult and personally draining. (His successive recommendations for the post of attorney general, Zoë Baird and Kimba Woods, proved to be especially fraught.)

The political novice's portfolio expanded in the following months. Soon, the burden of work and the fact of living in Washington apart from his family, still back in Arkansas, began to take its toll. In mid-May 1983, Foster experienced yet another setback. After news broke that multiple members of the White House travel office had been fired, the *Wall Street Journal* raised insinuating questions about whether Foster and other former Rose Law firm alumni, including Hillary Clinton herself, were somehow involved.[53] More depressed than ever, Foster consulted his doctor back in Arkansas and was prescribed an antidepressant. A day later, though, his body was discovered in Fort Marcy Park, a federal space in Virginia. A subsequent autopsy revealed that the forty-eight-year-old had shot himself in the mouth with his handgun.

Over the next four years, five separate investigations confirmed the findings of the autopsy report. On June 30, 1994, for example, Independent Counsel Robert B. Fiske Jr., who had initially investigated the Whitewater controversy, concluded from the evidence "that Vincent Foster committed suicide in Fort Macy Park on June 20, 1993."[54] Fiske's successor, Ken Starr, who would go on to investigate other Clinton controversies, including the Monica Lewinsky affair, reached the same conclusion.[55] And yet neither of these investigations, nor the three others, satisfied the growing legion of skeptics and conspiracy theorists who believed that Foster was likely murdered and that the Clintons were somehow involved. One of those skeptics was Irvine himself, who voiced his doubt in the *New York Times* after the Starr report was released in late 1997: "This is a joke, and a bad joke. . . . It's far worse than the Fiske report."[56]

A week after the Starr report was made public, Irvine and AIM hosted a conference on the Foster episode at the Army-Navy Club, in Washington, DC. Besides Irvine, panelists included John H. Clarke, a Washington, DC, attorney and Foster skeptic who had represented one of the witnesses in the Whitewater inquiry; Christopher Ruddy, a journalist who wrote a key book on the investigations, *The Strange Death of Vincent Foster: An Investigation* (1997); Patrick Knowlton, a private citizen who claimed his eyewitness testimony prior to the event was falsified by the FBI; and Hugh Sprunt, a CPA and amateur sleuth for whom uncovering the real story behind the Foster case had become a private obsession. In an attempt at some semblance of balance, AIM organizers also invited Philip Weiss, then a correspondent for the *New York Times Magazine* and self-described liberal who several months before had written a feature-length appraisal of the skeptics and conspiracy theorists titled "Clinton Crazy." (In his piece, Weiss had acknowledged the influence of the zealots: "The number of influential Clinton crazies is probably no more than a hundred, but their audience is in the tens of millions.)[57]

The conference aired on C-SPAN on October 20, 1987. In his opening remarks, Irvine made clear the conclusion that he and his AIM colleagues had reached: Based on the Starr report—or more precisely, based on inconsistencies and elisions in it—they were certain that "Foster's [dead] body had arrived at the park long before his car did." What he and his group had concluded, in other words, was that those responsible for Foster's death had murdered him off-site, transported his body to the park in a car that was not Foster's own, and finally driven his own car to the park to make it appear as if he had been at that site all along. The conference speakers that followed either supported this thesis, offered evidence for theories of their own, or in the case of Weiss explained that neither he nor anyone else knew what had happened that day. Nevertheless, he joined others on the panel lamenting the apparent media apathy. "I'm not optimistic about the truth emerging in this case," he said in his concluding remarks.[58]

Irvine thought he already knew the truth, however, and for years he continued to be frustrated by the press's unwillingness to follow his lead. In a 2001 *AIM Report*, for example, he marked the eighth anniversary of Foster's death with a renewed "effort to get the establishment media to examine the overwhelming evidence that proves Foster was murdered."[59] Once again, as he had in the past, he laid out the evidence that, he felt, supported his conclusion, including Patrick Knowlton's eyewitness account of seeing a suspicious brown car prior to Foster's death. Two years later, in a *Media Monitor* radio broadcast titled "Who Cares If Vince Foster Was Murdered?," Irvine discussed what he regarded as still newer evidence, a set of crime-scene photos of the dead White House official. A Foster skeptic and attorney was pressing for the release of the photos, while Foster family members argued in court that such a release would violate their privacy. Even some in the news media wanted to make the photos public. In its review of the case, though, the

US Supreme Court unanimously decided in favor of the Foster's family, causing Irvine to question the judgment of even the court's "most conservative justice," Antonin Scalia.[60]

MISREPORTING OPERATION IRAQI FREEDOM AND OTHER NEWS

By 2003, Irvine had been involved with AIM for more than three decades. At eighty-three, he had given up day-to-day involvement in the group and now held the honorary title of chairman emeritus. (AIM's new chairman was Irvine's son, Donald.) Meanwhile, AIM itself was thriving. Its assets totaled something above $5.5 million, with the Sarah Scaife Foundation continuing to be its biggest single funder, donating in the current tax year alone $425,000.[61] Moreover, with George W. Bush now in the White House after eight fraught years of the Clinton administration, the political landscape also seemed more congenial to the group's mission, although many of the old challenges remained. In 2003, with the help of several coauthors, Irvine published his final collection of media commentaries, *Why You Can't Trust the News*. As in his earlier works, he once again saw his task as nothing less than combating "mind pollution—the insinuation of misinformation and harmful ideas into people's heads via the media."[62]

The new self-published book was a modest affair. Pocket-sized, it contained advertisements for AIM merchandise appended to its back pages, along with a form for ordering extra bulk-rate copies. As for content, it collected, among other items, a variety of "Media Monitor" radio broadcasts from the past year or so, including many that had aired the various authors' perennial grievances: ongoing allegations of liberal news bias, given a boost with the recent publication of Bernard Goldberg's CBS News tell-all, *Bias* (2001); underreported failures of the FBI; fake news on global warming and pesticides; anti-Americanism in academia; and of course one of Irvine's ongoing pet peeves, the media's pandering to the gay agenda.

Also collected in the tiny book were a half-dozen radio transcripts about the major story of last year and now this one, "Operation Iraqi Freedom," official launched on March 20, 2003. In the run-up to the war, AIM had been critical of CNN and other cable news networks for giving what it deemed unwarranted airtime to Scott Ritter, the former Marine In-telligence officer and UN weapons inspector who had come to doubt that Iraq was actually stockpiling weapons of mass destruction, as the Bush administration claimed (*Trust*, 34).[63]

Following the monthlong war, AIM had criticized other critics of the operation. In an April 9 broadcast included in the book, for example, Notra Trulock, a former Energy Department intelligence official in the Reagan administration who had joined AIM as an editorial staffer, reprimanded retired CBS anchorman Walter Cronkite for denouncing the operation and labeling the Bush administration arrogant for pursuing it. Trulock charged that the eighty-six-year-old former newsman had a long-standing "leftist bias," beginning with his decisive turn against the Vietnam War following the Tet offensive. In light of such a history, she said, "it should be no surprise to find Cronkite echoing the far left in support of Saddam Hussein" (*Trust*, 88). In subsequent broadcasts, Trulock also leveled other charges. One was against former CNN newsman Peter Arnett for grant-ing an overly sympathetic interview to state-run Iraqi TV. Another was against the *Washington Post* and other "liberal media" for changing the tone of their coverage "at the first sign of casualties." And yet another was against the press generally for its use of anonymous sources in the ongo-ing post-war debate "over the accuracy of U.S. intelligence before the war in Iraq" (*Trust*, 91, 109).

A final item in the book had little to do with the Iraq War and was writ-ten by Irvine alone. It was a review of Hillary Clinton's recent memoir, *Living History* (2003), which recounted her eight years as First Lady and close adviser to the president.

The title of Irvine's review was "Hillary's Lies," an unsubtle signal to his readers what he thought about much of the former First Lady's recol-lections. He was especially exercised by what he regarded as her distorted retelling of what had come to be known as "Travelgate." In her memoir, Clinton had denied giving a direct order to fire the seven travel-office employees during the early days of the administration She did acknowl-edge, though, that her off-hand comment about the disorganized state of the office to some high-level White House staffers may have led to that unintended outcome.[64]

Irvine was having none of it. Pointing to a distant relative of Bill Clin-ton who had been installed in the office following the mass firings, he said in his review, "Hillary doesn't mention that they planned to have her [the relative] take charge of the operation with the expectation that she would steer the travel business to a firm in which their close friend . . . had an interest" (*Trust*, 105). In fact, a similar allegation following the incident had been investigated. Neither that investigation nor a later one by an independent counsel, however, had uncovered sufficient evidence against the former First Lady, who was never charged with a crime.[65] In her memoir, Clinton had dismissed the whole episode as minor, worthy at most of perhaps two to three weeks' attention by the press and others. "In a partisan political climate," though, it had morphed into a full-blown and fractious scandal.[66]

On November 16 of the following year, Irvine died from complications of a stroke at a hospice in Rockville, Maryland. In addition to Donald, his son and AIM chairman, he was survived by his wife, the former Kay Araki, and three grandchildren. At his funeral, one of those whom he had mentored, David W. Almasi, an official at the National Center for Public Policy Research, a bulwark of the conservative movement, spoke admiringly of his old friend and teacher. Summing up Irvine's importance to the movement, Almasi conjured a starkly vivid image: "Irvine was a thorn in the side of the liberal media for decades, and it will be a long time—if ever—before the aches he caused them go away."[67]

CONCLUSION

Following Irvine's death, friends and admirers continued to pay tribute to him, many, like Almasi at the funeral, commenting on his pioneering work and the vital importance of continuing it. In a posting on the AIM website November 26, 2004, for instance, Irvine's longtime colleague and collaborator, Cliff Kincaid, wrote that, in the thirty-five years since Irvine had founded AIM, he had so managed to blunt the impact of the big liberal media that they "have lost much of their stature and do not seem so big anymore." This was an ongoing war, however, as Kincaid reminded his readers, and "victory can only be achieved by continuing to make progress, by constantly maintaining and then elevating our standards of responsibility and accountability."[68]

Younger media critic L. Brent Bozell III voiced a similar theme. The founder nearly two decades earlier of the Media Research Center, in many ways the modern counterpart to AIM, Bozell celebrated Irvine "for inventing the field of professional conservative media criticism" and for offering a model for others "to correct the historical record if distorted by the press."[69] Politicians also joined in the eulogies. In a statement read on November 20 on the floor of the US Senate, then second-term Alabama senator Jeff Sessions credited Irvine for making clear for all to see "the liberal bias in media, Hollywood, and academia." Like others, the future embattled Trump attorney general, while braced for a long fight, was thankful to Reed Irvine for having equipped the voting public with the tools to watch and read the news with "a critical eye."[70]

Even mainstream news outlets, the very ones that had often come under fire from AIM, also ran obituaries that spoke, in part at least, of Irvine's considerable influence, not only in conservative circles but beyond. In the *Washington Post*, for example, the obit writer quoted Michael Hoyt, then executive editor of *Columbia Journalism Review* (CJR), who saw Irvine as representing "a resentment that was larger than him. Some people treated him as a kook, but others thought, 'Maybe he's got some points here.' That had a lasting impact."[71] In the *New York Times*, similarly, the obit writer quoted Alex S. Jones, then director of the Shorenstein Center on Press, Politics and Public Policy at Harvard's Kennedy School of Government: "I think AIM was the fountainhead of the effort to denounce the liberal media and create the image of the mainstream [press] as very liberal. And that effort has proved quite successful."[72]

A figure as outspoken as Irvine was bound, of course, to be criticized as well, even in death. In the same obituary in the *Washington Post* that quoted CJR editor Hoyt, for example, Ben Bagdikian, then professor emeritus at UC Berkeley, said, "He was a very doctrinaire, rather unchanging ultraconservative critic. In the years since the mid-1970s, a much more intellectually sophisticated conservative criticism of the news media began to emerge. . . . His criticisms were so stereotyped that they didn't carry the information that backed his accusations. It was an indictment without individual charges."[73] Irvine was perhaps a more dogged researcher than Bagdikian gave him credit for, but the claim that the late founder of AIM had espied the media world through a narrow lens, looking for instances to confirm and reconfirm his prevailing assumption of liberal bias, while hammering home his first principles of free market economics, patriotism, anti-communism, and Christian values, has persisted in the years since.

Consider for example a perceptive essay several years ago in the *Atlantic* by author Nicole Hemmer. A historian of the conservative movement whose books *Messengers of the Right* (2016) and *Partisans* (2022) are seminal texts, Hemmer has argued that, for media critics like Irvine and indeed for those who wrote for older publications like *Human Events*, the notions of objectivity and partisanship were in tension but ultimately not incompatible. In other words, explained Hemmer, while the stated mission of critics like Irvine was to correct the record, purging it of an alleged leftist slant, they saw no conflict in also infusing the record with their own conservative point of view.[74]

Examples abound. In his critique of Vietnam War news coverage, for one, Irvine not only made efforts to document where individual reporters or broadcast networks had distorted or ignored the facts. He also strove to make the case for a more pro-American brand of reporting, of the sort he fondly remembered from World War II. Similarly, when he criticized the mainstream media for its coverage of gays, he was not content to point out that news reports, many penned by homosexual writers, were one-sided or inaccurate. He also aimed to remind his readers and listeners than such a lifestyle was suspect, likely dangerous, and ultimately at odds with traditional Christian values.

Irvine's zeal to both correct the record and offer a counternarrative to it often overcame his judgment. The result was a variety of conspiracy theories that are also an undeniable part of his historical legacy. An illuminating case in point is the 1993 death of Clinton aide Vince Foster. Despite mounds of evidence to the contrary, Irvine and his co-conspiracy theorists persisted in the idea that Foster had died not by his own hand but by someone else's, most likely at the shadowy direction of the Clintons. As late as the 2016 wrap-up to the GOP presidential nomination, for example, Cliff Kincaid was keeping Irvine's theory alive, seconding candidate Donald Trump's characterization of Foster's death as "fishy." Wrote Kincaid, "Trump is right. Foster is the man who knew too much. He had knowledge of various Clinton scandals. . . . His body was found in a Virginia park on July 20, 1993, and the media accepted the verdict of suicide."[75] Irvine's theory about the downing of Korean Airlines Flight 007 was another instance of his zeal overtaking his judgment. Convinced that the plane had been deliberately targeted by the Soviets, he continued to cast doubts on US intelligence that had consistently indicated otherwise.[76] Such conspiracy theories have since become, if anything, more elaborate and widespread. Irvine and his colleagues are not solely to blame—the far left having conjured its own share of wild theories—but they have certainly contributed to our contemporary mistrust and paranoia. That is also part of Irvine's legacy.

To his supporters on the right, especially in the generation immediately following his, Irvine will likely remain a trailblazer, tenacious in his questioning of the so-called liberal media establishment, largely responsible for imputing to it the charge of bias, and successful in laying the groundwork for other conservative watchdogs and critics, including Bozell's Media Research Center, the National Center for Public Policy Research, and the Center for Media and Public Affairs. Some of Irvine's supporters also credit him with helping to create an audience for a new crop of conservative media outlets, including Fox News, Breitbart News Network, Liberty Broadcasting, Newsmax, the *New York Post*, the *Drudge Report*, and the now defunct WorldNetDaily.

To his detractors in the center and on the left, though, Irvine will be remembered as someone who hid zealotry behind a mask of media criticism, who often distorted rather than corrected the public record, who dismissed credible claims about global warming and other environmental problems, who gave a polite sheen to homophobia and other bigotries, and who perhaps most damagingly to public confidence trafficked in conspiracy theories. His successors, like Cliff Kincaid and Bozell, are frequently viewed by opponents through a similar lens.[77]

The politics of Irvine's legacy aside, however, he will almost certainly remain an important figure in the history of media criticism. First, he was a key link between an older group of conservative journalists and commentators, including those on *Human Events* and *National Review*, and a newer generation of media watchdogs and writers on the right, people like George Will, Charles Krauthammer, Peggy Noonan, Bill Kristol, L. Brent Bozell III, David Brooks, David Frum, Dinesh D'Souza, Ben Shapiro, and Charles Kirk. Second, almost singlehandedly at the start, he put Big Media on notice that it was being watched, under scrutiny for sins real and imagined by someone quite willing to call them out, demand equal time, hurl the charge of bias. And third, he proved surprisingly effective over time, keeping the press "leaning rightward for its respectability," as one observer has said of the general movement of which Irvine was the fountainhead.[78]

Irvine died knowing his criticism had made a difference. It had been a slow process, certainly, but it had had an effect.

NOTES

1. Reed Irvine, *Media Mischief and Misdeeds* (Chicago: Regnery Gateway, 1984), 8.

2. Ibid., 9. See also Accuracy in Academia, https://www.academia.org/.

3. Accuracy in Media, "Who We Are," https://www.aim.org/about/who -we-are/.

4. "Reed Irvine: America's Original Media Watchdog," Biography, http://www.reedirvine.net/biography.html. See also, "Reed Irvine," NNDB, 2019, https://www.nndb.com/people/692/000120332/.

5. Ibid.

6. For information on the now defunct University Professors for Academic Order, see Steven Alan Samson, "University Professors for Academic Order: Background," 1990, Digital Commons, Liberty University, Helms School of Government, https://digitalcommons.liberty.edu/cgi/viewcontent.cgi?referer=https:// www.google.com/&httpsredir=1&article=1284&context=gov_fac_pubs.

7. "Arthur G. McDowell, Union Leader, Dies after Automobile Crash," *New York Times*, October 8, 1966, Times Machine, 26, https://timesmachine.nytimes .com/timesmachine/1966/10/08/issue.html.

8. See, for example, William L. O'Neil's classic work, *Coming Apart: An Informal History of America in the 1960s*, with a new introduction by the author (1971; repr., Chicago: Ivan R. Dee, 2005).

9. See William F. Buckley Jr., *God and Man at Yale: The Superstitions of Academic Freedom*, with a new introduction by the author (1951; repr., Washington, DC: Regnery Publishing, 1999) and Russell Kirk, *The Conservative Mind* (1953; repr., Washington, DC: Regnery Gateway, 2016.)

10. See Nicole Hemmer, "The Conservative War on Liberal Media Has a Long History," *Atlantic*, January 17, 2014, https://www.theatlantic.com /politics/archive/2014/01/the-conservative-war-on-liberal-media-has-a-long-his

tory/283149/. Also, Matt Grossman, "Media Bias (Real and Perceived) and the Rise of Partisan Media," Niskanen Center, November 6, 2017, https://www.nis kanencenter.org/media-bias-real-perceived-rise-partisan-media/.

11. John B. Judis, William F. Buckley Jr., *Patron Saint of the Conservatives* (New York: Simon & Schuster, 1998), 114.

12. For an example of the right's continuing criticism of liberal bias during the 1964 presidential campaign, see Harry Stein, "The Goldwater Takedown," *City-Journal Magazine*, The Manhattan Institute, Autumn 2016, https://www.city-journal.org/html/goldwater-takedown-14787.html.

13. Irvine, *Media Mischief*, 8.

14. Quoted in Daniel Allen, "Anthony Lewis and AIM," March 26, 2009, https://www.academia.org/anthony-lewis-aim/.

15. Irvine, *Media Mischief*, 9.

16. John Cory, "TV: 13-Part History of Vietnam War on PBS, *New York Times*, October 4, 1983, 66, Times Machine, https://timesmachine.nytimes.com/timesmachine/1983/10/04/207299.html?pageNumber=66.

17. "Television's Vietnam," narrated by Charlton Heston, "Part One: The Impact of Media," YouTube video, 58:59, from a July 26, 1985, airing on PBS stations, posted by federal Expression, February 23, 2017, https://www.youtube.com/watch?v=iaECqmMYtxM; See also Fox Butterfield, "A Critique on PBS on Vietnam Sets Off a Dispute," *New York Times*, June 13, 1985, front page, Times Machine, https://timesmachine.nytimes.com/timesmachine/1985/06/13/issue.html.

18. Later historians have called Tet a "strategic victory" for Hanoi because it challenged the myth of American progress and caused key advisers to rethink continuing the war. See, for example, James H. Willbanks, *The Tet Offensive: A Concise History* (New York: Columbia University Press, 2007), 83.

19. Ibid., 21, 105.

20. Ibid., 55.

21. See, for example, Daniel C. Hallin, "The Media, the War in Vietnam, and Political Support: A Critique of the Thesis of an Oppositional Media," *Journal of Politics*, vol. 46, no. 1 (February 1984), 2–24. In a compelling article, Hallin argues that the change in Vietnam coverage *"seems best explained as a reflection of and response to a collapse of consensus—especially of elite consensus—on foreign policy* [italics in original]" (5).

22. See "The Media and War: An Interview with Daniel Hallin," March 5, 2018, Oxford Research Group, accessed June 13, 2020, https://www.oxford researchgroup.org.uk/blog/the-media-and-war-an-interview-with-daniel-hallin. More than three decades later, some critics on the right were also displeased with

The Vietnam War, a ten-part documentary by Ken Burns and Lynn Novick, and written by historian Geoffrey C. Ward, that appeared on PBS. See, for example, Mark Moyar, "What Ken Burns Omits from The Vietnam War," *Providence Magazine*, May 2, 2018, Providence Institute on Religion and Democracy, https://providencemag.com/2018/05/ken-burns-omits-vietnam-war/; also, Andrew Friedman, "Burns's 'Vietnam' Recites a Leftist Consensus," *Stanford Review*, October 24, 2017, https://stanfordreview.org/burnss-vietnam-recites-a-leftist-consensus/. The documentary was also criticized on the left, however: see, for example, Alex Shephard, "The Insidious Ideology of Ken Burns's *The Vietnam War*," *New Republic*, September 19, 2017, https://newrepublic.com/article/144864/insidious-ideology-ken-burnss-vietnam-war.

23. Irvine, *Media Mischief*, 34. All further references will be to this edition and quoted parenthetically in the text.

24. "The Uncounted Enemy: A Vietnam Deception," Parts I, II, and II, YouTube video, 1:16, originally aired on *CBS Reports* on January 23, 1982, posted by Michael Hiam, January 4, 2016, https://www.youtube.com/watch?v=PFXTCfY5qME, https://www.youtube.com/watch?v=F58OibBx2cI&t=4s, https://www.youtube.com/watch?v=GjyPlSCG4BQ&t=1s.

25. Ibid. See also, Mike Moravitz, "Westmoreland vs. CBS: The Military, the Media, and the Vietnam War," George Mason University, accessed June 14, 2020, https://mason.gmu.edu/~mmoravit/clioiiwebsite/westmoreland/about.html.

26. Dan Kowet and Sally Bedell, "Anatomy of a Smear: How CBS 'Got' General Westmoreland," *TV Guide*, May 29, 1982, 2–15.

27. Quoted in Moravitz, Westmoreland. See also, Burton Benjamin, *CBS, General Westmoreland, and How a TV Documentary Went Wrong* (New York: Harper & Row, 1988).

28. *Westmoreland v. CBS Inc.*, 596 F Supp. 170 (SDNY, 1984), Justia, https://law.justia.com/cases/federal/district-courts/FSupp/596/1170/1676298/.

29. In fact, Crile was not so much made to depart ship as temporarily restricted to his quarters, a move presumably intended to show the network was taking even technical lapses seriously. In 1985, he joined another CBS program, *60 Minutes*, where he produced segments for several of the top correspondents, including Wallace. See Douglas Martin, George Crile, "CBS Documentary Producer, Dies at 61," *New York Times*, May 16, 2006, https://www.nytimes.com/2006/05/16/obituaries/16crile.html.

30. "Texts of Statements on the End of Westmoreland's Libel Suit against CBS," *New York Times*, February 19, 1985, https://www.nytimes.com/1985/02/19/movies/texts-of-statements-on-the-end-of-westmoreland-s-libel-suit-against-cbs.html.

31. "Transcript of President Reagan Address on Downing of Korean Airliner," *New York Times*, September 6, 1983, https://www.nytimes.com/1983/09/06/world/transcript-of-president-reagan-s-address-on-downing-of-korean-airliner.html.

32. The accident claim was first made by investigative journalist Seymour Hersh in *The Target Is Destroyed: What Really Happened to Flight 007* (London: Faber & Faber, 1999).

33. See Celestine Bohlen, "Tape Displays the Anguish on Jet the Soviets Downed," *New York Times*, October 16, 1992, https://www.nytimes.com/1992/10/16/world/tape-displays-the-anguish-on-jet-the-soviets-downed.html.

34. Michael Getler, "U.S. Airforce Plane Crossed Path of Jet," *Washington Post*, September 3, 1983, https://www.washingtonpost.com/archive/politics/1983/09/05/us-air-force-plane-crossed-path-of-jet/69172ba5-232c-4650-b40c-7fc7666fad7a/.

35. David Shribman, "U.S. Experts Say Soviet Didn't See Jet Was Civilian, *New York Times*, October 7, 1983, https://www.nytimes.com/1983/10/07/world/us-experts-say-soviet-didn-t-see-jet-was-cililian.html.

36. Ibid. Other reports had the RC-135 over international waters at the time of the incident.

37. "Media Mischief," an interview with Reed Irvine on his new book, *Media Mischief and Misdeeds*, by Brian Lamb, C-SPAN, August 8, 1984, https://www.c-span.org/video/?102976-1/media-mischief.

38. There have been several well-regarded books on Iran-Contra that consider who knew what and when. See, for instance, Malcolm Byrne, *Iran-Contra: Reagan's Scandal and the Unchecked Use of Presidential Power* (Lawrence: University Press of Kansas, 2014) and Lawrence Walsh, *Firewall: The Iran-Contra Conspiracy and Cover-Up* (New York: W.W. Norton, 1997).

39. See, for example, R. W. Apple Jr., "The Iran Affair: A Presidency Damaged," November 26, 1986, *New York Times*, https://www.nytimes.com/1986/11/26/world/the-iran-affair-a-presidency-damaged.html; Fox Butterfield, "Helping the Contras," *New York Times*, May 17, 1987, https://www.nytimes.com/1987/05/17/weekinreview/iran-contra-affair-the-unfolding-story.html; and Jack Anderson and Joseph Spear, "Who Got the Contra Money?" *Washington Post*, March 31, 1987, https://www.washingtonpost.com/archive/local/1987/03/31/who-got-the-iran-contra-money/4b486913-bcd5-48eb-aef1-929136a1a58a/.

40. Cliff Kincaid, "How Bradlee Attacked Republicans for Fun and Profit," NoisyRoom.net, October 31, 2014, http://noisyroom.net/blog/2014/10/31/how-ben-bradlee-attacked-republicans-for-fun-and-profit/.

41. "Presidential Approval Ratings—Gallup Historical Statistics and Trends," Gallup, https://news.gallup.com/poll/116677/presidential-approval-ratings-gallup-historical-statistics-trends.aspx; see also, Haynes Johnson and Tracy Thompson, "North Charges Dismissed at Request of Prosecutor, *Washington Post*, September 17, 1991, https://www.washingtonpost.com/archive/politics/1991/09/17/north-charges-dismissed-at-request-of-prosecutor/d6b5b3dc-d164-40f2-a579-c23521f66686/.

42. "Accuracy in Media," Donor List, Conservative Transparency, accessed June 16, 2020, http://conservativetransparency.org/basic-search/?q=accuracy+in+media&sf%5B%5D=candidate&sf%5B%5D=donor&sf%5B%5D=recipient&sf%5B%5D=transaction&sf%5B%5D=finances; see also Jane Mayer, *Dark Money: The Hidden History of the Billionaires behind the Radical Right*, with a new preface (2016; repr., New York: Anchor, 2017), 73–111.

43. "Reed Irvine, Watchdog, " Biography.

44. Stephen Engelberg, with Jeff Gerth, "Officials Say Bush Heard '85 Charge against Noriega," *New York Times*, May 8, 1988, front page, TimesMachine, https://timesmachine.nytimes.com/timesmachine/1988/05/08/246788.html?pageNumber=1; Jim McGee and David Hoffman, "Rivals Hint Bush Understates Knowledge of Noriega Ties," *Washington Post*, May 8, 1988, https://www.washingtonpost.com/archive/politics/1988/05/08/rivals-hint-bush-understates-knowledge-of-noriega-ties/4226c789-bc77-460a-91ca-f539985490e9/.

45. Reed Irvine and Cliff Kincaid, *Profiles of Deception: How the News Media Are Deceiving the American People* (Smithtown, NY: Book Distributors, 1990), 95. All further references will be to this edition and cited parenthetically in the text.

46. McGee and Hoffman, "Rivals Hint."

47. "Envoy Offers No New Data on Bush Briefing and Noriega," *New York Times*, May 10, 1988, D24, TimesMachine, https://timesmachine.nytimes.com/timesmachine/1988/05/10/709188.html?pageNumber=95.

48. Texas Republican Senator John Tower had developed a reputation in Washington as a womanizer and an alcoholic. See, for example, Elizabeth King, "This Is What Happened Last Time a Cabinet Nomination Was Rejected," History and Politics, Time.com, February 3, 2017, https://time.com/4653593/cabinet-rejection-john-tower/.

49. "Crocker's Triumph, Reagan's Loss," *New York Times*, December 15, 1988, A38, TimesMachine, https://timesmachine.nytimes.com/timesmachine/1988/12/15/012588.html?pageNumber=38; Eloise Salholz and Shawn Doherty, "Shanties on the Green," *Newsweek*, February 3, 1986, 63.

50. Reed Irvine, Joseph C. Goulden, and Cliff Kincaid, *The News Manipulators: Why You Can't Trust the News* (Smithtown, NY: Book Distributors, 1993),

xvii. All further references will be to this edition and quoted parenthetically in the text.

51. On the epidemiology of AIDS at the time, see Dennis H. Osmond, "Epidemiology of HIV/AIDS in the United States," HIV InSite, University of California, San Francisco, 2003, accessed June 17, 2020, http://hivinsite .ucsf.edu/InSite?page=kb-01-03#:~:text=CDC%20estimated%20that%20 the%20peak,peaked%20around%20the%20mid%2D1980s.

52. On February 28, 1994, the Clinton administration instituted its "Don't Ask, Don't Tell" policy. The policy lasted until September 20, 2011.

53. "Who Is Vincent Foster," August 6, 1996, *Wall Street Journal*, https:// www.wsj.com/articles/SB839344430467171500.

54. United Press International, "Fiske Report on Foster Released," UPI Archives, June 30, 1994, https://www.upi.com/Archives/1994/06/30/Fiske-report -on-Foster-released/1784772948800/; also, "Whitewater: The Foster Report," 1994 Fiske Investigation, 1998, Washingtonpost.com, https://www.washington post.com/wp-srv/politics/special/whitewater/docs/fosterii.htm#IIB.

55. Ibid. Also, Susan Schmidt, "Starr Probe Reaffirms Foster Killed Himself," *Washington Post*, October 11, 1997, A4, https://www.washingtonpost.com /wp-srv/politics/special/whitewater/stories/wwtr971011.html.

56. Stephen Labaton, "A Report on His Suicide Portrays a Deeply Troubled Foster," *New York Times*, October 11, 1997, A8, TimesMachine, https://times machine.nytimes.com/timesmachine/1997/10/11/562050.html?pageNumber=1.

57. Philip Weiss, "Clinton Crazy," *New York Times Magazine*, February 23, 1997, https://www.nytimes.com/1997/02/23/magazine/clinton-crazy.html.

58. "Vincent Foster Case," panelists discuss their theories on the death of Vincent Foster, Accuracy in Media, C-SPAN, 1:18:00, October 18, 1997, https:// www.c-span.org/video/?93446-1/vincent-foster-case.

59. Reed Irvine, "Evidence Proving Foster Was Murdered," *AIM Report*, Accuracy in Media, July 1, 2001, https://www.aim.org/aim-report/aim-report -evidence-proving-foster-was-murdered/.

60. Reed Irvine, "Who Cares If Vince Foster Was Murdered?" *Media Monitor*, Accuracy in Media, December 18, 2003, https://www.aim.org/media-mon itor/who-cares-if-vince-foster-was-murdered/; see also, "Supreme Court Rules for 'Survivor Privacy' in Favish," The United States Department of Justice, April 9, 2004, https://www.justice.gov/oip/blog/foia-post-2004-supreme-court -rules-survivor-privacy-favish#:~:text=Favish%2C%20124%20S.,FOIA%20 Exemption%207(C).

61. "Accuracy in Media," Conservative Transparency, American Bridge 21st Century Foundation, accessed July 3, 2020, http://conservativetransparency.org /org/accuracy-in-media/.

62. Reed Irvine, Cliff Kincaid, and Notra Trulock, *Why You Can't Trust the News* (Washington, DC: Accuracy in Media, 2003), Preface, n.p. All further references will be to this edition and cited parenthetically in the text.

63. Ritter had earlier discussed his views on Iraq in a book. See Scott Ritter, *Endgame: Solving the Iraq Problem—Once and for All* (New York: Simon & Schuster, 1999), 34.

64. See Hillary Clinton, *Living History* (New York: Simon & Schuster, 2003), 172.

65. Charles Babington, "Hillary Clinton Cleared in Travelgate," *Sun Sentinel*, June 23, 2000, https://www.sun-sentinel.com/news/fl-xpm-2000-06-23-0006220924-story.html.

66. Clinton, *Living History*, 172.

67. David W. Almasi, "Tributes," November 18, 2004, "Reed Irvine: America's Original Media Watchdog," http://www.reedirvine.net/tributes_david_almasi.html.

68. Cliff Kincaid, "Reed Irvine's Legacy: Truth in Journalism," *AIM Report*, November 26, 2004, Accuracy in Media, https://www.aim.org/aim-report/aim-report-reed-irvines-legacy-truth-in-journalism-december-a/.

69. L. Brent Bozell, III, "Reed Irvine, RIP," *NewsFlash*, January 2005, vol. 12, no.1, 8, The Media Research Center's Monthly Members' Report, https://cdn.mrc.org/newsletters/watchdog-newsletter-01-05.pdf.

70. "Senate Floor Statement of Senator [Jeff] Sessions," November 20, 2004, "Reed Irvine: America's Original Media Watchdog," http://www.reedirvine.net/tributes_jeff_sessions.html.

71. Quoted in Patricia Sullivan, "Media Watchdog Reed Irvine, 82," *Washington Post*, November 18, 2004, https://www.washingtonpost.com/wp-dyn/articles/A58852-2004Nov17.html.

72. Quoted in Michael Kaufman, "Reed Irvine, 82, the Founder of Media Criticism Group, Dies," *"New York Times*, November 19, 2004, https://www.nytimes.com/2004/11/19/us/reed-irvine-82-the-founder-of-a-media-criticism-group-dies.html.

73. Quoted in Sullivan, "Media Watchdog."

74. Hemmer, "Conservative War on Liberal Media."

75. Cliff Kincaid, "Something Stinks: The 'Fishy' Vince Foster Case," AIM Column, Accuracy in Media, May 26, 2016, https://www.aim.org/aim-column/something-stinks-the-fishy-vince-foster-case/.

76. Another theory that Irvine and others clung to was that crash of TWA Flight 800 off Long Island on July 17, 1996, was the result of a rocket. See National Transportation Safety Board, Executive Summary, "Aircraft Accident Report: In-flight Breakup over the Atlantic Ocean Trans World Airlines Flight

800 Boeing 747-131, N93119 Near East Moriches, New York July 17, 1996,"
xvi, accessed July 4, 2020, https://www.ntsb.gov/investigations/AccidentReports
/Reports/AAR0003.pdf.

77. See, for example, Larry Keller, "Cliff Kincaid Takes on 'Liberal Media'
Gays," *Intelligence Report*, February 23, 2011, Southern Poverty Law Center,
https://www.splcenter.org/fighting-hate/intelligence-report/2011/cliff-kincaid
-takes-liberal-media-gays.

78. Michael Parenti, "The Politics of News Media," *Sacred Heart University
Review*, vol. 19, no.1, 2, https://digitalcommons.sacredheart.edu/cgi/viewcontent
.cgi?referer=https://www.google.com/&httpsredir=1&article=1045&context=shu
review.

Neil Postman, 1985

Chapter Six

Neil Postman

News as Entertainment

We are presented not only with fragmented news but news without context, without value, and therefore without essential seriousness; that is to say, news as pure entertainment.

—Neil Postman, *Amusing Ourselves to Death*, 1985

Neil Postman was, like Reed Irvine, a nonpracticing journalist who went on to become a leading media critic. A native New Yorker, Postman grew up in the 1930s in the largely Jewish borough of Brooklyn, after which he spent most of his adult life as a teacher at the New York University School of Education, later the Steinhardt School of Education. Here he chaired the department of Culture and Communication and founded a program in media ecology. Throughout his academic career, he was also a prolific writer, authoring or coauthoring some twenty books about subjects as various as education, linguistics, general semantics, technology, and most famously media studies. In both his published works on the subject and his teaching, he was not indifferent to politics. Unlike Irvine, however, Postman's focus was less on the political content or alleged bias of various media than on their effect on American public discourse and democracy.

Television drew most of his attention. In his best-known book, *Amusing Ourselves to Death: Public Discourse in the Age of Show Business* (1985), he examined television as if he were an alien from another planet taking stock of a strange new phenomenon, one that had the power to present the events of the day in a surprisingly novel way. Setting out the essential historical background, he traced the process by which, toward the end of the nineteenth century, America's older typographic culture

161

had begun to fade, giving way to telegraphy and the new image-centered technologies, epitomized first by photography and film and then by television. For Postman, this evolution was not simply a matter of one technology replacing others. Rather, like the Canadian media theorist Marshall McLuhan, to whom he was indebted, he also saw it as the advent of a new epistemology. Over time, it had formed the social and intellectual environment in which viewers were compelled to view both themselves and their culture.

Postman the historian could trace this transition with a measure of scholarly dispassion; Postman the moralist was not as sanguine: Like another of his mentors, the English writer and philosopher Aldous Huxley, he believed that the biggest threat to Western democracies was not external, as George Orwell had foreseen, but internal, most powerfully in the form of their dominant media: "I will say once again that I am no relativist in this matter," he wrote in his most famous book, "and that I believe the epistemology created by television not only is inferior to a print-based epistemology but is dangerous and absurdist.[1]

The differences for him were stark: while America's former typographic culture had helped to shape a certain rational and orderly quality of mind through a slow and methodical mode of exposition, television's rapid and often discontinuous presentation of images resulted in just the opposite: a habit of mind addicted to stimulation and amusement. And because amusement and entertainment were core values for commercial television—ways of delivering a mass viewership to advertisers—even the presentation of news had to be, first and foremost, packaged and presented in a pleasing way, whatever other informational or educational goals its producers had in mind.

Wise TV news consumers could not therefore, indeed should not, remain passive viewers. They needed to be active, engaged, and often skeptical critics. In *How to Watch Television News* (1992), which he coauthored with Steve Powers, his former pupil and a onetime broadcast journalist himself, Postman offered a primer on television news: how it was assembled and produced, how its pictorial biases worked subliminally to shape viewers' knowledge of their immediate and more distant reality, and what measures might be adopted to counteract the medium's pernicious effects. Nearly two decades after the original book, and five years after Postman's early death from lung cancer, his coauthor put out an updated edition. In the interim, new digital-based technologies had emerged, each with their own epistemologies, and these had steadily eroded television's once-dominant influence. It was yet another "news paradigm" shift, said Powers, who saw both the benefits and dangers of having what he viewed as unmediated news beamed directly not just "to our television screens but to an array of devices."[2]

The very idea of unmediated news is now, of course, difficult to sustain. In many ways, we have simply traded the older television gatekeepers for algorithms that filter what we see and hear on a variety of digital platforms, often confirming our biases or exploiting our cognitive weaknesses. Had he lived long enough, Postman might well have begun an investigation into new media. And as before, he would have adopted the twin stances of curious outsider and moral crusader. Less certain is whether this man of Enlightenment values who believed passionately in rationality—his final book looked back appreciatively to the eighteenth century—would have been as alert to the more Orwellian threats posed by the new media.

GROWING UP IN BROOKLYN

Postman's Brooklyn childhood both reinforced his ethnic identity and offered him a peek, albeit indirectly, into the broader American culture. Born on March 8, 1931, in the early years of the Great Depression, Neil Milton Postman grew up in the borough's Flatbush neighborhood, which he later described as "a little shtetl," one of those Jewish towns in Eastern and Central Europe before the Holocaust.[3] Both his parents spoke Yiddish. His father, Murray Postman, was a truck driver, and his mother, Bea, a homemaker with an unusual flair for writing. At the start of World War II, Postman's older brother, Jack, entered the army, while he and his sister, Ruth, a few years his senior, continued in school. It was also during this period that Postman began to publish a family newspaper, *The Postbox*. The paper, composed mostly of family gossip and summaries of previously condensed novels, was distributed to relatives at home, as well as to the forty or so male family members who were now serving in either the army or navy.[4]

His Brooklyn neighborhood largely circumscribed his day-to-day life. Here he passed and frequently patronized the bakeries, delis, candy stores, and Chinese restaurant "catering to the Jewish clientele." Here too he went to P.S. 99, attended by Christian as well as Jewish children; enrolled in Hebrew School in preparation for his bar mitzvah, entered Midwood High School, where in 1949 he graduated several years before another famous Midwood alumnus, Woody Allen; played sports on the public playgrounds; and in general absorbed the sights, sounds, and smells of a self-contained but richly textured world. Later in life, Postman would recall that this Brooklyn boyhood and sense of Jewishness helped to give him "a certain solidity in who I am." At the same time, being a Jew, even in the relative safety of America, made him something of an "outsider," which proved personally difficult at times but also provided Postman the writer a "unique perspective" from which to examine his culture.[5]

For a glimpse of the wider world, Postman and his friends turned to movies. Together, he and they would head down Ocean Avenue to Avenue J, where the Midwood Theatre showed many of the popular movies of the day. Among these were the Andy Hardy series, staring Mickey Rooney and set in the fictional Midwestern town of Carvel, a world apart from Brooklyn. Despite this, such idealized representations of American life struck a chord: "There was a sweetness to those movies that we related to," Postman would later recall in interviews conducted for *Growing Up Jewish in America: An Oral History.*[6]

Following high school, he entered the State University of New York at Fredonia, southwest of Buffalo, which several years earlier had become one of the state's teachers' colleges. His goal was a bachelor of science degree in education, with an emphasis on English instruction. He also joined the varsity basketball team. At just six feet, he was not among the team's taller players, even in an era when the average college player was shorter than today. Nevertheless, over three full seasons as a varsity player, he was a prolific point machine. In 1986, more than three decades after his graduation, the college inducted him into the Fredonia State Athletics Hall of Fame, the only member of the 1953 graduating class to be so honored.[7]

The Korean War, begun in mid-1950, was still being fought by the time Postman earned his BS degree. Like many of his family members during the last war, he enlisted in the army and was sent overseas. But his tour of duty came to an abrupt end several months later after China, North Korea, and the United States signed an armistice. Back again in New York City,

Postman enrolled in Teachers College, Columbia University, where over the next five years he completed both a masters and a doctoral degree in education. Having completed his academic training, and now married to the former Shelley Ross, he accepted a job in the English department of what was then San Francisco State College, a teacher-training institution that later became part of the California State University System.[8] His time in San Francisco lasted, though, just a single academic year, 1958–1959.

He and Shelley returned to New York for his new position at New York University's School of Education, now the Steinhardt School of Culture, Education, and Human Development. The school would be his academic home for the next thirty-nine years. A very capable administrator as well as brilliant teacher, he was eventually elected chair of the department of Culture and Communication, a position he held until a year before his death. In 1971, he established, along with his colleague and sometime collaborator Terence P. Moran, the graduate programs in media ecology. (Moran went on to found the undergraduate program in 1985.) In 1993, Postman was appointed University Professor, at the time the only teacher in the school of education to hold this title. And five years later, in honor of the American film star, producer, and NYU benefactor, he was named the Paulette Goddard Professor of Media Ecology.[9]

THE ACADEMIC AS POPULAR WRITER

Postman's arrival at NYU also marked the beginning of a prolific writing career, one not limited to a scholarly audience. In 1961, *Television and the Teaching of English* appeared. A guide for instructors, it was aimed in part at teaching teachers how to make their students better, more discerning viewers of television. Several other books on education followed during the next two decades: *Linguistics: A Revolution in Teaching* (1966), with coauthor Charles Weingarten, a professor of education at the University of South Florida with whom Postman would collaborate on his next three books; *Teaching as a Subversive Activity* (1969), which championed what became known as the "inquiry method" of education; *The Soft Revolution: A Student Handbook for Turning Schools Around* (1971), published a year after the campus shootings at Kent State and Jackson State; *The School Book: For People Who Want to Know What All the Hollering Is About*

(1973); and *Teaching as a Conserving Activity* (1979), which encouraged classroom teachers to provide a language- and history-centered antidote to what Postman saw as an American culture "overdosing on change."[10]

That change was being visually represented each night on television, which in turn had led to further disruptions. In *The Disappearance of Childhood* (1982), for instance, Postman argued that while the concept of childhood seemed valid in an age when reading literacy served to divide children from adults, that concept no longer made sense at a time when television's imagery was accessible to all, whatever a person's age or stage of development. In the Age of TV, in other words, the concept of childhood had become a quaint relic of another era.[11] Other books on the effects of television, and technology more broadly, followed, including *Conscientious Objections: Stirring Up Trouble about Language, Technology, and Education* (1988); *Technology: The Surrender of Culture to Technology* (1992); *The End of Education: Redefining the Value of School* (1995); and Postman's final book, *Building A Bridge to the 18th Century: How the Past Can Improve Our Future* (1999).

Amid this impressive output, he released two additional books, which in their different ways confirmed his public reputation as a critic who had cast a keen eye on his culture's most popular technology, identified its little-noticed but potent effects, and yelled an emphatic "No."

NEWS IN THE AGE OF SHOW BUSINESS: *AMUSING OURSELVES TO DEATH* (1985)

The origin of the 1985 book was an address Postman gave on October 2, 1984, to an audience at the Frankfurt Book Fair. In a nod to one of the twentieth century's most chilling dystopian novels, published in 1949, the theme of this year's fair was the forward looking "Orwell in the year 2000." The theme was intended to offer fairgoers a variety of views on what the Orwellian vision would look like at the beginning of the next century, and Postman had been enlisted to give the keynote address.

In his actual remarks, though, he demurred: "There is no doubt that Orwell's prophecies and parables have application to half the countries of the world," he explained at a time when the Cold War was still ongoing. "But the fact is as far as the Western democracies are concerned,

Orwell missed the mark almost completely."[12] As Postman saw it, such democracies were not likely to be overcome "by an externally imposed oppression," as Orwell had predicted in *1984*. Instead, the real threat to their citizens lay not in some Big Brother or some reality-bending Ministry of Truth but in the people themselves, as Huxley had predicted almost two decades earlier in *Brave New World* (1932). In the Huxleyan vision of the future, as Postman explained, "The people will come to love their oppression, to adore the technologies that undo their capacities to think." In short, while Orwell foresaw citizen-slaves being "marched single file and manacled into oblivion," his English counterpart "thought we would dance ourselves there, with an idiot smile on our face.[13]

All Western democracies were susceptible to this form of oblivion through distraction, Postman believed. Still, his own country was leading the way as the result of its "consuming love affair with television," the perfect technology of distraction and the reason why "America has given the world the clearest available glimpse of the Huxleyan future, 2000."[14] In the remainder of his address, he offered examples to illustrate his point, thereby giving his audience members a preview of a future that in many ways had already come to pass in America. His remarks that day also offered a précis, a synopsis, of what, a year later, would be his fully elaborated case against television and its unsalutary effects on public discourse.

That case was divided into two parts. In the first part, Postman laid out the theoretical and historical framework of his argument about television; in part 2, he cited the practical application of this framework in areas such as religion, politics, teaching, and of course television news. Throughout, he adopted a tone that was equal parts scholarly and polemical, measured but morally engaged.

Theory and History

In a chapter titled "The Medium Is the Metaphor," an intentional play on the medium-is-the-message concept explored in McLuhan's seminal 1964 book *Understanding Media: The Extensions of Man*, Postman reminded his readers what the Canadian media theorist had in mind when he coined his famous phrase: "Each medium, like language itself, makes possible a unique mode of discourse by providing a new orientation for thought, for expression, for sensibility."[15] The medium of photography, for example, might be perfectly suited for arousing certain emotional effects in the viewer through the artful representation of some object, place, or person, but it was eminently unsuited for laying out a complex philosophical argument. And precisely because each medium made certain "messages" possible and others less so, the introduction of a novel medium into society had profound and often overlooked effects.

In laying the theoretical groundwork for his discussion, Postman was also careful to clarify what McLuhan meant when he used the term "message" in his "medium-is-the-message" catchphrase. In McLuhan's usage, the term was not intended to mean "a specific, concrete statement about the world," which even in the harder sciences was always subject to certain epistemological limitations. Rather, message referred to some symbolic representation of reality—some metaphor that sought to approximate the actual world: "Whether we are experiencing the world through the lens of speech or the printed word or the television camera, our media-metaphors classify the world for us, sequence it, frame it, enlarge it, reduce it, color it, argue a case for what the world is like" (*Amusing*, 10).

A good way to understand this metaphorical process, Postman thought, was by looking at different cultures. While all cultures used media-metaphors or "symbolic forms" to express their most fundamental beliefs about the world—how it came to be, how it operated, where it was tending—cultures at various stages of technological development necessarily expressed these cherished truths differently. And thus oral-based cultures tended to rely on proverbs, sayings, chants, and recitations to express their most fundamental beliefs, their "messages," about the world; print-based cultures (the traditional university, say) tended to convey much of their world knowledge via written lectures, scholarly articles, monographs, and books; and image-based cultures through visual representations. Did this mean, then, that all was an epistemological muddle and that one culture's preferred medium for expressing "truth" was as good as another's? Not so, Postman insisted: "Some ways of truth-telling are better than others, and therefore have a healthier influence on the cultures that adopt them." In effect, he was throwing down the epistemological gauntlet, declaring himself no cultural relativist in the matter of ways of seeing and understanding the world. The literate man was declaring his unequivocal preference (*Amusing*, 24).

Postman's sly move into the murky theory of knowledge was risky, of course, especially in a book aimed at a popular audience. Still, while acknowledging the risk, he insisted that the move was nevertheless necessary if his critique of the visual-based medium of television was to be seen as more than just the standard aesthetic or educational indictment. Certainly, TV was a world-class purveyor of "junk," he thought, but it was also much more than this and thus much more dangerous (*Amusing,* 16–17).

How dangerous was illustrated by the effects of the nation's gradual metamorphosis from a print-based culture, what Postman called "typographic America," to an image-based one. The earlier culture had its origins in Colonial America, which was peopled by immigrants "who were as committed to the printed word as any group of people who ever lived." To give ballast to his claim, Postman cited a variety of facts and statistics, albeit somewhat selectively his critics would later charge. Among these data points was the relatively diffuse activity of reading in the early colonies, as evidenced by the widespread popularity of Thomas Paine's *Common Sense* (1776), a runaway hit that sold by some estimates between four hundred thousand and five hundred thousand copies in its first year of publication. And this in a land of just 2.5 million people (*Amusing*, 31–34).[16]

Newspapers and other printed material were also widely read. "By 1730, there were seven newspapers published regularly in four colonies, and by 1800 there were more than 180" (*Amusing*, 37). Beyond newspapers, the colonists also enjoyed reading pamphlets (*Common Sense* was among the first) and broadsides, typically single sheets of various sizes that publicized news and information of different kinds.[17] So great, in fact, was this "immersion in printed matter" that a wave of foreign visitors— French diplomat and historian Alexis de Tocqueville, among them—took special note of the colonies' high and widespread level of literacy. Visitors to America also took note of the "near universality of lecture halls," where people of all classes could hear printed lectures by well-known writers, humorists, and intellectuals (*Amusing*, 37–39).

The dominance of the printed word persisted well into the nineteenth century. And it was not just print's ubiquity that accounted for its survival but the absence of most alternative media, as Postman made clear: "There were no movies to see, radio to hear, photographic displays to look at, records to play. There was no television. Public business was channeled into and through and expressed through print, which became the model, the metaphor and the measure of all discourse."

The result of this general immersion in print was a culture that placed a high premium on "serious and rational public conversation" and all the qualities of mind—order, logic, fluency, precision—that make such public discourse possible (*Amusing*, 41–43). Individual thinkers, of course, were eminently capable of analytic thought prior to the dominance of the written word. (Socrates rejected writing, for instance, and identified with a form of the oral tradition.) Postman was careful not to push his thesis too far, making clear that his notion of a typographical mind referred not to individuals per se but to cultures, where "public discourse tends to be characterized by a coherent, orderly arrangement of facts and ideas" (*Amusing*, 51).

Such reading-enabled discourse also reinforced for people within the culture the view that the world was "a serious, coherent place, capable of management by reason, and improvement by logical and relevant criticism." As evidence for this, Postman cited, among other examples, the Lincoln-Douglas debates of 1858, a series of seven public discourses between Illinois GOP senatorial contestant Abraham Lincoln and Democratic contestant Stephen Douglas. While these debates certainly had their "carnival-like" atmospheres, they also placed extraordinary demands upon listeners' patience, their "capacity to comprehend lengthy and complex sentences aurally," and their knowledge of public issues. Despite these challenges, the debaters nevertheless pressed on, reasonably confident that their view of the world as "a serious, coherent place, capable of management by reason" was shared by most of their audience (*Amusing*, 45, 47, 62).

In time, such confidence would be sorely tested. The initial culprit, as Postman saw it, was the telegraph. Harnessing electricity in the service of communication, it had initially solved the knotty problem of conveying information rapidly across large amounts of space—in the case of America, across a vast continent. Now, for the first time, citizens could engage in a "continentwide conversation." But the telegraph also altered the nature of that conversation, especially after it became wedded to the printing press. For one, information no longer needed to be locally significant. In fact, it was now possible for a person in Maine to learn the same thing as a person in Texas, regardless of whether that information was relevant to either of them. Second, precisely because of its questionable relevancy, news from away did not necessarily require a response, action, or reply. It was often, in other words, information divorced from personal need. And finally, because telegraphic information was distinguished by its speed and not its capacity to look deeply into things, eye-catching headlines and punchy, often sensational stories became the order of the day, as illustrated in the Yellow Journalism of the mid-1890s. "To the telegraph, intelligence meant knowing *of* lots of things," wrote Postman, summarizing the effect of the new medium, "not knowing *about* them" (*Amusing* 64, 69–70).

And yet for all this, telegraphy's influence and effect might well have diminished over time had it not been joined to another technology, photography. Asserting its own value proposition—namely, to reproduce reality through the manipulation of light—the medium of photography conjured images isolated from their wider contexts for the purposes of making the viewer discern those images in a novel way. It was just this process of "dismembering" and reintroducing reality that made photography a natural fit for telegraphy, which also presented the world as a "series of idiosyncratic events" with no discernable beginning, middle, or end. And because photography not only had the capacity to reproduce reality but to replicate it infinitely, its effect on culture when paired with telegraphy was profound. Soon, newspaper editors began to marry far-flung telegraphic headlines and reports with photographs, seemingly anchoring such "news" to the real world and forever changing what Americans deemed as worth their attention. In fact, these disembodied, far-flung, and electrically generated images and words were, more often than not, *not* newsworthy. They were what Postman, echoing American historian Daniel Boorstin before him, called "pseudo-contexts," a structure invented to give fragmented, irrelevant information a seeming use and relevance (*Amusing*, 74–77).[18]

To be sure, all these technological changes did not alter America's typographic culture overnight. They did provide, however, the foundation for what came next, the newer technologies of film, radio, and eventually television. Not unlike the child's game of peek-a-boo, these technologies expressed a world in which "now this event, now that, pops into view for a moment, then vanishes again." In such a self-contained, self-referential world, coherence and sense mattered little. The essential point now was, not unlike the child's game, diversion and amusement, and never more so than when television became the dominant medium of the day (*Amusing*, 77–78).

In his critique, Postman was speaking, of course, as not only an observer but as an inhabitant of this new electronic culture. Indeed, writing in the mid-1980s, he had seen two generations come of age during a period when American life was so dominated by television that its presence was simply assumed, much like the medium of water for fish or air for humans. And precisely because the medium of TV was so pervasive, so taken for granted, it had easily and stealthily infiltrated all subjects of public interest—politics, education, religion, science, sports, and not least news.

The TV News Show

Television news, Postman thought, posed a unique set of problems for viewers. Unlike most print news, where the consumer could reexamine if necessary what he or she had just read and where at least a measure of context was believed necessary for comprehension, commercial news broadcasts offered up the world in a series of rapid and rapidly disappearing bite-size pieces, typically augmented by arresting visuals and largely devoid of any broader context.[19] The result was an epistemology of randomness, incoherence, and trivia, which for Postman was succinctly captured in the television (and radio) commonplace, "*Now . . . This,*" the catchphrase employed by anchors to link typically unrelated stories and segments. Television news did not intend, in short, to add to viewers' knowledge of the world; it was designed to offer them arresting, fleeting, and disembodied impressions of it.

For this reason, argued Postman, many television news producers paid almost as much attention to showmanship as their counterparts in entertainment did. Among other things, new producers regularly gave "prominence and precedence" to news stories with strong visuals; tended to cast their main anchors with an eye toward credibility, likeability, and above all facial appeal; placed a high premium on pace, making it incumbent on newscasters and reporters to adopt a snappy, no-superfluous-information delivery; and, in the local markets at least, surrounded their main players with an assortment of audience-pleasing types, including the comely weatherperson, the rapid-fire, slangy sportscaster, and the intrepid consumer watchdog (*Amusing*, 103).

There was, however, an inevitable price to be paid for such a steady stream of lively and entertaining news: Americans were drowning in a sea of "disinformation." By that term, Postman did not mean false or intentionally erroneous information, at least not in the conventional definitions of those terms.[20] Rather, he was referring to "misleading information"—information that is fragmented, random, and superficial but that contains just enough truth to give the illusion of knowledge rather than the real thing" (*Amusing*, 107). In effect, news as entertainment had blurred the line between ignorance and knowledge; it had altered people's sense of what it meant to be well informed. And the most alarming part of all this was that most Americans were already too mesmerized to notice or care.

The Reviews and Reviewers

Amusing Ourselves to Death went on to become Postman's most popular book. In time, it was translated into multiple languages and reissued in an anniversary edition twenty years after its original publication. Its initial critical reception was mixed, however. Reviewers generally agreed that Postman's critique of television, and especially its version of the news and politics, was insightful and essential, but many of these same reviewers faulted him for variously overstating his thesis, romanticizing print, and making a variety of outright factual mistakes.

Among the reviewers who largely favored the book was the *Washington Post*'s Jonathan Yardley, a Pulitzer Prize–winning book critic. In a review cleverly titled "The Vacuum at the End of the Tube," Yardley called Postman's examination of television a "powerful, troubling and important book."[21] There was little doubt that, as Postman's dominant metaphor expressed, the values of show business had become the standard measurement in so many areas of national life, including television news. The evidence seemed "irrefutable," and the general indictment "brutal," though Yardley nevertheless had a few quibbles. He disagreed, for instance, with the author's interpretation of the television commonplace, "Now . . . this," which struck him less as an epistemological signal of discontinuity than a "a euphemistic announcement that the viewer is about to be subjected to a commercial." Still, minor criticisms like this aside, Postman's book was a "brilliant" work, no less "provocative" than his previous one, *The Disappearance of Childhood*.[22]

Somewhat less effusive, though still largely positive, was a review in the *Los Angeles Times* by comparative culture scholar Laurien Alexandre.

Like Yardley, Alexandre praised Postman for offering a "thought-provoking" look at the relation of media to cultural content." Calling attention to television news as "the target of Postman's most stinging commentary," she reiterated his thesis that American culture "has become so adjusted to this world of fragmented events stripped of authenticity or connection, that all assumptions of coherence have vanished," thereby jeopardizing the healthy pursuit of democracy. Alexandre was less impressed, though, by some of Postman's historical claims. About his idea of the colonists having created something of "classless reading culture," for instance, she raised several complaints: first, the population of the merchant centers tended to be more literate than the colonies in general; second, enslaved Africans were not only prohibited from reading but punished for trying to learn how; and third, despite the general print-oriented culture, illiteracy was not uncommon among women, indentured servants, and the semi-skilled workers employed in early manufacturing shops. These historical gaffes aside, though, Alexandre ended by praising Postman's book for "a thoughtful exploration of contemporary culture, public discourse in the Age of Show Business."[23]

There were two other semi-complimentary reviews that week, both of which appeared in the *New York Times*. In one appearing in the daily paper (November 21, 1985), then *Times* television critic Walter Goodman praised Postman as "a sharp guide" when he "contents himself with analyzing television's treatment of public affairs, politics, religion and education." It was when the author strayed into the broader terrain of cultural criticism, though, that Goodman became impatient: "'Amusing Ourselves to Death' is best when its author helps us see what is happening on the screen. That picture is gloomy enough without apocalyptic prophecies of 'culture-death.'"[24]

Later in the same week, in the *Sunday Book Review* (November 24), writer and literary critic Anatole Broyard also pointed to Postman's elegant and perceptive critique of television, but like Goodman, he was impatient with the author's "apocalyptic" tendencies: "Like many brilliant writers, Mr. Postman . . . flings his argument as widely as possible," thereby ignoring "those inconvenient qualifications that real life always requires." One essential qualification, as Broyard saw it, was the degree to which the public had actually been hoodwinked: "He [Postman] talks as if we watched television naively, without irony or reservation, accepting its 'metaphors' at face value. Reading him, you would think there were no movies, sports or BBC productions on television. You'd suppose that nobody opens newspapers, magazines or books."[25]

Postman's critics were not entirely wrong: In his look at how public discourse and broadcast news had been debased in the age of show business, he had in fact too often flung his argument as widely as possible, sometimes ignoring nuance and qualification. His historical claims about colonial-era literacy are a case in point, and so too are his claims of a thoroughly stupefied public. These and other criticisms are too obvious to be overlooked.

Still, Postman was not simply writing as a scholar, though he was certainly that, but as a popular author and something of a moral crusader. If he tended in *Amusing Ourselves to Death* to overstate his case, he seems to have done so in order to drive home his point, which he believed needed to be heard over the deafening din of entertainment and show-biz-style news. In this sense, his analysis had an undeniable rhetorical aspect, designed not just to inform but to persuade skeptics of the rightness of his vision. Not all were convinced, of course. Enough eventually were, though, so that over time his critique of television has remained popular, even after television itself has ceded its former dominance to an even more ubiquitous digital culture.[26] Seven years after the publication of *Amusing Ourselves to Death*, Postman and a former student would continue his crusade, offering the public a how-to manual for becoming smarter TV news viewers.

THE SKEPTICAL VIEWER: *HOW TO WATCH TELEVISION NEWS* (1992, 2008)

In the early 1990s, Postman teamed up with former student Steve Powers, a onetime radio and TV newsperson who had gone on to get a PhD in media studies, to work on the guide for television news viewers. The choice of Powers as his coauthor made sense, augmenting as it did Postman's more limited experience with the behind-the-scenes nuts-and-bolts aspects of television news production.[27]

The pair's first order of business was to issue a caution: it was bordering on useless to try to learn how to watch television news without a solid grounding in print—newspapers, magazines, and books. Why? Because just as television held the edge in immediacy, print was better at offering a more nuanced and comprehensive view of the world. Viewers ignorant of this would find it difficult to gauge what they were seeing and, more crucially, missing on television. The authors cited the events of Tiananmen Square—the student uprising that took place in Beijing, China, in the spring of 1989—to illustrate their point. Television news may have done a good job of conveying the chaos and horror of the unfolding event. Still, because of the constraints of the medium, even those television news reporters on the ground had a limited capacity on air to discuss the historical and political context of the uprising. And so, unless viewers of these reports had augmented their knowledge of the uprising by also reading about it beforehand or afterward, they would be left largely in the dark about its historical context and significance.[28]

In the chapters that followed, Postman and Powers offered uninitiated readers a primer on the nature and practices of television news. Their survey included separate chapters on, among other things, audience tracking, consolidation, the news director, high-impact visuals, commercials, and so forth. Even in 1992, at least some of the ground they covered must have seemed obvious to more than a few readers. In the newer version of the book, published in 2008, following Postman's death, Powers took pains to update and expand a portion of the material, aware that during the almost fifteen-year interim a new contemporary audience had access to an almost unlimited menu of news "platforms" beyond television, platforms that could more and more easily track their every click. Nevertheless, even the revised edition left much of the original text intact, a sign perhaps that what the authors had written in 1992 still resonated.

In an early chapter titled "What Is News?," for example, they stressed a fact of news gathering that even sophisticated consumers sometimes forget: what constitutes "news" is in many ways a subjective determination. Certainly, there are events that by their very nature are consequential and therefore command widespread interest: a pandemic, a would-be insurrection, and a war certainly fall into this category. But most events are not so neatly categorized. If they are deemed newsworthy, it is in part at least because someone who is paid to have his or her finger on the public pulse has said so. In television, that person is typically the news director, as Postman and Powers pointed out in a latter chapter. News directors rely on their journalistic instincts, of course. But as key members of a commercial broadcasting team, they must also rely on their sense of what will maintain and ultimately expand audience share. And because the race for ratings is intrinsically competitive, in some markets fiercely so, events of the day that are complex, difficult to condense, and perhaps lack visual appeal make for poor television, almost certain to drive viewership down not up (*How to Watch*, 13–18, 75–78).

The alternative is not only a greater focus on lighter fare—softer features, for example—but an all-out effort to package even consequential news in a crowd-pleasing, quick-paced, entertaining way, as Postman had previously explained in *Amusing Ourselves to Death*. Such successful news packaging was far from easy. For one, it usually required a small army of people, everyone from the on-air staff to the scores of behind-the-scenes personnel.[29] Even in a small local station, it also called for an assortment of complex, expensive gear, which in the years since has only become more sophisticated.[30] Finally, a well-packaged story required a near-maniacal attention to the clock, lest even an important story drag or fail to hold viewer attention. So great in fact are the technical demands of television news, Postman and Powers pointed out, that more often than not "it is a case of technique triumphing over substance" (*How to Watch*, 74).[31]

The upending of journalistic values had had a perverse effect: for while Americans now had greater access than ever before to news, the quality of that news had eroded. The worst part was that most Americans were apparently not even aware that their fund of knowledge was, in the popular phrase, a mile wide and an inch deep. Certainly, chided Postman and Powers, "we know *of many* things (everything is revealed) but *about* very little (nothing is known)." In the updated edition of their book, Powers made clear that the intervening years had done little to change the state of things. In many ways, in fact, they had become worse. Though digital news platforms had proliferated, the quality of news that too many people received was even more of a mixed affair. If more than ever was being revealed, less than ever was truly known (*How to Watch*, 151).

Postman and Powers ended their original book with a list of viewer-saving reforms. Among other things, they urged TV news consumers to read more, to give greater thought to what is and is not news, to be wary of implicit messaging in ads, to get to know something of the "lords" behind commercial TV, to be alert to the framing and language of the news, to press for more TV literacy courses in school, and most urgently to reduce one's television news viewing by at least a third (*How to Watch*, 154–61). Some of these recommendations have been adopted in the years since, most famously in the "digital detox" movement that encourages the electronically addicted to withdraw temporarily from their various tech devices, including not only television but also smartphones, headphones, tablets, and computers.[32]

The Reviews and Reviewers

The Postman and Powers guide was not widely reviewed, either initially or in its revised edition. The reasons are unclear, but potential readers may have thought (incorrectly) that it was simply a rehash of Postman's earlier work or that there had already been earlier works on the market like it.[33] Whatever the case, those outlets that did review the book were positive, albeit with reservations.

In the *Chicago Tribune*, for example, the paper's then television critic, Clarence Petersen, no fan himself of the medium, praised *How to Watch TV News* as a book "that the television generation sorely needs to read." The authors are prone to developing their themes "in details that sometime belabor the obvious," Petersen cautioned, but they leave their readers with a clear sense of what they believe.[34] The anonymous review in *Publishers Weekly* also applauded the original book for offering "a brief, helpful analysis of America's most popular news source." The analysis covers both "theoretical issues" and more practical ones in "a sober but accessible style," though some areas could have been better addressed, including "what television news does well." The review ended with an additional suggestion: "The book would have been much richer if Powers had included anecdotes from his own career and reflected from his own experience on in-house decision-making."[35]

The last criticism rings true: given his long tenure in first radio news and then television news, Powers might well have included some instructive anecdotes drawn from his own career, including any battles with management over news content. Less persuasive is the complaint by *Publishers Weekly* that the authors completely ignored what television does well. As Postman made clear in his most famous book, and as he and Powers did as well in *How to Watch TV News*, the impact of the television moving image is a powerful one, conveying an undeniable and difficult-to-replicate immediacy and emotional impact. The problem was that television's greatest asset was also its primary weakness, as they made clear: "The fact that television news is principally made up of moving pictures prevents it from offering lengthy, coherent explanations for events. A television news show reveals the world as a series of unrelated, fragmentary moments." To expect otherwise was foolish, unless one came to the viewing experience with a "prepared mind," fortified by self-reflection and educated by an immersion in print (*How to Watch*, 114).

As card-carrying members of the latter camp, Postman and his broadcast colleague left no doubt where they stood.

CONCLUSION

Postman died on October 5, 2003, at age seventy-two, in Flushing, New York, where he and his wife, Shelley, had raised their family. A lifelong smoker, he succumbed to lung cancer and was buried in Cedar Park Cemetery, Paramus, New Jersey, along with other Jewish celebrities and notable writers, including Delmore Schwartz and Isaac Bashevis Singer. Among his immediate survivors were Shelley Ross Postman; their two sons, Marc, an astronomer, and Andrew, a writer; and their daughter, Madeline, a New York City elementary school teacher. His headstone, unveiled in the Jewish tradition a year later, read "Beloved Husband Father Grandfather Brother and Teacher."[36]

In his eulogy, Andrew Postman remembered his father as not only brilliant but very kind and optimistic: "He never lamented, never regretted, never wallowed in the dark land of What If. You can't possibly do that and also write twenty books.[37] Many of those books are still in print, and several, in particular *Amusing Ourselves to Death*, are still widely read and discussed. In 2007, four years after his passing, organizers at New York University's Steinhardt School of Media, Culture, and Communication established the Neil Postman Graduate Conference, a forum for students, faculty, and guest scholars to present their original research. Past conference themes have included "Loose Canons: The Requirements of Media Studies," "The Urban and the Rural," and "Thinking Through Collapse."[38]

In the popular media—and throughout his life, his books were directed more to a general audience than to an academic one—Postman's name and ideas seem to surface whenever commentators try to put the current media environment into a coherent context. Writing in 2015 in *Salon*, for example, former cultural journalist Scott Timberg reminded his readers that much of the superficiality decried by contemporary critics—cable news, comedy news shows, reality television—were anticipated three decades earlier by Postman. To illustrate, he quoted, among others, American journalist Matt Bai, who said his own inquiry into the changing values of television news coverage (*All the Truth Is Out: The Week Politics Went Tabloid*, 2014) had taken *Amusing Ourselves to Death* as "'a kind of a North star."[39] A couple of years later, in a piece in the *Atlantic* titled "Are We Having Too Much Fun?," staff writer Megan Garber also praised Postman for anticipating a time when "many Americans get their news filtered through late-night comedy and their outrages filtered through *Saturday Night Live*."[40] And in a piece that followed the next year on Vox, the news website, author Scott Illing, referring to Postman's 1985 study of "the Age of Show Business," argued why contemporary news and political consumers would be wise to "read this 30-year-old book."[41]

For commentators in the *post*-Postman era, though, one event perhaps more than any other best illustrates the merging of public discourse and show business: the rise and presidency of real estate mogul and former reality television star Donald J. Trump. In an early 2017 feature in the *Guardian* titled "My Dad Predicted Trump in 1985," for example, Andrew Postman wrote, "Colleagues and former students of my father . . . would now and then email or Facebook me, after the latest Trumpian theatrics, wondering, 'What would Neil think?' or noting glumly, 'Your dad nailed it.'"[42]

The gloomy assessment was accurate in many ways. Even for detractors, Trump's early theatrics were amusing, offering not only comic relief from the once serious business of electing a new president but a television spectacle difficult to turn away from. Once that novelty waned, however, at least half the country grew alarmed over the ongoing disinformation, the public complicity, and the commercial media's eagerness to highlight Trumpian antics in order to boost "circulation, online traffic, and ad revenue," as the younger Postman noted. His dad had left no surefire remedies for such systemic disruption, although he had also never given up on rationality or the salutary effects of a rigorous education, especially if begun in the early grades.[43] Many traditional conservatives were equally alarmed by the Trumpian spectacle and eager to pay homage to the author of *Amusing Ourselves to Death*. Writing in the *National Review* (September, 13, 2020), for example, commentator Cameron Hildith applauded Postman for explaining "how the man who headlined WrestleMania 23 got access to the nuclear codes." When all was said and done, concluded Hildith, perhaps Donald Trump "was made in a lab to be the Postman's postmortem rebuke to us all."[44]

What Postman might have thought about the forty-fifth president is, of course open to speculation. In the current era, prone to irrationality and easy violence, as the January 6 insurrection demonstrated, he would have found it necessary perhaps to revise his show-business metaphor to include something more ominous, as author and commentator Evan Osnos has argued in the *New Yorker*.[45] Though Postman the optimist may have rejected the darker view, there appears to be enough contemporary evidence to justify it. On a variety of social platforms, for instance, the tendency to create an unstable admix of news, entertainment, and rage-venting has led some commentators to see Americans as trending more in the direction of Orwell's *1984* than Huxley's *Brave New World*.

In a provocative essay in the business and technology magazine *Fast Company*, for example, author and businesswoman Maelle Gavet drew current-day analogies with two features of that dystopian novel. The first is "Two Minutes Hate," a daily ritual of denunciation for the revolving door of enemies of Orwell's Outer Party of Oceania. "Today, inflammatory hashtags and hoaxes are regularly promoted by fake accounts until they become official trends and are picked up by real people and even the mainstream media, Gavet explained." The other contemporary echo of *1984* is Newspeak, the Party's semantic manipulation of language for the purpose of hobbling complex expressions of feelings, ideas, and perceptions of reality. In social media's sharply circumscribed linguistic environment, noted Gavet, "nuance is not rewarded. And by allowing any opinion (no matter how fringe) to take on the appearance of fact, social networks have made it harder for us to comprehend our reality.[46]

His affinity for Huxley over Orwell aside, Postman might well have found much here to agree with. Certainly, new media has fueled rage, licensed irrationality, and reduced the need and indeed the desire for qualified, nuanced thinking. Still, as Postman might have rejoined, social media is not yet totalitarian, at least not in America and other Western democracies. If such platforms regularly arouse in us certain bad habits of mind and action, these are still largely "induced in ourselves," as Huxley might have put it.[47] America, at least in this view, is a long way from having a state-controlled media and Thought Police.

But unfettered access to news and information, if that is what it is, does not change the dynamic that Postman cautioned about decades ago. Fragmentation, discontinuity, and misinformation are still with us in the Digital Age as they were in the Age of Television. And as before and perhaps even more so now, the corrosive, sometimes dangerous effects on public discourse and democracy are palpable and alarming.

NOTES

1. Neil Postman, *Amusing Ourselves to Death: Public Discourse in the Age of Show Business* (1985; 20th Anniversary Edition reprinted with a new introduction by Andrew Postman. New York: Penguin, 2006, 27.

2. Neil Postman and Steve Powers, *How To Watch Television News* (1992; revised edition reprinted with new and updated material by Steve Powers (New York, Penguin, 2008), 162.

3. Myrna Katz Frommer and Harvey Frommer, *Growing Up Jewish in America: An Oral History* (New York: Harcourt Brace, 1995), 88.

4. Ibid., 111, 189–90.

5. Ibid., 242.

6. Ibid., 89.

7. "Hall of Fame," Men's Basketball, Neil Postman, Fredonia State University of New York, accessed December 14, 2020, https://fredoniabluedevils.com/honors/hall-of-fame/neil-postman/85; see also, "Athletic Hall of Fame," Fredonia State University of New York, accessed December 14, 2020, https://www.fredonia.edu/alumni/athletic-hall-fame.

8. "Our History," Department of History, San Francisco State University, accessed December 14, 2020, https://history.sfsu.edu/our-history.

9. New York University, "NYU Professor Neil Postman, 72, Social Critic and Educator," news release, September 25, 2003, https://www.nyu.edu/about/news-publications/news/2003/september/nyu_professor_neil_postman_72.html.

10. Neil Postman, *Teaching as a Conserving Activity* (New York: Delacorte, 1979,) 26; also published during this period was Postman's introduction to general semantics, *Crazy Talk, Stupid Talk: How We Defeat Ourselves by the Way We Talk and What to Do about It* (New York: Delacorte, 1976).

11. Renzo Llorente, "Neil Postman: American Educator, Media Theorist, and Social Critic," in Britannica.com, October, 1, 2020, accessed December 14, 2020, https://www.britannica.com/biography/Neil-Postman.

12. Address reprinted in Neil Postman, "Amusing Ourselves to Death, *ETC: A Review of General Semantics*, vol. 42, no. 1 (1985), 13, https://www.jstor.org /stable/42576719?read-now=1&seq=1.

13. Ibid., 14.

14. Ibid.

15. Postman, *Amusing*, 10. All further references will be to this edition and cited parenthetically in the text.

16. "America Counts: America behind the Numbers," United States Census Bureau, last revised July 2, 2019, https://www.census.gov/library/stories/2019/07 /july-fourth-celebrating-243-years-of-independence.html#:~:text=places%20 and%20economy.-,The%20U.S.%20population%20was%202.5%20million%20 in%201776.,Series%20B%2012%20table%20below.

17. "American Broadsides: History on a Sheet of Paper," Ian Brabner, Rare Americana, accessed December 14, 2020, https://www.rareamericana.com/ articles/american-broadsides/.

18. See Daniel Boorstin, *The Image: A Guide to Pseudo-Events in America* (1962; 50th anniversary edition, reprinted with a new afterword by Douglas Rushkoff (New York: Vintage, 2012).

19. Here Postman was endorsing and expanding on the view put forth two years earlier by PBS *NewsHour* host, Robert MacNeil. See Robert MacNeil, "Is Television Shortening Our Attention Span?" *New York University Education Quarterly*, vol. 14, no. 2 (Winter 1993), 2.

20. For a primer on different types of information, see, for example, "'Fake News,' Lies and Propaganda: How to Sort Fact from Fiction," University of Michigan Library Research Guides, last updated July 24, 2020, https://guides.lib .umich.edu/fakenews.

21. Jonathan Yardley, "The Vacuum at the End of the Tube," review of *Amusing Ourselves to Death: Public Discourse in the Age of Show Business*, by Neil Postman, *Washington Post*, November 3, 1985, https://www.washingtonpost .com/archive/entertainment/books/1985/11/03/the-vacuum-at-the-end-of-the -tube/790ab5db-51ee-4bd9-94ec-e2f2c7f1baeb/.

22. Ibid.

23. Laurien Alexandre, review of *Amusing Ourselves to Death: Public Discourse in the Age of Show Business*, by Neil Postman, September 25, 1985, *Los Angeles Times*, https://www.latimes.com/archives/la-xpm-1985-09-29-bk -18485-story.html.

24. Walter Goodman, review of *Amusing Ourselves to Death: Public Discourse in the Age of Show Business,* by Neil Postman, *New York Times*, November 21, 1985, Books of the Times, https://www.nytimes.com/1985/11/21/books /books-of-the-times-169933.html.

25. Anatole Broyard, "Going Down the Tube," review of *Amusing Ourselves to Death: Public Discourse in the Age of Show Business*, by Neil Postman, *New York Times*, November 24, 1985, Sunday Book Review, https://www.nytimes.com/1985/11/24/books/going-down-the-tube.html.

26. Amazon has consistently ranked the revised edition of the book, for example, at the top of several categories of readership: "Video and Television Engineering," "Television History and Criticism," "Media and Internet in Politics," https://www.amazon.com/Amusing-Ourselves-Death-Discourse-Business/dp/014303653X.

27. Wikipedia, s.v. "Steve Powers," last edited September 16, 2020, https://en.wikipedia.org/wiki/Steve_Powers.

28. Postman and Powers, *How to Watch*, x. All further references will be to this edition and cited parenthetically in the text.

29. For a catalog of contemporary broadcast careers, for instance, see, Dawn Rosenberg Mckay, "Television News Careers," *The Balance Careers*, updated November 20, 2019, https://www.thebalancecareers.com/television-news-careers-525690.

30. See "What Equipment Do I Need to Start a Television Station," Open-Broadcaster, accessed December 15, 2020, https://openbroadcaster.com/products/television-station-equipment-list.

31. On the issue of time, see, for example, "Video Length," Pew Research Center, Journalism and Media, July 16, 2012, accessed December 15, 2020, https://www.journalism.org/2012/07/16/video-length/.

32. Among the scores of articles on this movement, see Kendra Cherry, "What Is Digital Detox?, VeryWellMind, updated on September 21, 2020, https://www.verywellmind.com/why-and-how-to-do-a-digital-detox-4771321#:~:text=What%2Is%20a%20Digital%20Detox%3F,-By&text=A%20digital%20detox%20refers%20to,tablets%2C%20and%20social%20media%20sites.

33. See, for example, Mark Fishman, *Manufacturing the News* (Austin: University of Texas Press, 1980); Linda Ellerbee, *And So It Goes* (New York: G.P. Putnam, 1986); and Ken Auletta, *Three Blind Mice: How the Television Networks Lost Their Way* (New York: Vantage, 1991).

34. Clarence Petersen, review of *How to Watch Television News*, by Neil Postman and Steve Powers, *Chicago Tribune*, September 13, 1992, https://www.chicagotribune.com/news/ct-xpm-1992-09-13-9203230673-story.html.

35. Unsigned review of *How to Watch Television News*, by Neil Postman and Steve Powers, *Publishers Weekly*, September 1, 1992, https://www.publishersweekly.com/978-0-14-013231-1.

36. Wolfgang Saxon, "Neil Postman, 72, Mass Media Critic, Dies," *New York Times*, October 9, 2003, https://www.nytimes.com/2003/10/09/nyregion

/neil-postman-72-mass-media-critic-dies.html. See also, "Neil Milton Postman," *Find A Grave*, December 7, 2016, accessed December 15, 2020, https://www .findagrave.com/memorial/173609220/neil-milton-postman.

37. Andrew Postman, "Eulogy for Neil Postman," October 8, 2003, delivered at Parkside Chapel, Forest Hills, New York, posted on Neil Postman: An Online Archive, accessed December16, 2020, http://neilpostman.blogspot.com/.

38. "The Neil Postman Graduate Conference," New York University, Steinhardt School of Media, Culture, and Communication, http://postmanconference.org/.

39. Scott Timberg, "Meet the Man Who Predicted Fox News, the Internet, Stephen Colbert, and Reality Television," *Salon*, January 5, 2015, https://www .salon.com/2015/01/04/meet_the_man_who_predicted_fox_news_the_internet _stephen_colbert_and_reality_television/.

40. Megan Garber, "Are We Having Too Much Fun," *Atlantic*, April 27, 2017, https://www.theatlantic.com/entertainment/archive/2017/04/are-we-having-too -much-fun/523143/.

41. Sean Illing, "How Television Trivialized Our Culture and Politics," Vox, May 18, 2018, https://www.vox.com/conversations/2017/5/8/15440292/donald -trump-politics-culture-neil-postman-television-media.

42. Andrew Postman, "My Dad Predicted Trump in 1985—It's Not Orwell, He Warned, It's Brave New World," February 2, 2017, *Guardian*, https://www .theguardian.com/media/2017/feb/02/amusing-ourselves-to-death-neil-postman -trump-orwell-huxley.

43. Ibid.

44. Cameron Hilditch, "Still Amusing Ourselves to Death," *National Review*, September 13, 2020, https://www.nationalreview.com/2020/09/neil-postman -still-amusing-ourselves-to-death/.

45. Evan Osnos, "Pulling Our Politics Back from the Brink," *New Yorker*, November 8, 2020, https://www.newyorker.com/magazine/2020/11/16/pulling -our-politics-back-from-the-brink.

46. Maelle Gavet, "How Social Media Is Pushing Us toward 1984," *FastCompany*, September 1, 2020, https://www.fastcompany.com/90545787/how-social -media-is-pushing-us-toward-1984.

47. On this, see George Packer, "Doublethink Is Stronger Than Orwell Imagined," review of *The Ministry of Truth: The Biography of George Orwell's 1984*, *Atlantic*, July 2019, https://www.theatlantic.com/magazine/archive/2019/07/1984 -george-orwell/590638/.

Noam Chomsky in 1977.
Source: Hans Peters / Anefo. CC0 1.0 Universal Public Domain Dedication.

Chapter Seven

Noam Chomsky
News as Propaganda

The propaganda model describes forces that shape what the media does.

—Noam Chomsky, *Manufacturing Consent*, 1988

The seemingly boundless range of Noam Chomsky's intellectual interests can be divided conveniently, if perhaps a bit too neatly, into three major areas: First, in an early series of influential academic works, including *Syntactic Structures* (1957), *Current Issues in Linguistic Theory* (1964), *Aspects of the Theory of Syntax* (1965), and *Cartesian Linguistics* (1966), he set the linguistics establishment back on its heels with his bold theories. Whereas earlier practitioners saw their work as largely taxonomic—an effort to classify language by either its development in time or structural properties—Chomsky sought to investigate, in a formally logical way, what he regarded as the innate mental faculty that, among other things, made language acquisition in children so seemingly effortless.[1]

The idea of an innate capacity also touched on a second area of Chomskian interest: the philosophy of mind. In books like *Language and Mind* (1968) and *Reflections on Language* (1975) he argued that, far from being a tabula rasa, the human mind comprised, in addition to the language faculty, a series of other innate "modules," neural structures that interact with each other to generate a virtually unlimited range of thoughts, perceptions, and similar "cognitive products."[2]

In the popular imagination, though, Chomsky is perhaps best known for a third sphere of work: politics, economics, and social criticism. While absorbed in radical politics from an early age, he felt compelled to write his first book on the subject, *American Power and the New Mandarins* (1969), in response to the Vietnam War. Other books on related topics followed every few years. In *The Political Economy of Human Rights* (1979), he, along with coauthor Edward S. Herman, a professor of finance at the Wharton School of the University of Pennsylvania, continued a critique of US policy in Vietnam and Indochina generally; in *The Fateful Triangle* (1983), he examined relations between the United States, Israel, and the Palestinians, with a particular focus on the 1982 Lebanon War; in *Profit Over People* (1999), he outlined what he regarded as the harmful effects of neoliberalism, the embrace in the twentieth century of nineteen-century classical liberalism and free-market capitalism; in *Failed States* (2006), he argued that, in abusing its considerable power, the United States was not only imperiling its own democracy but other governments and people around the world; in *Requiem for the American Dream* (2017), which was preceded by a documentary film of the same name, he mapped the uneven concentration of wealth in the United States from the 1970s forward; and in *Consequences of Capitalism: Manufacturing Dissent and Resistance* (2021), he and coauthor Marv Waterstone explained how the capitalist system had stifled efforts to address key issues such as social justice and the environment.[3]

This third area of Chomskian concern also included books on the mass media. In *Necessary Illusions: Thought Control in Democratic Societies* (1989), *Media Control: The Spectacular Achievements of Propaganda* (1991; 2nd ed., 2002); and, most fully, in the first and revised editions with coauthor Herman of *Manufacturing Consent: The Political Economy of Mass Media* (1988, 2002), Chomsky laid out a contrarian view of the democratic press. If the press historically had been idealized as the "watchdog of democracy"—the institution tasked with speaking truth to power—he and Howard regarded it, and the mass media generally, as complicit in the effort by the money and power elites to consolidate and perpetuate establishment control. The press did this through a process the authors referred to as "the propaganda model"—a series of "filters" through which news and information typically had to pass before it reached the public.[4]

The result was "self-censorship without significant coercion"—a clear inversion of the autocratic formula by which news and information were

controlled through crude state intervention.[5] In America, a seeming democracy, such crudeness was not necessary, as the authors saw it, because
the news had been sifted for unfit or subversive content beforehand.[6] At
the same time, while the propaganda model was capable of molding public opinion without coercion, it was not always successful in doing so,
especially in societies like America's with competing sources of information. Nevertheless, the "effectiveness" gauge was largely beside the point,
Chomsky and Howard argued. What mattered more than the overall success of the model was what it managed to reveal: a largely unseen process
that, in a deeply structural way, tended to shaped what media do—in other
words, their performance. To demonstrate how this performance worked
in practice, the authors sifted through recent history and identified a series
of illustrative case histories.

Chomsky's media criticism, and in particular the propaganda model,
has generated considerable debate over the years. From the onset, its proponents regarded it as an incisive examination of how the press works in
practice rather than in its typically idealized formulations. Accordingly,
Chomsky supporters have consistently argued for his ongoing relevance,
even in a social media age when seemingly limitless channels are available for circumventing elite control. Chomskian skeptics have been less
impressed. Among some academics, his contributions have been ignored
or treated cursorily; and even those academics and nonacademics who
have taken his thinking seriously have faulted it for being, among other
things, too simplistic, too conspiratorial, and too inattentive to the evolving standards of journalistic professionalism. At least one detractor has
gone even further, charging that, were it not for Chomsky's status as a
linguist and cognitive scientist, his critique of media would be passed over
almost entirely. Still, for many, the Chomskian media critique remains
relevant, a testament perhaps to both the doggedness of those who have
embraced it and the continuing usefulness of the critique itself.

EARLY BACKGROUND AND EDUCATION

Avram Noam Chomsky was born on December 7, 1928, in an ethni-
cally diverse neighborhood in Northwest Philadelphia. His parents,

Elsie Simonofsky and Zeev (William) Chomsky, were both Jewish immigrants, she from Babruysk, modern-day Belarus, and he from what is
now Western Ukraine but then part of Czarist Russia. In America, both
Elsie and William taught at the Mikveh Israel School, in Philadelphia,
where they met. In time, Dr. Chomsky—he had earlier earned a graduate
degree in medieval Hebrew from Johns Hopkins University—was also
appointed to the faculty of Gratz College, a teacher-training institution
sharing space with the Mikveh Israel School. Eventually elected faculty
president in 1932, William Chomsky also went on to become a world-
famous Hebrew grammarian and the author of influential books on
language history and teaching. The young Noam was profoundly influenced by his father, with whom he regularly discussed scholarly topics,
including nineteenth- and twentieth-century Hebrew literature. But Elsie
Chomsky's left-wing Zionism, her spirited community involvement,
and her social activism also left their mark on young Noam, perhaps as
much as his father's scholarly influence.[7]

Doing Something Important

Just prior to his second birthday, Noam's parents placed him in Oak Lane
Country Day School, which he would attend until he was twelve years
old. Only recently affiliated with Temple University, the progressive pre-
school and elementary school stressed creativity and self-exploration in a
multicultural, noncompetitive environment. The precocious child thrived
in it, as he recalled in a later interview: "It was a lively atmosphere, and
the sense was that everybody was doing something important."[8] One of
the activities that came to engage him was writing for the school newspaper. Published just before his tenth birthday, his first piece of writing was
a heartfelt editorial about the deep disappointment he felt over the fall of
Barcelona and the defeat of the various antifascist groups at the hands of
the Nationalists. In many ways, the editorial signaled the beginning of his
fascination with radical movements, in particular anarcho-syndicalism
and libertarian socialism. A few years after this, he began attending the
Mikveh Israel School in preparation for his bar mitzvah. Perched in the
front row, close to his teachers, he often led class discussions, putting on
display the kind of intellectual curiosity and liveliness he had developed
both at both home and at Oak Lane.[9] (Oak Lane closed in 2010.)

The Blur of High School

In 1940, Noam entered Central Park High School, about two miles from his home. Then as now among the best public schools in the nation, Central Park was known for its high academic standards. For Noam, though, the culture shock was almost immediate. Suddenly, he not only discovered that he was an especially gifted student but that his academic status alone was enough to elevate him in the school's hierarchy, its "system of prestige and value." The revelation was not a happy one. Having thrived in the loosely structured, intellectually freewheeling, and non-competitive atmosphere of Oak Lane, he had now entered an intensely competitive and regimented one. He participated in a number of clubs, was well liked by his classmates, and early on was even a school football booster.[10] And yet, looking back years later, he acknowledged remembering "virtually nothing about high school," except, that is, its "emotional tone, which was quite negative."[11]

An Extension of High School

In 1945, at the age of sixteen, Noam entered the University of Pennsylvania. Like other children in the Chomsky circle of families, he was able to attend the expensive Ivy League school on certain conditions—that he live at home, commute to campus, and work to help out financially. (He taught Hebrew school in the afternoons and on Sundays.) Nevertheless, he entered college with the expectation that a new world of learning would soon open up to him.[12] And initially at least, this is what happened. As a freshman, he took an "exciting" course in the philosophy of logic with C. West Churchman, a young assistant professor who would go on to make major contributions to systems theory.[13] He also became immersed in several college courses in Arabic, which coincided with his and his father's shared interest in Semitic linguistics. Over time, though, the university came to feel to him "pretty much like an extension of high school." By the end of two years, he had grown restless, eager "to drop out to pursue my own interests, which were then largely political." One possibility was to go "to Palestine, perhaps to a kibbutz, to try to become involved in efforts at Arab-Jewish cooperation within a socialist framework."[14]

He then met a teacher whose personal charisma, along with his intellectual and political interests, tempered his feelings about school. The teacher was Zellig Sabbettai Harris, a leading figure in modern linguistics who since his own undergraduate days at the University of Pennsylvania was active in left-wing Zionism. Soon, the now eighteen-year-old Chomsky began taking Harris's graduate courses in linguistics, often held off campus in unlikely places like the local Horn & Hardart Automats. Chomsky also read proofs of his teacher's forthcoming book, *Methods in Structural Linguistics*, which laid the theoretical groundwork for the idea of an innate grammatical structure. And at Harris's suggestion, he enrolled in courses in philosophy and mathematics with such leading figures as Nelson Goodman, Morton White, and Nathan Fine. College now seemed more exciting, not unlike his first school experience at Oak Park.

Eventually, Chomsky would earn both a BA degree and a MA degree from the university.[15] For his BA, he submitted an honors thesis titled "Morphophonemics of Modern Hebrew," which drew on both his own early knowledge of the language and Harris's linguistic theories. For his MA, awarded in 1951, he submitted a revised version of his undergraduate thesis, which anticipated some of his later theories and would eventually be published in book form.[16] During this period, he also married Carol Doris Schatz, a physician's daughter from Oak Park whom he had known since childhood.[17]

Society of Fellows at Harvard and MIT

In 1951, following a recommendation from philosopher Nelson Goodman, Chomsky was admitted to the Society of Fellows at Harvard, in Cambridge, Massachusetts. For someone of his lower-middle-class background, it was a unique opportunity. Now with generous financial support and no teaching or administrative responsibilities, he could finally devote himself to study and research. He took full advantage of the opportunity. Working with sustained intensity, he completed the first draft of a nearly thousand-page manuscript in the nascent field of theoretical linguistics. Later published as *The Logical Structure of Linguistic Theory* (1975), he in time presented a chapter of the manuscript to Penn in fulfillment of his PhD requirements.[18] Like his BA and MA degrees, it was a "quite unconventional" PhD, as he would later say, and he was right: Besides his ongoing correspondence with Harris and Goodman, he had had no real involvement with the university since 1951.[19]

But he had few real job prospects in linguistics. For one, his formal training included as many courses in logic and philosophy as it did linguistics. For another, the theoretical work he was doing "was simply not recognized as related to the field," which at this point was dominated by the structuralists and behaviorists.[20] Certainly, he had taken steps toward enhancing his professional status, but he had not yet taken some essential ones, such as publishing in *Language*, the key publication of the Linguistic Society of America. As for his sprawling manuscript, he had submitted selected portions to the then Technology Press of MIT, but they had been summarily rejected, and not unreasonably given his novice status in the field, as he would later recall.[21]

Despite this, in 1955, he landed his first full-time university position, thanks to a good word from his friend Roman Jakobson, the Russian-born Harvard linguist.[22] The job would split Chomsky's time between a research project in machine translation and undergraduate teaching. The former interested him not at all, and he admitted as much to the lab director, but he found that he actually enjoyed teaching: in his language course, he was able to air his theory of a generative grammar, while in his philosophy courses, he could explore the sorts of theoretical issues that not only underlay his own work but that in time laid the foundation for MIT's future Department of Linguistics and Philosophy, officially established in 1976.[23]

It was also during this period that his first book, *Syntactic Structures* (1957), was published. The book, actually a monograph, was a revision of some of his undergraduate course notes, which in a roundabout way had caught the eye of editors at Mouton & Co., a Dutch publisher producing a series on general linguistics. Reworking some of Zellig Harris's ideas on generative grammar, *Syntactic Structures* not only set modern linguistics on a new path but argued for a more precise theory of grammar expressed in contemporary mathematical terms.[24] Officials at MIT were impressed by their young and audacious scholar. In 1961, they asked Chomsky and a fellow linguist, the Latvian-born Morris Halle, to set up the university's first graduate program in linguistics. The program, initially housed within the Department of Foreign Languages and Literatures, attracted other important scholars and soon developed an international reputation. In 1965, just four years after its founding, it produced its first crop of PhDs.[25]

Meanwhile, Chomsky had begun to publish in earnest. In 1964, he put out *Current Issues in Linguistic Theory*, a revision and expansion of an earlier paper he had delivered at the ninth International Congress of Linguistics. The following year, he wrote *Aspects of the Theory of Syntax* (1965), an elaboration of the ideas first presented in *Syntactic Structures*. And that same year, he produced *Cartesian Linguistics: A Chapter in the History of Rationalist Thought* (1965), which traced the historical basis for his idea of a universal grammar. Other books on linguistics soon followed, including *Language and Mind* (1968); *The Sound Pattern of English*, with Halle (1968); *Reflections on Language* (1975); *Lectures on Government and Binding* (1981); and *The Minimalist Program* (1995). Collectively, Chomsky's scholarly contributions roiled the field, although a few of his books—*Cartesian Linguistics*, for instance—were reviewed critically. Still, Chomsky now found himself at the center of an international and "rational debate," as he later called it, one not dissimilar from the ongoing intellectual exchange in the physical sciences. For linguistics, he believed, it was a hopeful sign of the future.[26]

TOWARD A PROPAGANDA MODEL

The situation was considerably different in the area of contemporary affairs. Here too there was a need for clarity and rationality, but too often, as he saw it, discussions of domestic and international affairs were marred by distortion, misrepresentation, and ideology. Even worse, the "privileged minority" best equipped by training and status to seek the hidden truth was often either disengaged or complicit in the deception. In a powerful 1967 essay in *The New York Review* titled "The Responsibility of Intellectuals," he criticized a minority that he counted himself among for its failures, especially concerning the Vietnam War. His essay was a rallying cry to his fellow intellectuals and to himself. Henceforth, there would be the need to put forth a credible counternarrative to the official one.[27]

In a series of books, beginning with *American Power and the New Mandarins* (1969), he elaborated on this thesis. Finally, in *Pirates and Emperors, Old and New: International Terrorism in the Real World* (1986), published two years before *Manufacturing Consent*, he made explicit a premise that had been expressed more or less implicitly all along. Drawing partially on an existing liberal critique, he pointed out that, while the United States as a nominal democracy imposed relatively few restraints on freedom of expression, it had become unusually adept at manipulating thought:

> The less the state is able to employ violence in defense of the interests of elite groups that effectively dominate it, the more it becomes necessary to devise techniques of "manufacture of consent," in the words of Walter Lippmann sixty years ago, or "engineering consent," the phrase preferred by Edward Bernays, one of the founding fathers of the American public relations industry.[28]

In America, in other words, the task of ensuring that the voice of the people voiced the right ideas was less an act of bullying, as it was in outright autocracies, than an act of public relations. Certainly, an overly compliant intellectual community was playing a role in this PR charade, as Chomsky had stressed a decade and a half before. But so too were the mass media, which had in many cases abrogated their traditional role of speaking truth to power for an incautious seat at the official propaganda table.

HOW THE PRESS PERFORMS: A THEORETICAL MODEL

In *Manufacturing Consent: The Political Economy of the Mass Media* (1988), Chomsky and coauthor Edward S. Herman, a soon-to-be-retired professor of finance at the University of Pennsylvania, devised a model to explain how the mass media carried out its new propagandistic role. Among other things, the model took into account both the media's external relationships and its internal institutional structures. Externally, the media functioned largely to "serve, and propagandize on behalf of, the powerful societal interests that control and finance them."[29] Internally, the media operated not through heavy-handed corporate tactics but rather through "the selection of right-thinking personnel"—key employees who could be counted on to internalize the institution's codes of "newsworthiness." Pick and acculturate the right editors, writers, and other personnel, in other words, and they will end up monitoring and censoring themselves, as Ben Bagdikian among others had earlier pointed out. Other internal elements—consolidated ownership, an ad-based business model, and the often parasitical relations between news makers and news outlets, also enabled commercial media to carry out their primary function. Incorporating these and other components into an "analytical framework," the authors arrived at their descriptive "propaganda model" of media conduct (*Manufacturing*, xi).

News Filters

If one drilled down still further, the Chomsky and Herman model could also be understood as a series of conduits or "news filters" through which information had to flow in order to be considered newsworthy. Numbering five in all, these filters reiterated the main elements of the propaganda model, while adding a few more, including "flak" or negative feedback that seeks to discipline the media when they move too far afield, and "anticommunism," at the time still an effective mechanism for controlling what were deemed radical political sentiments. In passing "the raw material of news" through such screens, large newspapers, wire services, and broadcast media were complicit in the effort to ensure that whatever the public eventually read, heard, or saw would be, in effect, properly scrubbed. In this way, whether wittingly or unwittingly, the media contributed to marginalizing or suppressing news that was insufficiently establishment, that questioned the economic status quo, or that otherwise provoked dissent or discord (*Manufacturing*, 2). And while such goals were not always achieved—and certainly not in cases in which the public had sufficient access to independent news—the propaganda model was nevertheless a good analytical tool for understanding media performance (*Manufacturing*, xii).

A Real-World Application: The Plot to Kill the Pope

In the final several chapters of *Manufacturing Consent*, Chomsky and Herman applied their analytical framework to a series of case studies. Among the "lessons" of these studies, the authors believed, was the tendency of US media to treat news differently when it aligned with official interests and when it did not. And so, for example, when Polish Roman Catholic priest and anti-communist Solidarity activist Jerzy Popielusko was murdered in 1984, the event was covered far more widely than when, around this same time, priests who protested US involvement in Latin

America were assassinated. The Solidarity activist, in the authors' parlance, was deemed a "worthy" victim, while the dissident Latin American priests were deemed "unworthy."

A similar phenomenon was at work, it seemed, in the case of international elections. Whenever such elections were held in US-favored countries (Dominican Republic, El Salvador, Guatemala), the press typically followed the official line and portrayed them as "legitimate." In contrast, whenever elections were held in countries the United States regarded unfavorably (Nicaragua under the Sandinistas, for example), they were usually viewed in both Washington and the establishment press as "meaningless" or, worse, a farce (*Manufacturing* 37, 87–88). In such instances, the press followed rather than set the official agenda. There were also times, however, when mass media had played a more active role, setting rather than following the official agenda. One of these instances came to be known as the "KGB-Bulgarian plot," a putative conspiracy in May 1981 to kill Pope John Paul II, presumably for his support of Poland's Solidarity movement. Here, as the authors saw it, the mass media not only initiated the claims of a conspiracy but, as part of the anti-communist, anti-Soviet ideology of the time, kept "the pot boiling from inception to the conclusion of the case" (*Manufacturing*, 143).[30]

The key facts of the shooting have largely faded from public memory: As John Paul II was passing through St. Peter's Square in an open car at the start of his weekly general audience, a lone gunman fired four shots. Two of the shots injured the Pope—one shot hitting his abdomen, just missing vital organs, the other his left hand. (The remaining two shots injured a pair of bystanders.) Those near the pontiff disarmed and retained the gunman, who was later identified as Mehmet Ali Agca, a twenty-three-year-old escapee from a Turkish prison who was serving a sentence for the murder of a liberal journalist. Meanwhile, Pope John Paul was taken by ambulance to Rome's Gemelli Hospital, where he underwent extended emergency surgery. He emerged from the operation in critical but stable condition.[31]

The apparent motive for the attempted assassination was at first unclear, beyond a few tantalizing clues. In its initial report of the shooting, for instance, the *New York Times* (May 14, 1981), cited unnamed Italian police who claimed to have found several notes handwritten in Turkish in Agca's pocket, one of which supposedly said, "I am killing the Pope as a protest against the imperialism of the Soviet Union and the United States and against the genocide that is being carried out in El Salvador and Afghanistan."[32] The notes seemed to point to some sort of left-wing association, perhaps with Palestinian Marxists, but Italian police officials were soon doubtful, and so was the *Times* based on its independent investigation. With contributions from a team of correspondents, the investigation indicated "a clear pattern of connections between the gaunt, taciturn Mr. Agca and an international alliance of not Palestinian Marxists but right-wing Turkish extremists.[33]

This right-wing narrative came to dominate early media coverage, but then, Chomsky and Herman point out, a very different counternarrative took hold, one that resurrected the idea of a left-wing plot. It was initiated in large part by the *Reader's Digest*, which since its founding in the early 1920s by the Wallace family had maintained a clear anti-Communist editorial stance.[34] The publication hired two people with impeccable anti-Soviet credentials to investigate the shooting: Claire Sterling, whose book *The Terror Network* had argued that the Soviets were engaging in terrorism through proxies, and Paul B. Henze, a broadcaster and former CIA operative.[35] Based on their joint research, Sterling wrote a piece for the magazine titled "The Plot to Kill the Pope" (September 1982), which argued that the conspiracy had been coordinated through Bulgaria, at this point still part of the Soviet Bloc. According to Sterling, Bulgaria's motive for its involvement was twofold—first, to weaken NATO by implicating a Turk in the attempted assassination and, second, to undermine the Solidarity movement by eliminating its most high-profile supporter, the Pope. A follow-up TV special on NBC, narrated by veteran correspondent Marvin Kalb, followed a similar story line.

In their discussion of the alleged communist-led plot, Chomsky and Herman began by poking holes in what they saw as the flawed narrative. On the Bulgaria connection, there was certainly circumstantial evidence that pointed to a link between Agca and this Soviet satellite. For one thing, Agca's prior travels had for a short time landed him in Bulgaria, where he became friendly with Turkish drug dealers involved in the Bulgarian drug trade. Did this establish a solid connection between Agca and Bulgaria, as the would-be conspiracists Sterling, Henze, and Kalb claimed? Not really, argued Chomsky and Herman, who regarded the evidence as at best circumstantial (*Manufacturing*, 144). The trio had also erred, Chomsky and Herman believed, when it charged that one of the key rationales of Agca's supposedly Soviet-inspired mission was to undermine support for Solidarity. Ignored here was that the first time Agca had threatened to kill the pope was in 1979, the year *before* Solidarity was formed. In fact, far from being a communist sympathizer, "Agca was a committed rightist, and therefore not a likely candidate for service to the Communist powers," unless in the unlikely event he had participated in a false-flag operation to implicate them. If such inconvenient details were being willfully explained away or worse ignored, the authors concluded, it was probably because they were out of sync with the broader narrative then being promoted by the Reagan administration and others in the West: the Soviet Union was a major state-sponsor of "international terrorism" and used dupes like Agca to carry out its nefarious destabilization plan (*Manufacturing*, 145–48).[36]

It was a powerful narrative, one that the *Reader's Digest* and some other right-tilting media had eagerly embraced. But what about other media? Had they been too uncritical—or worse, complicit—in their own coverage of the alleged KGB-Bulgarian plot? Some had been, charged Chomsky and Herman, who believed from their research that several of the largest media outlets had persisted in the idea of a Soviet-orchestrated plot, in some cases even after conclusive evidence to the contrary had emerged.[37] Such media had variously failed to explore and test other theories, had relied on putatively expert sources whose background suggested an axe to grind, and had participated unwittingly or not "in a classic propaganda campaign that got the message of Bulgarian-Soviet guilt over to the public" (*Manufacturing*, 155).

For one, they pointed a finger at *Newsweek*, at this point the second most widely read US newsweekly behind *Time* magazine. Reviewing *Newsweek*'s January 3, 1983, cover story, "The Plot to Kill Pope John Paul II," the authors cited numerous instances when both writers and editors had simply parroted the received story line. Magazine readers were informed, for example, that "investigators now think" Agca was using his right-wing affiliations as a cover, when in fact this was an unsubstantiated assertion by Paul Henze, the broadcaster and former CIA operative. Readers were also told that Bulgaria and the Soviet Union had had a long-standing campaign "to destabilize Turkey through terrorism," which was a direct quote from Henze, for whom, like Claire Sterling, Soviet terrorism by proxy was an article of faith. Finally, without substantial evidence, the story had reported as "established fact" that "Agca had help from a huge set of Bulgarians," both in his country and in Rome. (Italian prosecutors would later find no solid evidence for this claim.) Such reporting followed a subtle but undeniable pattern, Chomsky and Herman thought; largely because of the newsweekly's generally confident tone, along with "its quotes from many authorities supporting the charges," its story was undeniably "powerful," but a closer examination revealed it to be "a piece of uncritical propaganda" (*Manufacturing*, 156).

The authors also pointed to reporting failures by the *New York Times*. In reviewing thirty-two *Times* reports written between November 1, 1982, and January 31, 1983, Chomsky and Howard found that twelve stories contained not hard news but rather someone's opinion or speculation, and another twenty *Times* stories were on "peripheral subjects, such as smuggling in Bulgaria or papal-Soviet relations." Among the remaining sixteen stories, only one included "a solid news fact," while the rest were either soft news or trivia. As Chomsky and Howard viewed it, this farrago of speculations, tangential reports, trivia, and minor details ended up producing "a lot of smoke," which served to keep "the issue of possible Soviet involvement before the public," while at the same time staying safely "clear of substantive issues that bore on motives, quality of evidence," and the story's broader anti-communist context (*Manufacturing*, 157).

If the media's failures in this instance were blatant, they were nevertheless indicative of how the press actually operated according to the propaganda model. Indeed, contrary to the popular movie image of the press as cantankerous and uncompromising, it was in fact more often than not complicit in inculcating and defending "the economic, social, and political agenda of the privileged groups that dominate the domestic society and the state," Chomsky and Howard claimed (*Manufacturing*, 298). In the real world, newspapers and other media did not buck the system. They were participants in keeping it going.

HOPEFUL SIGNS

Despite this gloomy assessment, Chomsky and Howard were not ready to give up on the idea of a free and independent press. For one thing, press propaganda, if that is what it was, did not always achieve its desired effect. The so-called Vietnam syndrome, for instance, had made the public hesitant to endorse later US excursions abroad, however they had been portrayed in the press. Reagan had discovered this new reality in the 1980s after his efforts to destabilize the leftist Nicaraguan government encountered strong headwinds. Other "counterforces" had also served to diminish the commercial media's effect. The authors cited several of these at the end of the original edition of *Manufacturing Consent*: the proliferation of local public-access channels; the emergence of local nonprofit television and radio stations, such as Pacifica Network in California; the ongoing presence of public radio and TV, above all NPR and PBS; and other such developments. Nearly a decade and a half later, in the revised edition of their study, they reiterated their belief "that democratic politics requires a democratization of information sources and a more democratic media" (*Manufacturing*, xlix). Urging grassroots groups and others to continue agitating for such a media, they also encouraged them to explore newer channels of information, including the internet, which at the time at least seemed to augur a new age of independent and widely sourced journalism.[38]

REVIEWERS REACT TO THE MODEL

Reviewers largely ignored *Manufacturing Consent* when it first appeared. There were undoubtedly many reasons for this, but some supporters have cited the book's harsh and wide-ranging critique of both US foreign policy and the mainstream media. Whatever the actual case, commentators who did weigh in tended to be warily appreciative but far from uniformly complimentary.

Writing in the *New York Times*, for instance, diplomatic historian Walter LaFeber said the book highlighted the challenge faced by the US government in the waning days of the Cold War: Was the United States capable of forming a post–Cold War policy based on an informed and morally aware public consensus? To this question, said LaFeber, the authors had responded with a resounding no, and they had documented their response with a series of recent case studies. These studies were well researched, said the reviewer, but Chomsky and Howard had weakened their argument on occasion by "overstatement" and omission. How was it possible, for example, that at times grassroots oppositional movements, with relatively limited access to the media, had prevailed over the elite propaganda system, as had happened when the Reagan administration attempted to supply military aid to the right-wing Contras that opposed the Sandinistas? For the authors, complained LaFeber, the explanation for such an unlikely victory lay in the simple fact that the propaganda system was not all-powerful. But such an explanation failed to satisfy, since it raised as many questions as it answered. In a book that was otherwise effectively damning in illustrating "the news media's role in covering up errors and deceptions in American foreign policy of the past quarter-century," noted LaFeber, elisions of this sort were "unfortunate"[39]

The updated edition of the book was also not widely reviewed, although the few reviews that did appear covered a range of opinions. Among the most favorable reviews came from overseas. In the *European Journal of Communication*, for example, Jeffrey Klaehn, an independent scholar who in time edited two collections of essays on the propaganda model, argued that the book was more relevant than ever "in an era in which corporate ownership of media has never been as concentrated, right-wing pressure on public radio and television is increasing, the public relations industries are expanding exponentially, and advertising values dominate the news production process." Klaehn concluded by encouraging his fellow commentators and academics to make a greater push to consider the propaganda model as part of their "scholarly debates on media performance."[40]

Among the harshest US reviews was an essay collected for a book titled *The Anti-Chomsky Reader* (2004), an anthology of critical pieces about the author's work, including his media criticism. Written by Eli Lehrer, a former editor of the house organ of the conservative American Enterprise Institute, the essay was titled "Chomsky and the Media: A Kept Press and a Manipulated People." In it, Lehrer issued what amounted to a blanket condemnation of *Manufacturing Consent*. Largely ignoring the book's coauthor, the former editor complained, among other things, that Chomsky's analysis was "very much that of an outsider who knows relatively little about the media"; that "his theories are based on illogical, flawed or fallacious arguments"; and that "his assertions about media control seem increasingly antique in the [new] information age." To the superficial eye, Lehrer concluded, Chomsky seemed like a "vulgar Marxist," forever discovering new evidence of the pervasive "ideas of the ruling class." And yet even this comparison did not hold up, since, unlike the dyed-in-the-wool Marxist, he "has too much contempt for the American people to hold out even a vague hope for revolution."[41]

A FURTHER EYE ON THE US MEDIA

Manufacturing Consent was immediately followed by two other media-related books: *Necessary Illusions*: *Thought Control in Democratic Societies* (1989), a collection of five lectures Chomsky had delivered on Canadian radio the year before, and *Media Control: The Spectacular Achievements of Propaganda*, first published in 1991.

NECESSARY ILLUSIONS: THOUGHT CONTROL IN DEMOCRATIC SOCIETIES

Here Chomsky reiterated his view of modern mass media, applying his and Herman's original analytical framework to both older and newer case histories. Accompanying each of the five chapters, moreover, was a detailed, multipart appendix covering additional information that might have easily overwhelmed even the most attentive of his Canadian radio audience. In appendix I of the published book, though, he discussed something that was probably of more than passing interest to his current readers: the idea animating at least some of the negative comments directed toward his previous book, *Manufacturing Consent*. As he saw it, those comments were driven, at least in part, by the notion that both he and Herman had crossed certain standard boundaries of permissible discourse, and thus they had to be called on it. Even some of the more temperate and reasonable reviews, as he saw it, had faulted the authors for their difficult conclusions.

A prime example of this later group was the *Times* review by historian Walter LaFeber. Untangling the logic of LaFeber's review, Chomsky thought, was worth the effort, since it was "one of the very rare attempts to evaluate a propaganda model with actual arguments instead of mere invective, and is furthermore the reasoning of an outstanding and

independent-minded historian"[42] With that in mind, he examined three of
the reviewer's criticisms. Two were included in LaFeber's original *Times*
analysis, and one was added subsequently after Herman complained in a
letter to the editor about that original analysis.

Chomsky took exception, for instance, to LaFeber's complaint, expressed first in his *Times* review, that the authors had provided an inadequate explanation for the propaganda model's occasional failures. "By the
same logic," Chomsky said, "an account of how [then official Communist
Party newspaper] *Pravda* works to mobilize bias would be undermined
by the existence of dissidents. Plainly, the thesis that *Pravda* serves as an
organ of state propaganda is not disconfirmed by the fact that there are
many dissidents in the Soviet Union" (*Necessary Illusions*, 148). He also
objected to LaFeber's claim, voiced in his published reply to Herman's
letter to the editor, that the authors of *Manufacturing Complaint* had overstated the press's problems, thereby undermining their critique. "If the
news media are so unqualifiedly bad," LaFeber had said in his reply, "the
book at least needs to explain why so many publications . . . can cite their
stories to attack President Reagan's Central American policy."[43] Such stories did indeed exist, Chomsky acknowledged, especially if one searched
diligently for them. But once again citing the Soviet Union, he pointed
out their existence no more weakened the essential thesis of *Manufacturing Consent* than the presence of dissident material in the Soviet Union
refuted the fact that its "press transmits government propaganda and tries
to 'mobilize bias'" (*Necessary Illusions*, 150).

Media Control: The Spectacular Achievements of Propaganda

The second book following *Manufacturing Consent* was a much slimmer
one. Despite its brevity, though, the pocket-size publication, published
in 1991 and updated in 1997 and 2002, distilled in simple language and
terms the political assumptions undergirding much of Chomsky's (and
Herman's) media critique up to this point.

In *Media Control*, Chomsky began by framing the discussion that would
follow around two different conceptions of democracy. The standard
conception, found in most dictionaries, was of a "representative" system
of governance in which the public elects its leaders but retains essential
control of both the means and the information required to play a part "in

the management of their own affairs."[44] Most mainstream commentators, he believed, would rely on some version of this definition to describe the US system. And yet, as commentators from Franklin to Churchill to Lippmann to Robert Kennedy had described, such a democracy was frequently messy, difficult, and frustrating, never more so than when some unified action was required or felt to be required by elected officials or other powerful interests. For this reason, explained Chomsky, there was a long history, going back as far as seventeenth-century England, of an alternative theory of democracy, one in which the public must be inhibited from managing its own affairs "and the means of information must be kept narrowly and rigidly controlled." This description of democracy, he readily acknowledged, might well sound "odd," given all we have learned about how the democratic system of government is supposed to work. And yet, he insisted, it was in fact the more common form of democracy, nowhere more so than in the modern United States (*Control*, 10).

The prevailing system posed a challenge, however. Since the United States was still nominally a democracy—in Lincoln's words, a government "of the people, for the people, by the people"—the public could not be bludgeoned into agreement, as they would be in an autocracy or totalitarian state. If public consent was to be achieved, it would have to be through more subtle means, using the available tools and channels of communication to convey certain information—that is, propaganda. Chomsky summed up this approach in a cynical phrase: "Propaganda is to democracy what the bludgeon is to a totalitarian state" (*Control*, 20). In the remaining short chapters of *Media Control*, he surveyed what he regarded as the "spectacular achievements of propaganda." Starting with President Wilson's successful effort to create a war fever after 1916—an effort powerfully assisted by not only the press but by the still nascent field of public relations, as Walter Lippmann had explained—the survey moved steadily through twentieth-century history to the first Bush administration's campaign to mobilize public opinion against Saddam Hussein.[45]

In this campaign, as in the previous ones, the press had played a vital role, as Chomsky saw it. Among other things, he pointed to its silence, in the buildup to the war, about the "Iraqi democratic opposition," the umbrella term for groups that were opposed to the regime of Saddam Hussein and in favor of a parliamentary democracy. Prior to the war, representatives of these groups had come to Washington seeking assistance for their cause, Chomsky explained. At the time, though, the Iraqi president was apparently still in Bush's good graces, and thus the representatives and their requests were ignored, and there was virtually no reporting in the press of that key fact.

Even when official Washington turned on Hussein following his invasion and annexation of neighboring Kuwait, the opposition's advice about how the conflict might be resolved peacefully and war with Iraq avoided was still largely ignored, not only by the Bush administration itself but by the national press. "That's the wrong view and therefore they're out," said Chomsky before the war had actually begun. "We don't want to hear a word about the Iraqi democratic opposition. If you want to find out about them, pick up the German press, or the British press. They don't say much about them, but they're less controlled than we are and they say something." It was for him another sobering illustration, in a long list of other ones, of an overly docile press, underreporting a story that ran counter to the official one, which in this case was that aggression could not be rewarded and therefore military intervention was justified. It was also a reminder of "a deeply indoctrinated population" that failed to notice the press lapses (*Control*, 55).

All this, Chomsky thought, raised a fundamental question: just what kind of democratic society do we want to live in? The choices were stark. If, on the one hand, it was the current one, then the masses would remain a "bewildered herd," by turns fearful and awestruck, and the intellectuals would dutifully "repeat the slogans they're supposed to repeat" while the larger society deteriorates (*Control*, 65). This was, in effect, the vision of a democratic society as "a form of self-imposed totalitarianism." If, on the other hand, aided by a free press and unencumbered intellectuals, enough people rejected this vision and reassumed both the means and information necessary to participate wisely and fully in the democratic process, then there was the prospect of a different future. Ultimately, it was left to the people to decide which vision of society held out the greater promise of a better life.

CONCLUSION

During his long and varied career, Noam Chomsky has placed himself outside the mainstream, whether in his academic work in linguistics and the cognitive sciences or in his role as social critic. His militant insistence on pushing the bounds of discourse as the price of progress has endeared him to many, while outraging and frequently confusing others. To his supporters, he is intellectually audacious and brave, indifferent if necessary to the niceties of decorum; to his detractors, he is contrarian, pessimistic, anti-American, self-righteous, too quick to impugn motives, assign blame, see conspiracies. Often their response has been not to engage him but to ignore him.

His media criticism—a central part of his critique of modern democratic society—has provoked the same dichotomous response. To those he has influenced, and there are many, his work alone and in collaboration with the late Edward Herman, and in particular their propaganda model, remains crucial. On the one hand, it aids our understanding of how mass media shapes the democratic narrative, and, on the other hand, it sets the stage for future research on the success of the mass media's influence. Certainly, new digital media has complicated the question of his ongoing significance, students of Chomsky acknowledge, but they reject the idea that such media have invalidated it. Others, meanwhile, see things differently. They characterize his and Herman's insistence on media control in the age of almost limitless news and information platforms as outdated, the intellectual product of another era, and they ridicule their methodology as too often simplistic and prone to overstatement. "If you think that the *New York Times* is *Pravda*, which is essentially what they're saying, then what vocabulary do you have left for Fox News?," the late media scholar Todd Gitlin said in an obituary after Herman's death, in 2017.[46]

Some Chomsky commentators have attempted, however, to walk a middle line. They are at once sympathetic to his basic project and yet aware that his analytical framework needs updating, especially in the age when so much media, social and otherwise, are directed to manufacturing not consent but distrust and resentment. In "The Propaganda Model and Manufacturing Consent: U.S. Public Compliance and Resistance," for example, political media scholar Anthony R. DiMaggio attempts to walk such a line. As a contributor to *The Cambridge Companion to Chomsky*, DiMaggio summarizes Chomsky and Herman's views on mass media and offers updated studies to support their joint thesis. In passing, DiMaggio also attempts to account for why so many "mainstream intellectuals" seem hesitant to comment on the pair's work. Certainly, part of the reason has to do with professional timidity, a hesitancy "to endanger their status by advocating theories questioning the foundation of American politics and media." At the same time, says DiMaggio, "one should also recognize shortcomings with the model."[47]

The most significant of these, he argues, is the model's failure to account for a contradictory trend in recent American history. Specifically, if the older propaganda model had successfully unmasked elite efforts to manufacture consent in *favor* of government policies and narratives, it had relatively little to say about elite efforts to manufacture dissent *against* government. The modern avatar of this distrust-in-government movement was, in many ways, Barry Goldwater, who had made the "revolt" against the welfare state a cornerstone of his 1964 presidential campaign.[48] Nearly two decades later, Ronald Reagan, with his characteristic flair and mediagenic personality, gave new voice to the message in his 1981 inaugural address, announcing famously, "In this present crisis, government is not the solution to our problem, government *is* the problem." The fortieth president's view of things was also among the founding principles of the Tea Party, the fiscally conservative movement that grabbed headlines during the second year of the Obama administration. (Reagan has been called "the original Tea Party candidate."[49]) Even progressive reformers like Ralph Nader had a hand in making citizens distrustful of their government, as some scholars have argued.[50]

In many ways, all this anti-government rhetoric culminated years later in the favorite slogan of Steve Bannon, the alt-right media executive and former investment banker who became Donald Trump's chief policy strategist and who vowed early on to fight daily for the "deconstruction of the administrative state."[51] Such an agenda also requires media participation and propaganda, of course, but not ostensibly for the purpose of shaping an elite consensus but for stoking public resentment against it. This was populism—but of a faux variety. For while the right-wing populists attempt to depress "trust and participation in the entire political process," in part by stoking voter resentment over "hot button" and fringe issues, their real intent is to legislate "in ways that support the agendas of the economic elite," DiMaggio argues.[52]

In the Trump era, for instance, administration officials and their allies adopted a media strategy aimed at inflaming voter resentment and mistrust over issues such as immigration, abortion, guns, policing, climate change, voting, civil rights, and even a worldwide pandemic. At the same time, they exerted their collective power to pass massive corporate tax cuts and derail years of sometime bipartisan regulation. The latter made many in the corporate community happy, while the resentment campaign and eventual cries of a "stolen election" led directly to the January 6, 2021, storming of the Capitol. In Chomsky's sardonic phrase, perhaps this failed insurrection was yet another spectacular achievement of propaganda.

Whatever the case, the propaganda of dissent seems in many ways like another fertile area of media research.[53] If some rise to the challenge, they will almost certainly owe a debt of gratitude to Noam Chomsky. Like few others before him, he applied a formidable intelligence, intellectual energy, and political commitment to the fraught but crucial question of the proper role of mass media in a democratic society.

NOTES

1. When children acquire a given language, they have been clearly influenced by a specific linguistic environment. But Chomsky argued that linguistic behavior, and indeed the "unconscious construction of a grammar," were fundamentally not a response to external stimuli but to the language faculty itself. See, for example, James A. McGilvray, "Noam Chomsky, American Linguist," *Encyclopedia Britannica Online*, updated December 17, 2020, https://www.britannica.com/biography/Noam-Chomsky/Linguistics.

2. Ibid.

3. See Noam Chomsky, *American Power and the New Mandarins*, rev. ed, with a new introduction by Howard Zinn (1969; repr., New York: New Press, 2002); with Edward S. Herman, *Political Economy of Human Rights*, 2 vols. (1979; repr., Chicago: Haymarket, 2014); *The Fateful Triangle: The U.S., Israel, and the Palestinians*, rev.ed., with a new foreword by Edward W. Said (1983; repr., Chicago: Haymarket, 2014); *Profit over People*: *Neoliberalism and Global Order*, with an introduction by Robert W. McChesney (New York: Seven Stories Press, 1999); *Failed States: The Abuse of Power and the Assault on Democracy* (New York: Owl Books / Henry Holt, 2006); and *Requiem for the American Dream* (New York: Seven Stories Press, 2017); Noam Chomsky and Marv Waterstone, *Consequences of Capitalism: Manufacturing Discontent and Resistance* (2021; repr., New York: Hamish Hamilton, 2021).

4. Edward S. Herman and Noam Chomsky, *Manufacturing Consent: The Political Economy of Mass Media*, rev. ed., with a new introduction by the authors (1988; repr., New York: Pantheon Books, 2002), 2.

5. Jeffery Klaehn, "A Critical Review of Herman and Chomsky's 'Propaganda Model,'" *European Journal of Communications*, vol. 17, no. 2, June 1, 2002, 147, https://journals.sagepub.com/doi/10.1177/0267323102017002691.

6. Noam Chomsky, *Media Control: The Spectacular Achievements of Propaganda*, rev. ed., (1991; repr., New York: Seven Stories Press, 2002), 9–10.

7. Robert F. Barsky, *Noam Chomsky: A Life of Dissent* (Cambridge: MIT Press, 1997), 9–14; see also Associated Press, "Dr. William Chomsky, 81, Hebrew Grammarian, Dies," *New York Times*, July 22, 1977, https://www.nytimes .com/1977/07/22/archives/dr-william-chomsky-81-hebrew-grammarian-dies .html, and "Elsie (Simonofsky) Chomsky," WikiTree, last modified August, 6, 2021, https://www.wikitree.com/wiki/Simonofsky-1.

8. "Interview," *The Chomsky Reader*, ed. James Peck (New York: Pantheon Books, 1987), 5.

9. Barsky, *Life*, 16–19.

10. Ibid., 22

11. "Interview," *Reader*, 6.

12. Ibid., 6–7.

13. In 1958, after leaving the University of Pennsylvania and holding several other academic appointments in the interim, Churchmen joined the faculty of the School of Business Administration at the University of California, Berkeley, where he taught, among other courses, the philosophy of systems science. See Kathleen MacClay, "C. West Churchman Dies," news release, *UC Berkeley News*, March 31, 2004, https://www.berkeley.edu/news/media /releases/2004/03/31_chrch.shtml.

14. "Interview," *Reader*, 6–7.

15. Ibid., 7–8.

16. See Noam Chomsky, *Morphophonemics of Modern Hebrew* (1979; repr., New York: Routledge, 2011).

17. Barsky, *Life*, 13.

18. Noam Chomsky, *The Logical Structure of Linguistic Theory* (New York: Springer, 1975).

19. "Interview," *Reader*, 8.

20. Ibid., 15.

21. Quoted in Barsky, *Life*, 83.

22. See, for example, *Roman Jakobson*, ed. Margaret Thomas (New York: Routledge, 2014).

23. "About Us," Department of Linguistics and Philosophy," Massachusetts Institute of Technology, accessed April 20, 2021, https://philosophy.mit.edu/; Barsky, *Life,* 87; and "Interview," *Reader,* 15–16.

24. See, for example, Pavle Ivić, John Lyons, et al., "Linguistics," *Encyclopedia Britannica Online,* updated September 11, 2020, https://www.britannica.com/science/linguistics/additional-info#history.

25. "Brief History of Linguistics at MIT," Department of Linguistics and Philosophy, Massachusetts Institute of Technology, accessed April 20, 2021, https://linguistics.mit.edu/274-2/; "Interview," *Reader,* 16.

26. Ibid.

27. Noam Chomsky, *The Responsibility of Intellectuals,* with a new preface by the author (1967; repr., New York: The New Press, 2017).

28. Chomsky, *Pirates and Emperors, Old and New: International Terrorism in the Real World* (1986; repr., Chicago: Haymarket Books, 2015), 25.

29. Herman and Chomsky, *Manufacturing Consent.* All further references will be to this edition and cited parenthetically in the text.

30. In a footnote, Chomsky and Herman point out, by way of qualification, that the press's three principal news sources in the Bulgarian story also had "long-standing relations with the [US] government," something the authors elaborate on further in the text (*Manufacturing Consent,* 364).

31. See, among other initial press reports, Henry Tanner, "Pope Is Shot in Vatican Square," *New York Times,* May 14, 1981, https://www.nytimes.com/1981/05/14/world/pope-shot-car-vatican-square-surgeons-term-condition-turk-escaped-murderer-seized.html.

32. Ibid.

33. R. W. Apple Jr., "Trail of Mehmet Ali Agca: 6 Years of Neofascist Ties," *New York Times,* May 25, 1981, 1, *Times Machine,* https://timesmachine.nytimes.com/timesmachine/1981/05/25/132317.html?pageNumber=1.

34. On the *Digest*'s anti-communism, see, for example, Joanne Sharp, *Condensing the Cold War: Reader's Digest and American Identity* (Minneapolis: University of Minnesota Press, 2000); on its long-standing conservatism, see, Patrick A. McGuire, "Doing the Right Thing: *Reader's Digest* Last Appeal, Condensed and Conservative," *The Baltimore Sun,* August 25, 1993, C1.

35. See Claire Sterling, *The Terror Network* (New York: Henry Holt, 1994) and Wikipedia, s.v., "Claire Sterling," last modified March 5, 2021, https://en.wikipedia.org/wiki/Claire_Sterling; also, Wikipedia, "Paul B. Henze," last modified February 9, 2021.

36. Sterling and her colleagues had asserted improbably that Agca had already been recruited in 1979 by the Soviets for future work and that his right-wing stance was merely a cover for the eventual operation.

37. In a trial held in Rome in March 1986, three Bulgarians and three Turks, including Agca himself, were acquitted of conspiracy charges because of "ambiguous evidence." Agca remained in prison for his assassination attempt until 2010. See John Tagliabue, "6 Acquitted in Ruling on Pope; Ruling Ambiguous," *New York Times*, March 30, 1986, https://www.nytimes.com/1986/03/30/world/6-are-acquitted-in-plot-on-pope-ruling-ambiguous.html.

38. For Chomsky's reservations about New Media, see Alex Henderson, "Noam Chomsky: Social Media Outlets Have 'Become Major Forces for Undermining Democracy,'" AlterNet, December 24, 2018, https://www.alternet.org/2018/12/noam-chomsky-social-media-outlets-have-become-major-forces-undermining-democracy/; Noam Chomsky, interview by Seung Yoon Lee, *Byline*, April 14, 2015, https://byline.com/2015/04/14/chomsky-i-dont-look-at-twitter-because-it-doesnt-tell-me-anything/; and Alan MacLeod, "Still Manufacturing Consent: An Interview with Noam Chomsky," *Transcend Media Service*, June 24, 2019, https://www.transcend.org/tms/2019/06/still-manufacturing-consent-an-interview-with-noam-chomsky/.

39. Walter LaFeber, "Whose News," review of *Manufacturing Consent: The Political Economy of Mass Media*, by Edward S. Herman and Noam Chomsky, *New York Times*, November 6, 1988, https://www.nytimes.com/1988/11/06/books/whose-news.html.

40. Jeffrey Klaehn, "A Critical Review and Assessment of Herman and Chomsky's 'Propaganda Model,'" *European Journal of Communication*, June 1, 2002, https://journals.sagepub.com/doi/10.1177/0267323102017002691.

41. Eli Lehrer, "Chomsky and the Media: A Kept Press and a Manipulated People," in *Anti-Chomsky Reader*, eds. Peter Collier and David Horowitz (New York: Encounter Books, 2004), 67–86.

42. Noam Chomsky, *Necessary Illusions: Thought Control in Democratic Societies* (1989; repr., Toronto: Anansi, 2003), 148. All further references will be to this edition and cited parenthetically in the text.

43. For both Herman's letter and LaFeber's reply, see Edward S. Herman, "Letter to the Editor, *New York Times*, December 1, 1988, 147, *Times Machine*, https://timesmachine.nytimes.com/timesmachine/1988/12/11/307488.html?pageNumber=147.

44. Noam Chomsky, *Media Control: The Spectacular Achievements of Propaganda*, 2nd ed. (New York: Seven Stories Press, 2002), 9. All further references will be to the edition and cited parenthetically in the text.

45. For a discussion of how PR helped to rouse the American people to support World War II, see, for example, Alan Axelrod, *Selling the Great* War: *The Making of American Propaganda* (New York: St. Martin's, 2009) and George Creel, *How We Advertised America* (1920; repr., London: Forgotten Books, 2012).

46. Harrison Smith, "Edward Herman, Media Critics Who Co-Wrote *Manufacturing Consent*, Dies at 92," *Washington Post,* November 16, 2017, https://www.washingtonpost.com/local/obituaries/edward-s-herman-media-critic-who-co-wrote-manufacturing-consent-dies-at-92/2017/11/16/7cab93ca-cade-11e7-aa96-54417592cf72_story.html.

47. Anthony R. DiMaggio, "The Propaganda Model and Manufacturing Consent," in *The Cambridge Companion to Chomsky,* 2nd ed., edited by James McGilvray (New York: Cambridge University Press, 2017), 276.

48. See, for instance, Frank Annunziata, "The Revolt against the Welfare State: Goldwater Conservatism and the Election of 1964, *Presidential Studies Quarterly,* vol. 10, no. 2 (Spring 1980), 254–65, https://www.jstor.org/stable/27547569?seq=1.

49. See Don Gonyea, "Ronald Reagan: 'The Original Tea Party Candidate,'" NPR.org., February 5, 2011, https://www.npr.org/2011/02/05/133506347/ronald-reagan-the-original-tea-party-candidate.

50. See, for example, Paul Sabin, *Public Citizens: The Attack on Big Government and the Remaking of American Liberalism* (New York: Norton, 2021).

51. Philip Rucker, "'Deconstruction of the Administrative State' Is the Plan, Bannon Tells Conservatives," *Washington Post,* February 23, 2017, https://www.mcclatchydc.com/news/politics-government/article134553909.html.

52. DiMaggio, "Propaganda Model," 291.

53. Ibid. Such research, DiMaggio and others have advocated, should engage "critical scholars, activists, and the public."

Chapter Eight

Contemporary Critics in the Post-Truth Era

The news we report is real. But so is the need to be even better at reporting it.

—Frank Bruni, the 49th Hays Press-Enterprise Lecture,
May 18, 2018, UC Riverside.

After more than a hundred years of American media criticism, much of it focused on the proper role of the press in a democratic society, a contemporary group of critics has not only raised new issues but explored older ones in novel ways. As in the past, many of this group are men, predominantly white men: Eric Alterman, L. Brent Bozell III, James Fallows, Bernard Goldberg, Mickey Huff, Alex S. Jones, Mark Levin, Robert McChesney, Ben Smith, Brian Stelter, and Charles J. Sykes, among others.

Contemporary media criticism is not, however, an exclusive white man's club. Women, people of color, the LGBTQ community, and members of various marginalized groups are responsible for some of today's most original and at times controversial commentary. Among these writers and commentators are Jill Abramson, Sharyl Attkisson, Eric Deggans, Brooke Gladstone, Amy Goodman, Sam Husseini, Janine Jackson, Ana Kasparian, Candace Owens, Jennifer Pozner, Alissa Richardson, Anita Sarkeesian, and Adrienne Shaw.

Today's media critics are also politically diverse, another reason for their ability to raise new issues while imaginatively engaging with older ones. Conservative critics like Attkisson, and Goldberg, for example, have drawn on their broadcast backgrounds—each was a well-regarded correspondent for CBS News—to add yet another chapter to the right's ongoing story of the mainstream press's liberal bias. Candace Owens also calls on her personal history, in her case as a Black conservative woman, to add a new twist to the right's charge. In *Blackout: How Black America Can Make Its Second Escape from the Democrat Plantation* (2020), Owens labels the major news outlets as "little more than a propaganda machine" engineered "to intensify black allegiance to the Democrat Party."[1] Alex Marlow, editor in chief of Breitbart, the far-right news and opinion site, is well steeped in this and other conservative criticisms of the press. And yet for Marlow, who embraces Donald Trump's conservative populism, even these criticisms inadequately address the press's alleged elitist agenda, including its unquestioning globalism.[2]

At the other end of the political spectrum, progressives have kept their own running account of alleged media sins. In a series of progressive critiques that includes *Blowing the Roof off the Twenty-First Century: Media, Politics, and the Struggle for a Post-Capitalist Democracy* (2014), for instance, communications academic and public radio host Robert W. McChesney argues for an independent, noncommercial media as the essential precursor to establishing "a plausible democratic socialist society"—that is, a "post-capitalist democracy."[3] (He dedicates his book to Noam Chomsky, among others.) A somewhat younger progressive critic, veteran broadcast journalist and investigative reporter Amy Goodman, focuses much of her critical energy on those "silenced" by the mainstream media—the reformers, resisters, and various other citizen activists.[4] And a still younger group of left-leaning commentators—Abigail Martin, Mickey Huff, Anita Sarkessian, Adrienne Shaw, among others—has pointed to other putative media lapses: censored and underreported news, anti-feminist tropes in popular culture, distorted images of queer and other groups in news and video games, and the like.[5]

Occupying a space somewhere between these political poles is a group of center to center-left critics. Many are working, or formerly working, journalists—commentators whose theories of a properly functioning press are usually tempered by the more practical considerations of news gathering and the business of journalism. Included in this group are Alex S. Jones, a former media reporter for the *New York Times* and retired director of Harvard's Shorenstein Center on Media, Politics and Public Policy; James Fallows, a longtime staff writer at the *Atlantic*; Jill Abramson, the former executive director of the *New York Times*; Eric Deggans, National Public Radio's first full-time TV critic; and Brooke Gladstone, a former journalist and current host of the syndicated WNYC radio show *On the Media*. This insiders' perspective is on display, for instance, in Abramson's book, *Merchants of Truth*: *The Business of News and the Fight for Facts* (2019). Noting that Trump's presidency had been a boon for her onetime employer, pushing "subscription orders to 4 million in 2018," the former executive editor made clear that the business windfall had come at a price: "the more anti-Trump the *Times* was perceived to be, the more it was mistrusted for being biased."[6]

Opinion versus reporting, profits versus journalistic integrity—it was a dilemma that not only the paper of record but other news outlets were forced to grapple with during the polarized Trump era. Issues like these and others are at the core of much of contemporary media criticism. At the same time, today's most insightful critics also regularly circle back to many of the classic press issues: Is the commercial model still the best one for journalism? What are the limits if any of a free press? At what point does information end and disinformation begin? When does news become propaganda? And finally, and in many ways bracketing all other concerns, is journalism with all its flaws still capable of being the foundation of a deliberative democracy?

PRESS CRITICS ON THE RIGHT

The conservative charge of press bias has, as we have seen, a long pedigree. In her seminal work, *Messengers of the Right*: *Conservative Media and the Transformation of American Politics* (2016), historian Nicolle Hemmer chronicled the movement's early media pioneers. These included broadcaster Clarence Manion; book publisher Henry Regnery; and William Rusher, a lawyer and GOP activist who in 1957 was hired by William F. Buckley to be publisher of *National Review*, which would become the leading organ of the nascent conservative cause.[7]

What united this small group, beyond its committed anti-communism, was its strong belief "that established media were not neutral but slanted toward liberalism," as Hemmer pointed out. Their accusation of "liberal bias," though, was not simply an observational conclusion but an attack on the very notion of neutrality or objectivity itself, which the pioneers believed "was a mask mainstream media used to hide their own ideological projects." In place of this flawed neutrality, they would offer other "outsiders" like themselves—that is, those who found neither their concerns nor voices reflected in the mainstream media—"ideological integrity," which is to say a different and better way of sifting evidence, evaluating sources, and gauging "truth-claims."[8]

A second-generation of messengers built on this platform. In 1987, for example, L. Brent Bozell III, son of first-generation conservative activist Brent Bozell Jr., founded the Media Research Center (MRC), modeled after Reed Irvine's Accuracy in Media, established a decade and a half earlier. The following year, conservative commentator Rush Limbaugh landed his first nationally syndicated radio show. In 1996, *Fox News* cofounder Roger Ailes hired thirty-five-year-old Sean Hannity to host his first television show, *Hannity & Colmes*. In their different ways, each of these commentators surveyed the world through a distinctively conservative lens, in the process taking what had been a minority point of view and pushing it further and further into the mainstream.

In the years since, still other hosts and commentators have arrived on the scene: Glen Beck, Hugh Hewitt, Laura Ingraham, Mark Levin, Alex Marlow, Candace Owens, Michael Savage, Ben Shapiro, and Tucker Carlson, among others. Like those who came before them, these conservative commentators have kept up the right's long-standing critique of liberal media bias. At the same time, under pressure from today's right-wing populism, many among this group have also waded into other waters, raising concerns about globalism, immigration, election integrity, race, and the press itself, among other issues, that have provoked reactions not only from the center- and progressive-left but also from the self-styled contrarian right.

The Liberal Press's "Fear Monopoly"

In 1990, L. Brent Bozell III, along with Brent H. Baker, then MRC executive director, edited a collection of research and essays titled *And That's the Way It Isn't: A Reference Guide to Media Bias*. For those old enough to remember, the book's title was clearly a sardonic echo of Walter Cronkite's famous sign-off at the end of the *CBS Evening News*. Despite the former anchor's claims of impartiality, Bozell and Baker believed that he had failed on a near daily basis to present the day's events even-handedly. He had, as they saw it, a discernable bias, which usually titled leftward. Starting out with the belief that an "'objective' news media" was a fiction, the authors set out to assemble essays, charts, surveys, studies, quotes, word-use analyses, and lists to document their thesis.[9]

In a chapter titled "Reporters and Politics: Cheerleaders for the Left?," for instance, Bozell and Baker dug into MRC's archive of incriminating media quotes. The first newsperson quoted, predictably, was Cronkite, who, among other things, was said to have assured an audience during the early years of the recently ended Reagan presidency that "liberalism isn't dead in this country" but "has temporarily, we hope, lost its voice." A second former news anchor, David Brinkley, was also cited for betraying his political bias. Asked to name the best presidents in his lifetime, Brinkley had reportedly listed only Democrats—Roosevelt, Kennedy, and Truman. Also drawing conservative ire was then ABC correspondent Sam Donaldson, who, in speaking of the right-wing opponents of the Nicaraguan Sandinistas, had reportedly said on *This Week with David Brinkley*, "I think the House was right to turn down aid to the Contras." These and similar statements were, as Bozell and Baker saw it, still "further evidence that liberals permeate the media."[10]

Bozell followed up his first book fourteen years later with a second, *Weapons of Mass Distortion: The Coming Meltdown of the Liberal Media* (2004).[11] Much had changed in the interim: after four years of the first Bush administration and eight years of Clinton, a Republican, George W. Bush, once again occupied the White House. Popular polls also indicated a continuing stasis in the viewership of the regular evening news, a partial effect of viewers' turn to cable and online news.[12] Perhaps adding to viewer disaffection were several flawed news reports, including Dan Rather's story on the new president's service in the Texas Air National Guard. So great was the fallout in certain circles from the story, in fact, that it would soon lead to a surprising result: Rather's resignation after a twenty-four-year tenure as *CBS Evening News* anchor.[13]

Bozell regarded many of these changes as hopeful, indicative of not only a public dissatisfaction with Democratic leadership but a growing mistrust of mainstream news outlets, which he took as a harbinger of their eventual meltdown. Still, for all the hopeful signs, the "liberals' fear monopoly on news coverage" remained strong, with the left poised to keep it that way. If that were so, Bozell and other conservative critics would need to remain vigilant, documenting the frequent instances of liberal distortion in hopes that even more of the news-consuming public would come to see how it had been duped.[14]

In part 2 of *Weapons of Mass Distortion*, titled "Bias in Action," he moved chapter by chapter through what he regarded as distorted single-issue coverage, beginning with abortion. The matter, he wrote, "receives more slanted news from the mainstream media than perhaps any other issue," in large part because the press had normalized the extremists, the abortion absolutists, for whom any check on reproductive choice was unacceptable.[15] He was only slightly less critical of how other hot-button issues had been treated: on taxes, the national press had become "flacks for the Democratic Party," which pushed for higher taxes to fund its social programs; on the environment, it had embraced "radical environmentalism" as a sort of religion; on gay rights, it had turned a story into a cause, promoting the gay-rights agenda; and on the subject of guns, it had treated the gun-control advocates sympathetically, while shunning what it regarded as the "Neanderthal perspective of the gun owners"[16]

Bias was even more evident, he believed, in the broader press stories. Once again, he reeled off what he regarded as the most egregious examples, including the national media's "love affair" with Bill Clinton, despite his personal and administrative scandals; its favorable treatment of "the other Clinton," Hillary, despite a record that established her "as a liar and relentless character assassin," especially concerning her husband's various paramours; its in-depth attention during the 2000 presidential election to pet liberal causes, while at the same time either disparaging issues of concerns to conservatives or ignoring them altogether; and its efforts to discredit and undermine the war on terrorism.[17]

There was a countermovement afoot, however. Fox News—which had been inaccurately dismissed by liberals as "right-wing media"—seemed to be gradually overtaking the left-leaning CNN. Clearly, viewers were eager for news coverage that was "fair and balanced"—the Fox slogan would remain until 2017—and they were registering their discontent by tuning out, both literally or figuratively, news outlets like CNN, ABC, NBC, CBS, and the *New York Times*.[18]

Three years before Bozell's *Weapons of Mass Distortion*, former CBS correspondent Bernard Goldberg had also taken aim at CBS's supposed liberal slant. In 2001, the twenty-two-year network veteran released the widely read *Bias: A CBS Insider Exposes How the Media Distort the News*, published by Regnery, the latter-day incarnation of Henry Regnery's original book company. In a personal narrative, Goldberg recalled how, in 1996, he had watched what he regarded as an unbalanced *CBS Evening News* report on the "flat tax," which was then being championed by conservative GOP presidential candidate Steve Forbes. Outraged, Goldberg decided to submit an editorial to the *Wall Street Journal*, calling out both his network and other "media elites" for their blatant "liberal bias." He knew his colleagues would resent his telling tales out of school, but the vehemence of their reaction surprised him. Suddenly, he "had become a nonperson at CBS," no more so than with the then anchor and managing editor of the *CBS Evening News*, Dan Rather, whom Goldberg referred to disparagingly as "The Don."[19]

The flat-tax episode had precipitated Goldberg's critique and the ensuing backlash. It was not, though, the network's coverage of the big political issues that revealed its bias but its handling of "the big social and cultural issues."[20] As Goldberg surveyed recent history, including the preceding eight years of the Clinton administration, he saw examples of topics that, he believed, would have been treated differently if media elites had not been so out of touch with middle America: homelessness, the AIDS epidemic, gay rights, Black-white relations, affirmative action, abortion, feminism, and the like. As it was, these topics had been covered from an elite perspective, with reporters and editors behaving like "flacks for liberal causes." TV as a result was losing viewers by the droves.[21]

In 2014, another CBS insider, Sharyl Attkisson, issued a similar critique of the network. By this point, Attkisson had been a journalist with CBS News for twenty-one years. During this period, she had served in a variety of roles and had even coauthored a college textbook for aspiring journalists, *Writing Right for Broadcast and Internet News* (2002).[22] To be sure, there had been frustrations along the way—stories Attkisson said she wanted to cover but was not permitted to, stories she did cover but not in the way she had hoped to. Those frustrations built over time, culminating during the Obama administration, which she believed CBS had coddled, despite some of Obama's domestic and international failures. She attributed the journalistic lapse not only to corporate timidity but to CBS's long-standing liberal bent.

In early March 2014, she and the network reached what Attkisson told *Politico*'s "On Media" reporter was an "amicable" parting of the ways.[23] Despite this, by year's end, she had released the first of what would be a trilogy of behind-the-scenes media tell-alls, *Stonewalled: My Fight for Truth against the Forces of Obstruction, Intimidation, and Harassment in Obama's Washington* (2014). Referring to herself in the book as "a political agnostic," she complained that all was fine when, earlier in her CBS tenure, she had examined "[George W.] Bush controversies," but all that changed "when I started digging into Obama Administration problems. I was suddenly a fanatic bent on destroying the president and all good things liberal."[24]

The Trump Effect (Part I)

With the election of Donald J. Trump in 2016, the conservative critique of mainstream media bias went into high gear. Here, after all, was someone who not only had the uncanny ability to drive the elite media to distraction but, as right-leaning critics saw it, cause them to exhibit their worst side: blatant bias, arrogance, tendentiousness, self-righteousness. And the more the elite press challenged Trump—the more it claimed its journalistic prerogative to correct his assertions or call out his lies—the more he was able to lash back. In so doing, the forty-fifth president succeeded in channeling "the anger of millions who despise the press," explained journalist and media commentator Howard Kurtz in *Donald Trump, the Press, and the War over Truth* (2018).[25]

Kurtz seemed to be troubled by the excesses on each side. Saying he was not pro-Trump but "pro-reality," the host of Fox News's *Media Buzz* first called his own profession to task: "I am increasingly troubled by how many of my colleagues have decided to abandon any semblance of fairness out of the conviction that they must save the country from Trump." He then turned his attention to the president and his "acolytes," noting how strategically they had counterattacked, using charges of "fake news" and other assaults "on the Fourth Estate to neutralize their own untruths, evasions, and exaggerations." The attack and counterattack may have resulted in great theater—the president's "supporters love his street talk and view the media critiques as nonsense driven by negativity"—but the political entertainment had come at a price: the further erosion of trust in both the press and the presidency, two historic institutions of American life.[26]

Despite his seeming twin focus, Kurtz was clearly more concerned with his own flawed institution than with that of the presidency. Throughout his book, he took pains to document how his fellow journalists had abandoned the "fundamental values" of their profession in covering Trump. Evidence was everywhere: the so-called Steele Dossier, which alleged various misdeeds by the Trump presidential campaign both before and after 2016; James Comey's testimony before the Senate Judiciary Committee, in which the former FBI director detailed Russian interference in the election; the allegations of collusion and obstruction included in the Robert Mueller Report; the pull-out from the Paris Climate Agreement; and the violent Charlottesville "Unite the Right" rally, followed by the presidential declaration of "good people on both sides." In surveying these and other stories, Kurtz said there was "simply no factual dispute that the coverage of Donald Trump has been overwhelmingly negative in tone, tenor, and volume." The tragedy of this coverage for the nation was clear: while Trump would not remain in office forever, "the media's reputation, badly scarred during these polarizing years, may never recover."[27]

The following year, Bozell also considered the media's Trump coverage.[28] In *Unmasked: Big Media's War against Trump*, coauthored with MRC staffer Tim Graham, Bozell, like Kurtz, claimed he was not a card-carrying member of the pro-Trump party. There was, for one thing, the policy failures up to this point, which from the conservative point of view were glaring: the national debt continued as a "national disgrace," no repeal of Obamacare, Planned Parenthood still existed, the administration's various import tariffs had been a "mistake," and North Korea remained a nuclear threat. And to top it all off, there was of course Trump's "obnoxious tweeting."[29]

But the title of Bozell's book signaled his real intent; like Kurtz, he had his eye on the media: "This is the story of a media that set out to destroy a president and his administration but destroyed themselves instead."[30] Bozell covered some of the same ground as Kurtz, including what he labeled "the Russian obsession." In keeping with the martial metaphor of his title, though, he also examined the arsenal of weapons, along with the tactics and strategy, that Big Media had seemingly deployed against the sitting president. Strategically, the goal was to minimize—indeed, often to deny outright—any Trump "good news," including his massive tax cuts and tough stance on immigration. For the liberal press and the pundit class, such news was no news for a good reason: "Journalists simply cannot admit that anything Trump has done or is doing or is thinking is good for the United States because it will reflect positively on him." And reflecting positively on a chief executive whom both the liberals and Never Trumpers made no secret of despising was simply not part of the war plan. If Trump had retaliated with "attacks on the 'fake news media'" and those attacks had resonated with the public, it is "because they're true, and demonstratively so."[31]

Bozell was not hesitant to name names, everyone from then MSNBC anchor Brian Williams to Univision's Jorge Ramos, the Mexican American journalist who in 2015 had been ejected unceremoniously from then candidate Trump's press conference on immigration. Without doubt, charged Bozell, these journalists had treated other Republican presidents unfairly, as the liberal media were wont to do. Trump was a singular case, however: journalists like Williams, Ramos, and others were clearly "on a jihad to remove him from office."[32]

Other conservative critics also considered the Trump effect, typically as part of an even broader criticism of the mainstream press. In 2019, the same year as Bozell's book appeared, for instance, attorney and radio host Mark Levin in *Unfreedom of the Press* pilloried the media's failure as the "bulwark of liberty." In place of its "old fashioned fact gathering and news reporting," Levin argued, the modern media now functions "as a propaganda tool for a single party and ideology," by which he meant, of course, the Democrats and liberalism. For this reason, Donald Trump was correct to denounce his negative press treatment. But the damage of such actions had gone considerably beyond Trump, Levin thought, because they "not only destroy their own purposes but threaten the existence of a free republic."[33]

Former CBS broadcast journalist Sharyl Attkisson made much the same point in the third book of her media trilogy, *Slanted: How the News Media Taught Us to Love Censorship and Hate Journalism* (2020). Noting that hers was "the story of what happens when reporters convince news consumers that the reporters' own opinions are more valuable than facts," Attkisson leveled a variety of old and new charges, along with a defense of Trumpian actions: If as president he pushed his own narra-

Candace Owens, cofounder of the BLEXIT Foundation, speaking at the 2020 Conservative Political Action Conference at the Gaylord National Resort & Convention Center in National Harbor, MD.
Source: Evan Golub/ZUMA Wire/Alamy Live News.

tives and acted in unconventional ways, he also "exposed bias, flaws, and weakness in the news media, causing its members to lose their collective minds and shed all pretense of objectivity."[34]

Both Candace Owens and Alex Marlow also make Trump part of the wider stories they tell. In Owen's *Blackout*, that bigger story concerns both the Democrats—whose hegemony and policies "have led to the erosion of the black community by fostering a persistent victim mentality"—and the media that have become the party's de facto propaganda arm. Even liberal media icons like Lyndon Johnson—"one of the most racist men ever to occupy the Oval Office"—were key in perpetuating this mentality, thereby keeping the Black community dependent on its "liberal saviors." Enter the alleged enemy of the Black community, Donald J. Trump. In stark contrast to the Democrats and their media backers, says Owens, Trump was not interested in fostering dependence, although as presidential candidate he was

understandably interested in soliciting Black votes. In fact, when talking to
such voters, he had famously said, "What the hell do you have to lose?" In
so doing, Owens explains, he was clearly signaling a new day: "Trump's
speech was a call to action for anyone who dared to abandon the status
quo in favor of real change." And as president, she insists, he mostly kept
his word, lowering the pre-pandemic Black unemployment rate to about
"5.5%, down from nearly 8 percent when he first took office." Despite this,
the liberal "propaganda machine" not only failed to credit the president but
maliciously attacked him for being a racist.[35]

In *Breaking the News: Exposing the Establishment Media's Hidden
Deals and Secret Corruption* (2021), Alex Marlow, Breitbart editor in
chief, also calls attention to the hostile attacks against Trump, both before
and during his presidency. For Marlow, Trump's coverage in the mainstream press was, in fact, part and parcel of an approach to news reporting that was so slanted, so unfair, that it forever changed the calculus of
the conservative media critique: "This is not a book merely about liberal
media bias. Since Trump descended that escalator and announced his candidacy for president in 2015, 'bias' is far too benign a word for establishment media's collective tendencies." Ideologically, Marlow argues, those
tendencies transparently embrace "leftism, globalism, and corporatism,"
which in turn "drive major content decisions by leading new outlets." His
aim, similar in many ways to Bozell's, is to expose the main outlets of this
allegedly ideologically driven coverage—Bloomberg News, MSNBC,
and the *New York Times*. The last two outlets were for Marlow especially
biased in their treatment of the forty-fifth president.[36]

In the case of the *New York Times* ("a family business run in concert
with powerful figures from Wall Street, Silicon Valley, and the Democrat Party"), Malow's list of putative offenses is long: included are "the
Habermans," both Clyde and his daughter Maggie, who proved relentless
in their negative Trump reporting and commentary; allegations of presidential racism, which had the effect of fanning "the flames of racial division"; the "1619 Project," the collaborative effort to reframe the nation's
historical narrative to give primacy to slavery and the unheralded contributions of Black Americans; the "canceling" of Senator Tom Cotton,
whose editorial calling for the military to restore order during the Black
Lives protests was first published and then retracted; and, even more
inclusively, the paper's relentless commingling of fact and "propaganda"

during the Trump era.[37] Conspicuously missing among Marlow's long list of *Times* offenses is its coverage of the 2020 election results, which he concedes showed that Trump had lost, albeit thanks largely to the prevalence of mail-in ballots during the pandemic. At the same time, the January 6, 2021, uprising at the Capitol is downplayed, despite graphic reporting and images to the contrary. Those who stormed the Capitol that day were, as Marlow sees it, "simply frustrated idiots," people who failed to see that this "was not the best way to help Donald Trump."[38]

The Contrarian Conservative Rejoinder

Both liberals and others on the left have pushed back against such commentary, as discussed below. More surprising, perhaps, is that this commentary has also provoked a strong reaction among some traditional conservatives, who remain fierce critics of the former president. Among the most reflective of the traditionalists is Charles "Charlie" J. Sykes, currently the editor at large of the website *The Bulwark*, which he has described as "a home for rational, principled, fact-based center-right voices."[39] In *How the Right Lost Its Mind* (2017), the self-described "contrarian conservative" argues that Trump's nomination and subsequent election not only changed the "face of conservatism" but led to "the implosion of conservative media, many of whose leading voices turned from gatekeepers to cheerleaders and from thought leaders to sycophantic propagandists."[40]

Among the worst offenders in this regard, Sykes charges, are those who promote the "politics of paranoia." He points specifically to two media personalities: Matt Drudge, the author, former radio and television host, and creator of the *Drudge Report*, an aggregator of mostly right-wing news; and Alex Jones, the creator of the far-right website *Infowars* and a well-known conspiracy theorist. "If you want to understand the nature of the Right's alternative reality, or its vulnerability to 'fake news,'" Sykes explains, "you need to start with Jones and Drudge."[41]

Only somewhat lower down Sykes's list of offenders are Fox News, Breitbart News, and then national radio host Rush Limbaugh, who died in early 2021. Each had so variously and successfully stoked voter resentment and outrage that an improbable—and in many ways, unqualified—candidate like Trump was made to seem not only less improbable but in fact inevitable. Limbaugh proved especially effective in this cause, Sykes says, because he offered "the loudest and most influential voice setting the table for a voter insurrection." And in the process, of course, he and other promoters of outrage—Sean Hannity, Glenn Beck, Michael Savage, Tucker Carlson, and Ann Coulter, among others—had become very rich.[42]

Sykes is not prepared to let the left off the hook, however. If "messengers of the right" had emerged early on, as historian Nicole Hemmer had described, there was a reason for their appearance: "real evidence of media bias," and a clear reluctance among mainstream media outlets to "take conservative ideas seriously."[43] The first-generation of conservative media helped to bridge that gap. A similar phenomenon was occurring today, Sykes thought: if too many right-leaning news outlets over time have become "deeply compromised," too beholden to a party or ideology, the left-tilting media have also overreached, nowhere more ferociously than in their coverage of the Trump election and presidency. The effect of all this ideological sniping was a highly polarized media environment, where different news outlets have their preferred set of facts, narratives, and truths. Meanwhile, the public itself has been forced, sometimes willingly, sometimes not, into a series of what the Associated Press termed "intellectual ghettos."[44]

Such "binary choices" are, says Sykes, not healthy for either party. In fact, just as the far left and its media are unrepresentative of liberalism, "crude populism" and its outlets are not representative of historic conservatism, a political philosophy rooted in the "ideas of freedom, limited government, and constitutionalism." Sykes ends his book on the populist right with some "modest advice" for his fellow traditional conservatives: abandon your current either/or mentality and reach beyond your "tribal loyalties." It is an about turn, he believes, that will not only prove salutary to democracy but to the conservative cause: "If you take your view of reality and your facts from Infowars and Breitbart or the other alternative reality sites, you will eventually find yourselves in a corner, isolated from people you need to persuade."[45]

THE PROGRESSIVE CRITIQUE OF THE PRESS

For sheer and often reckless audacity, few news sites on the left rival outlets like Infowars and Breitbart. And yet, like historic conservatives, traditional liberals have also been challenged by those on their ideological flank. In the area of media commentary, this challenge has come from critics who, not unlike their far-right counterparts, want to shake up the status quo and replace mainstream media with what they regard as better, more responsive alternatives. For those on the further left, this usually means a noncommercial, publicly funded media system.

Toward a Noncommercial News Media

Contemporary progressives have employed a variety of rhetorical strategies to criticize the mainstream news media. These range from irreverent memoirs, to exposés, to pointed scholarly analyses, to outraged reminders of what news stories have been underreported or completely ignored.

In *Cable News Confidential: My Misadventures in Corporate Media* (2006), for example, Jeff Cohen, cofounder of Fairness and Accuracy in Reporting (FAIR), the progressive media watchdog, wrote a playful chronicle of his time on cable as a left-oriented news pundit. In chronological order, Cohen had worked for CNN (1987–1996), Fox News (1997–2002), and MSNBC (2002–2003). Before accepting his first stint, at CNN, he faced a clear conflict of interest. On the one hand, he had founded FAIR the year before in order, as he would later write, "to document bias . . . expose corporate censorship, and advocate for minority and dissenting voices." Now he would be on the payroll, however modestly, of one of the cable news outlets he had criticized. On the other hand, he needed the money and, just as importantly, his appearances on TV would further a key FAIR goal: "to take progressive media criticism out of the of ghetto of small publications and propel it into the biggest media outlets we could access." CNN—and later Fox News and MSNBC—certainly fit the bill, and thus Cohen found himself, as he would later describe it, "embedded" within the enemy camp.[46]

And so began his sixteen-year tenure as a cable TV news pundit. During this period, he jousted with many luminaries of the right wing, including Patrick Buchanan, the former Nixon communications director who went on to become a TV commentator and perennial presidential candidate; MRC founder L. Brent Bozell; and Bill O'Reilly, the then Fox News host and future cable news megastar. Cohen's role was to offer the progressive slant on a range of topics, from domestic matters and foreign policy to, of course, the media. Looking back, Cohen recalled rewarding stretches on TV, and in particular his multiple appearances on Rupert Murdoch's newly hatched Fox program *Night Watch.* "I savaged corporate media week after week and got paid for it . . . by Darth Murdoch," Cohen recalled. In fact, compared with the alternatives, he found *Night Watch* smart and balanced and perhaps the best news show on cable.[47]

His time in corporate media also confirmed his worst fears, however. In their race for viewers and advertising dollars, the cable networks had transformed standard news coverage into entertainment, adopting classic Hollywood genres (crime drama, sex farce, suspense thriller, war movie) to make their broadcasts livelier and more enjoyable. As lurid crime, for example, cable had offered its viewers breathless and virtually around-the-clock coverage of the O.J. Simpson murder trial. As sex farce, it had played up the more ludicrous elements of the Bill Clinton–Monica Lewinsky affair. And for the classic war movie, it had put together sensationalized footage of the early "Shock and Awe" stages of the Iraq War. But, observed Cohen, the cable networks were less interested in airing controversial news, especially if it offended powerful interests and even more especially if those powerful interests tilted conservative. As other critics before him had pointed out, he saw that these corporate boundaries were largely internalized rather than spelled out: "The biggest fear is doing anything that could get you, or your network, accused of being liberal."[48]

Cohen ended his cable news chronicle with urgent advice for his readers: "Having been inside the TV news sausage factory, I can wholeheartedly recommend that you find alternatives to corporate-processed news." Many of the examples he pointed to are still around today: *Democracy Now!*, hosted by progressive journalists Amy Goodman and Juan Gonzalez; *Daily Kos*, founded by blogger Markos Moulitsas; AlterNet, established in 1998 by the Institute for Alternative Journalism; and *Mother Jones*, currently published by the Foundation for National Progress, a grantee of the MacArthur Foundation. Those seeking out such alternative media may question their "biases or limited resources," Cohen acknowledged, but they would never have cause to doubt "that corporate owners, agendas, or sponsors are obstructing the flow of information."[49]

A similar interest in alternative news media runs through the work of Robert W. McChesney. A professor emeritus of communication at the University of Illinois, a former radio broadcaster, and a longtime political activist, McChesney has been, on the one hand, an astute historian of American corporate media, and, on the other hand, a harsh critic of such media. Beginning with *Telecommunications, Mass Media, and Democracy: The Battle for Control of U.S. Broadcasting, 1928–1935* (1993), for instance, he has set forth his case for why commercial media has proven so inimical to democracy. In the updated preface to one of his best-known books, *Rich Media, Poor Democracy: Communications Policies in Dubious Times* (1999), he summarized his essential argument: "This book chronicles how monopolization and hyper-commercialism, all derived from the incessant pressure for profit, increasingly makes journalism and media writ large an undemocratic force."[50]

Neither monopolization nor hyper-commercialism were, McChesney believed, historically inevitable. They had come to seem so, however, because of several largely unquestioned "myths." In *The Problem of the Media: U.S. Communication Politics in the 21st Century* (2004), he described those myths, including the idea that the dominant form of American journalism and media was somehow a "natural" rather than a man-made phenomenon. Not so, McChesney argued: "Just as capitalism is not the 'natural' social system for humanity, so commercial media are not Nature's creation either." That the current media was not "Nature's creation" did not necessarily invalidate it, of course, especially if it were subject to debate and change on behalf of the public good. But too often discussions of the media proceeded not on behalf of the public good, as people imagined—this was the second myth—but as if fundamental change was unthinkable. And precisely because real change was dismissed, the status quo or "corporate-insider hegemony" persisted.[51]

This status quo was not serving the public, especially in the case of journalism. As McChesney and other progressives see it, journalism in a democratic society has three essential missions: to serve as a watchdog of the powerful, to sort truth from lies, and to offer facts and informed commentary on key issues. By these standards, he argued, US journalism was on the whole failing: indeed, in a system that rewarded caution and conformity and prized simplicity over comprehension, too many newsgathering professionals thought twice about challenging the powerful, relied on official and establishment spokespersons, reached for attention-grabbing "news hooks," and remained cautiously within the safe boundaries of permissible discourse. In some ways, of course, these were simply rational accommodations to the current system. But what if that system could be changed, McChesney asked, so that it was "no longer rational to produce what passes for journalism today"?[52]

His response was the subject of several of his later books. In *The Death and Life of American Journalism: The Media Revolution That Will Begin the World Again* (2010), for example, he and coauthor John Nichols argued for a public-funded alternative to commercial media. Such an alternative was especially crucial at a time when the internet was upending traditional business models, causing newspapers and other print outlets to go out of business. Such an alternative was also well-grounded in history: "The first generation of Americans understood that it was entirely unrealistic to expect the profit motive to provide for anywhere near the level of journalism necessary for an informed citizenry, and by extension self-government, to survive." And while the First Amendment expressly forbids state censorship, he noted, it says nothing that would impede "the public from using their government to subsidize or spawn independent media."[53] Certainly, the Public Broadcasting Service was a partial example of what he had in mind. Closer still perhaps were the more robustly state-supported public news organizations of other countries, including several of the leading democracies in Western Europe. In these countries, and especially in the UK, Germany, and Sweden, public news organizations were not only the main sources of news but, and this was key if the charge of state monitoring was to be avoided, the most trusted sources.[54]

The American version of this public news system would not be established easily. Ultimately, it would require that media reform and social reform move in a sort of lockstep, each trending in the direction of what McChesney described as a "post-capitalist democracy." In such a democracy, the normal incentives would no longer seem rational, whether in the larger society or in journalism. In *Blowing the Roof off the Twenty-First Century: Media, Politics, and The Struggle for Post-Capitalist Democracy* (2014), he explored his vision through a series of historical essays, a few dating to as early as 2001. Throughout, he was alert to any evidence that a postcapitalist society was becoming more likely, which often meant that events were trending in a prolabor, pro-government, pro-reform direction, as when the barriers to a "new new Deal" during the Obama administration appeared to be falling. Such events presumably also made the advent of a commercial-free, independent press more likely, just as the drive to such a press would help to realize the kind of society McChesney had in mind. It was a fundamentally synergistic vision of the press and society, and for McChesney it was reason enough to remain optimistic about real reform, despite all.[55]

In the final essay of the collection, he offered a few examples of what incremental but meaningful reforms might look like. Two of the reforms involved the internet, a medium that to this point at least had not only failed to remedy journalism's flaws, as he saw it, but had often "accelerated" them.[56] First, he proposed cashing out the big for-profit internet service providers (ISPs)—in 2014, Verizon, AT&T, and Comcast were the market leaders—and replacing them with a publicly owned network that would make cellphone and broadband access into a sort of "digital post office."[57] Second, he proposed that regulators move more aggressively against the monopolistic practices of the internet giants—Google, Facebook, Apple, Amazon, and Microsoft, among others. It would be an uphill battle, McChesney acknowledged, given how self-protective such giants had proven to be to this point. Still, it was urgent that we "think about how monopolized Internet services could be put in the public domain and guided by open-source protocol." In this way, "power would be in the hands of the users, who would control their own digital fate, rather than in the hands of the giant firms that are mostly unaccountable . . . except to their investors."[58]

McChesney ended his book of essays on a familiar note. As he had in *The Death and Life of American Journalism* years earlier, he called upon lawmakers, advocates, and concerned citizens generally to think of media, and the press specifically, as a "public good," not incidental to a thriving democracy but essential to it. For this reason, "the state must enter the field big-time," as it had with marked success in other countries. It might be funded in a variety of ways, as, for instance, by levying an annual fee on every American over eighteen years old. But, however it was ultimately funded, such an institution was "a necessary part, even a cornerstone, of the movement to democratize the United States."[59]

Underreported/Unreported: What the Mainstream Press Misses

Beyond pushing for independent media, today's progressive critics have also pressed for a more responsive and responsible media. Included among this group are Amy Goodman, an investigative reporter and host of *De-mocracy Now!*, the flagship of a nonprofit news organization by the same name; Janine Jackson, program director of FAIR and host and producer of its syndicated radio show; and Mickey Huff, president of the Media Freedom Foundation and director of Project Censored, which has taken as part of its twofold mission to report "the news that didn't make the news."[60]

In the introduction to her first book, *The Exception to the Rulers: Exposing Oily Politicians, War Profiters, and the Media That Love Them* (2004), which she wrote with the assistance of her brother, David, Amy Goodman made clear her journalistic credo: "Going to where the silence is. That is the responsibility of a journalist: giving voice to those who have been forgotten, forsaken, and beaten down by the powerful. It is the best reason I know to carry our pens, cameras, and microphones into our own communities and out to the wider world."[61] At the time, Goodman was a reporter at New York radio station WBAI, part of Pacifica Radio, an independent progressive media network. She was also, beginning in 1996, the of co-host, along with fellow journalist Juan Gonzalez, of a daily news show, *Democracy Now!*, which had begun as a Pacifica project. Each of

Amy Goodman, Principal Host, Democracy Now! addresses the 2010 Chicago Green Festival.
Source: Chris Eaves. CC BY 2.0.

these positions, and the latter one especially, Goodman believed, provided her with the freedom to pursue stories that she might not otherwise be allowed to pursue elsewhere. The rapid growth of *Democracy Now!*—which in time had split from Pacifica, becoming the flagship for a progressive media network—was evidence to her that people were "hungry" for a media that did not shirk the most serious issues of "war and peace, life and death."[62] Her first book, part summary of a few of her most important stories to date, part takedown of what she regarded as a cowed and craven US media, set the tone for both her journalism and media critique for nearly the next twenty years.

In her next book, *Static: Government Liars, Media Cheerleaders, and the People Who Fight Back* (2006), for which her brother was an official coauthor, Goodman took on the George W. Bush administration. Over its first five years, the authors believed, the administration had been responsible for a string of disasters—the National Security Agency's Terrorist Surveillance Program, the US invasion of Iraq, the government's feckless response to Hurricane Katrina, the extraordinary rendition of foreign nationals, the "enhanced" interrogation of enemy combatants, and the suppression of domestic dissenters, among other incidents. As bad as these events and episodes had been, though, the Goodmans argued that they had been made worse by the press's irresponsibility. Not only had it failed to reveal the lies behind the abuses (warrantless wiretaps, unlawful extradition, torture), it had actually been complicitous in them, sometimes unwittingly, sometimes not, by treating government propaganda uncritically. Independent media like *Democracy Now!* were making efforts "to create a universe of alternative information," despite the David versus Goliath battle. For such media to really succeed, though, they needed to expand their audience and the population of social activists generally. She knew full well that it would be a daunting struggle.[63]

Goodman's subsequent books continued to focus on those people and events that she believed had been underreported or ignored. In *Standing Up to the Madness: Ordinary Heroes in Extraordinary Times* (2008), also coauthored by David Goodman, she cited a series of historical events that had paved the way for today's social activism, including working-class efforts to reclaim New Orleans after Hurricane Katrina and engaged scientists warning about climate change.[64] In *Breaking the Sound Barrier* (2009), an anthology of her columns for King Features Syndicate, she reported on topics that the mainstream media had covered with little more than sound bites, including the global economic meltdown and grassroots activism.[65] Such activism was also the subject of her next book, with *Democracy Now!* colleague Denis Moynihan, *The Silenced Majority: Stories of Uprisings, Occupations, Resistance and Hope* (2012).[66] Four years later, she released, along with her brother and Moynihan, an anniversary collection of *Democracy Now!*'s best stories to date, from coverage of whistleblowers like Julian Assange, Edward Snowden, and Daniel Ellsberg to the LGBTQ revolution.[67]

Like Amy Goodman, Janine Jackson has established an auxiliary career in broadcasting. It is one of the many platforms she employs as program director of FAIR to not only get out her various media-reform messages but to cover neglected stories. In recent years, either as host of FAIR's syndicated weekly radio show *CounterSpin* or contributor to its newsletter *Extra!*, Jackson has focused on a number of these stories. In a May 7, 2021, broadcast of her radio program, for example, she cited the corporate news media's historically "rigid template" of reporting on Palestine and Israel. "That the frame can be rigid, but not balanced, is reflected in the Reuters report on Sheikh Jarrah—the East Jerusalem neighborhood where Palestinians were driven from their homes by court rulings favoring settlers. [The report] gets to the next-to-last paragraph before noting that 'most countries regard settlements that Israel has built there as illegal.'" Such "stale" storytelling was, she argued, still too often the norm, but domestic understanding of the situation in the Middle East of late had become more complex. This was due in large part to the work of Human Rights Watch but also to Palestinian rights groups, including the US Campaign for Palestinian Rights. Her guest that day, Ahmad Abuznaid, was the executive director of the group. After confirming Jackson's observation that reporting on the Middle East had become more nuanced, Abuznaid quickly added that there was yet a long way to go: "I don't think the average American truly understands what Israel is and what it's been doing to the Palestinian people, and how our tax dollars are actually aiding in human rights abuses."[68]

The third in the trio of prominent progressive media critics is Mickey Huff. In addition to chairing the journalism department at Diablo Valley College, in California, Huff also leads Project Censored, an organization with deep roots in the progressive movement. From its beginning in the mid-1970s, it has pursued a twin goal: to make students more media savvy while pointing out instances of media censorship. Regarding the latter goal, Project Censored has two main vehicles: *The Public Censored Radio Show*, a weekly public affairs program on the Pacifica network, and its annual yearbook, a compendium of the preceding year's best efforts to shed light on formerly underreported or censored stories. Of late, Huff has refreshed and streamlined the group's yearbook, which is now known as *Project Censored's State of the Free Press*.[69] Typically, collected stories are placed into a number of broad categories. In the 2021 edition of the annual yearbook, for example, there were articles on missing and murdered indigenous women and girls, corporate malfeasance, military bloat and pollution, GOP tax cutting, and the like.[70]

In their story for *The Conversation* (June 24, 2019), for example, a group of academic environmentalists drew on their own research, based on multiple Freedom of Information requests, to document the US military's "enormous" carbon "boot print." In 2017, they report, the US military bought almost 270,000 barrels of oils a day "and emitted more than 25,000 kilotonnes of carbon monoxide by burning those fuels." Of the main branches of the US military, the Air Force was the largest emitter, at least based on its purchase of fossil fuels: $4.9 billion. In total, the US military's consumption and emissions outrank those of most medium-size countries. If it were a country, in fact, "its fuel usage alone would make it the 47th largest emitter of greenhouse gases in the world, sitting between Peru and Portugal." Adding to the problem, noted the authors, is that the Pentagon, among other government departments, is wary of sharing its data. This led them to an inescapable conclusion: "It does no good tinkering around the edges of the war machine's environmental impact." To reverse it, lawmakers must assign other worthy policy priorities "a funding bump."[71]

The Trump Effect (Part II)

In addition to his work with Project Censored, Huff has also written at length about other media issues. In 2019, for example, he and fellow academic Nolan Higdon put out *The United States of Distraction: Media Manipulation in Post-Truth America (And What We Can Do about It)*. In it, the authors asked how the American public had allowed itself to become so distracted from some of the biggest issues affecting it.[72] Their answer, like many progressives before them, was to point a finger at the corporate media system, which had engaged in a tricky sleight of hand, switching journalism in the public interest for circulation-pumping entertainment and trivia. This tricky switch has been going on for many years, as Neil Postman had argued years before. But after Trump's arrival on the scene, it was easy to imagine that the former "tele-celebrity" had almost single-handedly created a new age of glossy showbusiness and "post-truth." Not so, argued the authors. While Trump had certainly exacerbated existing trends, the new age had clearly predated his entry into the politics: "Long before Trump's candidacy, ratings drove programming and news. In the process, celebrity, entertainment, scandal, crime, disaster, and spectacle clearly dominated over the substantive reporting, in-depth investigation, and public-interest advocacy capable of questioning and countering abuses of power and government authority." The situation seemed in many ways intractable, especially since so many people had been so thoroughly taken in.[73]

The authors were not without hope, however. In a clever twist on Trump's campaign slogan, there goal was to "Make America Think Again." Such a goal would require not only enhanced "critical media-literacy education," a long-standing Project Censored aim, but media changes: wider news framing, more local investigative journalism, more educational news programming, and more insiders willing to blow the whistle. Regarding story framing, for example, Huff and Higdon argued that news stories needed to include sources beyond the usual suspects in the two major political parties, all of whom were eager "to propagate a particular spin or party narrative." In a discussion of climate change, say, it would be far better to bypass those party loyalists and cite climate scientists and other experts who had less of an axe to grind. Similarly, whistleblowers should be better treated, especially in the commercial media, since they often help to expose "unethical and corrupt practices that they believe the public has a right to know." For this reason, it was urgent for more independent media to offer as much "space and safety" for such public citizens as possible. These and related reforms would be steps toward improving today's news system, the authors stressed, which after Trump was never more resistant to change or more critically in need of it.[74]

THE CENTER-LEFT CRITIQUE

Liberal media critics are similar in several ways to those further to their left: like the progressives, liberal critics are concerned with reforming the current media, countering conservative challenges to it, and guarding against the fabrications and manipulations of would-be authoritarians. Unlike their progressive counterparts, though, center-left critics are as a group less willing to upend the commercial media system, either as a good in itself or as a giant step toward a radically different society. As in many cases working or formerly working journalists themselves, they tend to anchor their concerns and reform ideas in not only a broader set of principles but in their real-world reporting experiences. Much of what they propose—renewed standards of objectivity, a closer observance to the boundaries between news and opinion, curbs on pack journalism, more useful news—reflects their general pragmatism. All of which is not to say they lack vision: if they are skeptical of utopianism, most are also committed to the idea that an engaged press is the cornerstone of a functioning democracy, just as a dysfunctional press is its nemesis.

Salvaging the Commercial Model

One of the first of today's liberal journalists to critique his own profession was James Fallows, the then editor of *US News & World Report*. In *Breaking the News: How the Media Undermine American Democracy* (1996), published in the same year Bill Clinton made his successful bid for a second term, Fallows presented what amounted to a report on the state of his profession, circa the latter 1990s. As he saw it back in that still quaint era, journalism was being affected by several cultural, technological, and other changes, including the multifaceted impact of television, modern image-over-style political campaigning, and the shifting of the "financial fundamentals of the business." The collective impact of these changes on the profession was he believed unsalutary, causing journalism to stray from its foundational if often aspirational values of objectivity, proportionality, and contextualization. Because of TV's influence, for instance, news had too often devolved into spectacle and reporters into pampered celebrities, at times given greater prominence than the stories they covered. Similarly, both broadcast and print news seemed infected by the marketing trend that had taken over political campaigns, especially those for the nation's highest office. In the recent Clinton-Dole race, for example, the press had tended to focus less on the crucial national issues than on the consultant-driven events and photo-ops, the backstage maneuverings, and the general political circus. Both campaigning and TV's effect were in turn linked to the third trend—the expectation that, like other industries, the best gauge of whether journalism was working was its quarterly financial returns.[75]

The public had taken note, said Fallows. Many now regarded the press as "too arrogant, cynical, scandal-minded, and destructive," charges not wildly dissimilar from those hurled at the time by many conservatives. Opinion polls had registered the public's hostility, but so too had a more troubling indicator: the "quiet consumers' boycott of the press," resulting in an ongoing loss of both readership and viewership. The loss portended a real tragedy for the democratic electorate, which was more and more deprived of information about "trends they don't happen to observe themselves" or about events in other countries or "even parts of their own town."[76]

There were no surefire remedies for what ailed journalism. Clearly, Fallows was not proposing that the existing commercial media be dismantled, as some of his more radical colleagues were. Despite its flaws, the commercial media was likely to continue and might even change journalism for the better, assuming the right market incentives. Even in the absence of these incentives, though, there were reform efforts afoot that offered him a measure of hope. One was the still nascent public journalism movement.

Spearheaded by Kansas newspaper editor Davis Merritt and New York University professor of journalism Jay Rosen, the movement attempted to break down what it regarded as the artificial barrier between news producer and consumer. Each, after all, inhabited the same society, and each therefore had a shared stake in the successful functioning of that society. And so, just as citizens were dependent on the press for vital information, the press was dependent on citizen feedback via polls and other mechanisms for what such news should be. In short, the public journalism movement envisioned the consumers of news and the press locked in a reciprocal relationship, one that ideally mitigated cynicism and apathy and kept news from devolving into spectacle or worse.[77]

This was the ideal, at least. But, as Fallows was aware, editors of some of the nation's largest and most influential newspapers were skeptical. Their main concern was that, in pursuing stories and projects in the public interest, journalists would forgo their professional objectivity and detachment. "I know there are times when individual feelings among reporters and editors may cause them to want to take a side," said Leonard Downie, the then executive editor of the *Washington Post*. "We work very hard here to try to drive that out of their work."[78] Even after *Breaking the News* appeared, the dispute over public journalism continued, surprising Fallows by its intensity. Certainly, the movement had its flaws and a few flawed practitioners, he acknowledged in the afterword to the paperback edition. Still, for all its defects, it held out the promise of "a journalism its creators can admire, journalism that gives citizens information they can use."[79]

Like James Fallows, former *New York Times* press critic Alex S. Jones also envisioned alternatives to the traditional press model. He was less hopeful, though, that over the long term these alternatives would prove a credible substitute for that model. In *Losing the News: The Future of the News That Feeds Democracy* (2009), the then director of Harvard's Shorenstein Center on Media, Politics, and Public Policy, began by examining what he saw as still other changes affecting the profession. The rise of digital technology especially interested him. In the thirteen years between his book and Fallows's, that rise had caused news organizations generally and newspapers in particular to reexamine both their core mission and economic viability. The reexamination worried Jones: "The book's focus is on the values of journalism at a time when those values are increasingly viewed as obsolete or unaffordable in a media world turned upside down by digital technology."[80]

Jones was not unsympathetic to the economic havoc wrought by digital technology. A for-profit champion who regarded "a strong bottom line as the best guarantee of first-class journalism," he believed that news organizations, and especially newspapers, needed both to innovate and enhance their efficiency in order to survive. At the same time, he regarded himself as a traditionalist, a champion of "fact-based accountability news," which was the "iron core" of not only the profession but also democracy. These twin perspectives, he said, made him a realist, neither as hopeful as the optimists who saw innovation as unerringly liberating nor as despairing as the pessimists who feared a "frightening new world" of "talk, advocacy, spin, trivia, and out-and-out propaganda"[81] His own project was to point out how journalism could survive in an era of innovation and rapid change but do so by offering serious and accurate news

In a chapter provocatively titled "Objectivity's Last Stand," for example, Jones considered what had happened to this older standard in the new digital era. Certainly, there had been defendable reasons for questioning the older standard. Foremost perhaps, it imposed an impossible ideal, since as almost every professional knew or should have known journalism required that hard reportorial and editorial choices be made, and such choices inevitably injected an element of subjectivity into even the most ethically balanced process. Those who denied that fact of journalistic life were kidding themselves, never more so than when they failed to acknowledge certain cultural and personal biases that may have guided their choices. At the same time, Jones was not ready to give up on objectivity. Doing so would cause more problems than it solved: among other things, it would further alienate an already cynical public. And it would also exacerbate the trend of opinion dressed up as news, especially in an era when more and more news outlets had calculated that it was cheaper to produce opinion-based content than news-based. Jones wanted none of this. If a degree of bias in news was inevitable, that was no excuse to throw in the towel and give up on professional standards and ethics. Perfect objectivity might be unattainable, but it was still an ideal worth pursuing: "I want my news to be delivered by someone acting as an honest broker whose goal is the best possible truth."[82]

Jones believed that digital news, at its best, could do some of this. But it was finally the commercial newspaper—he had come from a newspaper family in Greeneville, Tennessee—that would prove pivotal if the values of good journalism were to be preserved. Certainly, this model would need to be updated in order to sustain itself economically. Newspapers, both large and small, for example, would be wise to continue to expand their online presences, offering traditional journalism on another platform, as many went on to do. They would also be smart to collaborate more regularly with nonprofit news organizations like ProPublica and the Center for Public Integrity, on the one hand, and for-profit ones like GlobalPost, on the other hand. Again, some newspapers went on to do just this in subsequent years. In the end, though, while there was no single way to save newspapers, Jones knew it was crucial that the "reality-based press" survive, which would in turn make democracy's survival more likely.[83]

Another contemporary critic who thinks the commercial news model is salvageable is Jill Abramson, the former executive editor of the *New York Times*. In *Merchants of Truth: The Business of News and the Fight for Facts* (2019), released in the final year of the Trump administration, Abramson focused on two updated versions of older media—her erstwhile employer and the *Washington Post*—and two apparently successful versions of new media, BuzzFeed and Vice Media. Her portraits are hopeful ones, including her portraits of the evolution and prospects of the two updated versions of older media.

She offers the best insider's perspective on the *Times*, of course. Joining the paper in 1997, she served as executive editor from 2011 to 2014, a period during which growing numbers of people preferred to get their news digitally, initially on their computers and increasingly on their cell phones. The move to digital affected both newspaper circulation and ad revenue. Seeing the proverbial handwriting on the wall, she explains, many "newspaper families were calling it quits and cashing in, including the owners of Times Mirror, Knight Ridder, and Dow Jones." But the Ochs-Sulzberger family, in control of the *Times* since 1896, stayed the course, convening a group at one point tasked with considering new "revenue-producing" ideas, including a more aggressive push to paid online news and other services. At the same time, the company was investing in infrastructure, principally in the form of a new headquarters in Midtown Manhattan.[84]

The changes had the desired effect: while the paper's print circulation continued to decline, its online subscriber base grew, increasing both total subscription and the proportion of overall revenue derived from digital advertising and other products. (By the second quarter of 2020, the company for the first time reported "revenue that owed more to digital products than to the print newspaper."[85]) The election and presidency of Donald J. Trump also proved a big boost, especially to the paper's online readership, which like the paper's readers generally skewed liberal. And while Abramson's successor, Dean Baquet, had said, "he didn't want the *Times* to be the opposition party," there was, she acknowledges, "an implicit financial reward for the *Times* in running lots of Trump stories, almost all of them negative."[86]

The de facto editorial policy came with costs. "The more anti-Trump the *Times* appeared to be, the more it was mistrusted for being biased," said Abramson.[87] But if the paper's reputation suffered in the wider world, especially among traditional conservatives and even more so among pro-Trump Republicans, it seemed to be pleasing its rising number of readers. In time, the paper of record not only managed to right itself financially but, despite its tough editorial stance toward Trump and sometimes because of it, it continued to produce examples of significant, fact-based, deeply researched reporting. In 2018, four members of the reporting staff won a Pulitzer Prize for a series of stories on sexual predation that helped to prompt an international reexamination of women's sexual abuse. In 2019, another team of *Times* reporters was awarded a Pulitzer for explaining the tangled history of President Trump's finances. And in 2020, staffers from the paper received a prize in the international reporting category for covering the violence directed at perceived enemies within the Vladimir Putin regime.[88] In other words, six years after Abramson's tenure on the *Times* ended, and one year after she published her book, the paper was prospering. For this, she credited, among other things, an enlightened family ownership. It had not only enabled old media to learn new tricks but to remain vital in the new digital era.

Bad Blood, Media Style

Even those liberal critics who are most intent on salvaging the commercial news system acknowledge that modern media, and in particular cable news outlets, too often see discord as an essential component of their business model. In two books published several years apart, contemporary liberal critics Eric Deggans and Matt Taibbi make this case, offering suggestions on how the media's impulse toward conflict and discord can be tempered.

In *Race-Baiter: How the Media Wields Dangerous Words to Divide a Nation* (2012), Deggans, PBS's television critic, began from the premise that many members of the American media have "a bias towards conflict" because it has proven successful in boosting audience share, rais-

Eric Deggans, NPR TV Critic
Source: Courtesy Eric Deggans.

ing advertising revenue, and enhancing political influence. The default practice when covering an issue, therefore, is to find ways to pit one side against another, especially if the topic is already volatile, in which case the contest easily devolves into a Manichean struggle for survival. Crucial to all this is employing the right language to frame the issue—language that emphasizes rather than minimizes the cultural and social differences between the contesting parties. Not only do incendiary words and phrases help to build drama, but they also work "to feed our fears, prejudices, and hate toward each other," especially when the issue under debate is race.[89]

Deggans offered a variety of episodes to illustrate his thesis. Among them was the Trayvon Martin case, the fatal shooting in 2012 of an unarmed black Florida teenager by a member of a neighborhood watch program named George Zimmerman who claimed to have acted in self-defense. On Fox News, explained Deggans, the case had often been reported and commented on in ways that seemed calculated to emphasize its underlying racial tensions, despite network denials to the contrary. In fact, even before Zimmerman had gone on trial for the shooting, some of the network's most famous personalities weighed in. On the morning show *Fox & Friends*, for instance, news host and commentator Geraldo Rivera spoke of the teen's dress that evening as provocative: "I think the hoodie [he wore] is as much to blame for Trayvon Martin's death as George Zimmerman was." Then Fox News host Bill O'Reilly devoted one of his commentaries to the apparent rush to judgment by supporters on each side. He issued an especially ominous warning, however, about Martin's champions, whom he accused of injecting race into the matter and thus inciting the very real prospect of "racial violence" should Zimmerman be acquitted, as he eventually was.[90]

If Fox News had done its part to inflame the situation, so too had its liberal counterpart, MSNBC. Deggans was especially critical of the network's decision to anchor so much of its Trayvon Martin coverage around host Reverend Al Sharpton, the longtime civil rights activist. In his off-air comments, Sharpton had specifically framed the case and its ultimate disposition as a matter of long-overdue racial justice, although in his role as MSNBC host he was more measured, giving at least the appearance of evenhandedness. Nevertheless, Deggans believed that in ceding so much airtime to Sharpton, MSNBC had created more than just the appearance of conflict: "Sharpton sometimes pivoted from leading rallies or press conferences for Martin's parents to interviewing them and their attorneys for his MSNBC show on the same day." Sharpton's attempts to balance his twin roles notwithstanding, the whole episode, thought Deggans, was indicative of the networks' metamorphosis from straight reporting "to political punditry operations."[91]

Journalist Matt Taibbi made something like this charge in his *Hate Inc.: Why Today's Media Makes Us Despise One Another* (2019). Early on, Taibbi laid out his mission to both his liberal and conservative readers: "To people of both persuasions . . . this book is intended to start a conversation about how much of our disdain for each other is real, and how much of it is a product of the media machine." Like Deggans and other critics who had examined the contemporary news landscape, Taibbi argued that a disproportionate amount of the contempt, indeed hatred, that Americans increasingly now feel for one another was the product of a media system under unprecedented economic and competitive pressures "to serve up mountains of highly politicized, vituperative content."[92]

The son of an award-winning TV and print reporter, Taibbi found support for his assertion in examples drawn from his own reporting and the reporting of others. For the former, he drew especially on his coverage, for *Rolling Stone*, of the 2016 presidential election campaign between Hillary Clinton and Donald Trump. During that campaign, he readily acknowledged, a key goal for both him and others in the press corps was to generate good copy or arresting visuals, often by creating drama and dissent where none or little existed. And in a perverse way, the strategy worked: focused less on issues and more on the clash of personalities, the name calling, the childish antics, and the increasingly rowdy rallies, the public audience for news expanded. So too did public cynicism, however: "People believed us less, but watched us more."[93]

Taibbi was especially critical of Fox News under Rupert Murdoch, its founder. Alert to what built audience share, the network had drifted away from traditional news and increasingly centered its business model on deeply politicized programming. To symbolize this programming, the front cover of Taibbi's book included a picture of one of Fox's star conservative commentators, Sean Hannity, a fixture on the network since 2009. But to demonstrate that Fox was not alone in stoking divisiveness, the front cover also included a picture of MSNBC's most popular liberal commentator, Rachel Maddow, whose eponymous TV show (now airing weekly) dated to September 2008. In an appendix to his book explaining Maddow's inclusion, Taibbi noted that she had also come to embody a dangerous media trend, "transforming [herself] from a sharp-minded, gregarious, small-time radio host to towering patriotic media cudgel, a depressingly exact mirror of Hannity." For Taibbi, neither the Fox nor the MSNBC model would do: each was exacerbating divisions in the country, causing many decent Americans not just to disagree but to demonize one another. A step in reversing this trend, if there was one, was to tone down the hate and return to a news system that encouraged balance, distance, and independence. An apt touchstone for this alternative model was, he suggested, the job of journalism "as my father had done it."[94]

The Trump Effect (Part III)

The polarized—and polarizing—media that Taibbi and other liberal critics described reached something of an inflection point during the Trump era. If media's tendency to sow division predated Donald Trump, his appearance on the scene seemed to ratchet it up exponentially. From the announcement of his candidacy on the Trump Tower elevator on June 16, 2015, to the calamitous end of his presidency five and a half years later, the press, and especially the cable press, seemed to cover his every appearance, rally, tweet, and outrageous comment. His gravitational pull was so enormous that he seemed for a time to be at the center of almost every news story. Liberal critics took notice, not unlike their counterparts at the political extremes. And in a series of books, some focused primarily on Trump, others that placed him in a wider narrative context, they offered yet another perspective on how the forty-fifth president twisted the American media into sometimes unrecognizable shapes.

The origin of the Trump era is the subject of an earlier book by Matt Taibbi with the comic title *Insane Clown President: Dispatches from the 2016 Circus* (2017). Recalling his own experiences on the 2016 campaign trail, Taibbi described how the media's cynical habit of fomenting conflict to attract viewers reached an apogee of sorts with the appearance of the carnival-like candidacy of Donald J. Trump. "Trump sold hate, violence, xenophobia, racism, and ignorance, which oddly enough had long been permissible zones of exploitation for American television entertainment," Taibbi wrote. Sensing a potential windfall at a time of declining profits, the media latched on to Trump, offering him almost unlimited coverage and airtime, not despite his divisiveness but because of it. If cable TV could have filled all 8,760 hours of its on-air programming with Trump and his assorted antics, it would have certainly done so, Taibbi quipped.[95]

The arrangement in many ways worked. Certainly, it benefited Trump, who even as a relative political novice gained a disproportionate amount of media coverage. The various news outlets also benefited, of course, in the form of both expanding audiences and bigger profits.[96] And in a perverse but undeniable way, even large segments of the American people gained by being drawn into and amused by the 2016 campaign and its circus-like atmosphere. And yet the longer-term effects of that big-tent show eventually proved damaging, Taibbi argued. In time, more and more Americans took the clown show they were seeing as reality, their preferred reality in fact, and voted Trump into office: "Sixty million people were announcing that they preferred one reality to another. Inherent in this decision was the revolutionary idea that you could choose your own set of facts."[97] In sending Trump to the White House, in other words, his legions of enthusiastic voters had not only split America along sharply drawn political lines but along sharply drawn epistemic ones as well. None of this might have happened if large swaths of the media had not been ready and willing to assist.

In her brief but lucid book also published in 2017, *The Trouble with Reality: A Rumination on Moral Panic in Our Time*, Brooke Gladstone explored a similar point. The host and managing editor of New York Public Radio's nationally distributed *On the Media*, Gladstone considered how the Trump phenomena, abetted by the media, had eroded America's traditional belief in a shared reality. Certainly, there were times in our history—the Civil War, the division over civil rights, the fierce debates over America's engagements abroad—when the notion of a shared reality had been severely tested and even fractured. And yet at most other times and despite our ongoing differences, "our common culture and environment" had enabled us to reach a widespread agreement over "fundamental principles" and facts. Gladstone offered a range of examples: the broadly common fight to save democracy during World War II, the passage of major pieces of social and economic legislation, the space race, the historically bipartisan support of massive public works and infrastructure programs. With the media-assisted candidacy and election of Donald Trump, though, much of what was left of the nation's common codes, and therefore its claims to legitimacy as a functioning republic, were shattered: "By degrading the very notion of a shared reality, Trump has disabled the engine of democracy."[98]

A centrist reformer at heart, Gladstone believed the situation was dire but not irremediable. Some consensus over fundamentals might well be recovered if people were willing to do hard things. One was to become acquainted with other people's experiences without the aid of a media filter. Such direct, unmediated encounters with people were admittedly difficult in a media-saturated culture in which much of what we know about other people and the world, or think we know, comes to us secondhand and often in distorted form. But steps such as this were essential to salvaging a shared "democratic code." Unless we are willing to embrace another, perhaps illiberal code, wrote Gladstone, "our obligation as citizens is to repair and improve the nation in which we live."[99]

Several later books also considered how the media-abetted Trump phenomenon had split America along several fault lines. In *Audience of One: Donald Trump, Television, and the Fracturing of America* (2019), for example, James Poniewozik, the chief TV critic of the *New York Times*, narrowed his lens from the broader media landscape to Trump's favorite medium. Poniewozik argues that, throughout his life, Trump has been so immersed in the popular culture of television that, in very real ways, "his story is its story, and vice versa."[100] The *Times* critic begins with the former president's childhood, speculating on all the ways that the television shows of the early- and mid-1950s instilled a lifelong addiction to the medium. From here, Poniewozik goes on to describe Trump's own efforts at character creation, specifically the part of the artful and successful businessman, which was reinforced first by *The Apprentice* and then by *The Celebrity Apprentice*, his successful NBC show that began airing in 2004. With his mega-businessman persona established, Trump found it easy to create another role for himself, that of the outspoken political pundit. Indeed, well before he made his political intentions clear, his frequent appearances on *Fox & Friends* and other Fox shows had already burnished his personal political brand. During these appearances, he would simultaneously entertain and outrage the network's conservative audience with all manner of accusations and conspiracy theories, including claims about President Obama's actual birthplace.[101]

Candidate Trump had still other tricks up his sleeve. With his campaign up and running, he and his team turned its most "defining events," the MAGA rallies, into loud and unruly TV spectacles, which borrowed heavily from the staged clashes produced by World Wrestling Entertainment, the integrated media and entertainment company. Here hecklers would be physically removed from the audience, typically at the urging of the man at the podium, and the press, a favorite target of his ridicule, would be cordoned in special Trump Press Pens. When the red light of the camera lit, explains Poniewozik, the candidate knew what producers craved—conflict and drama—and he was a master at providing it, while largely monopolizing the camera's attention.

There was a curious shift, though, when candidate Trump became President Trump. Gradually, explains Poniewozik, the medium that he had controlled so skillfully began to control him. The very cable news shows that he consumed hour after hour still motivated him but they also "enraged him" with many of the stories they ran. He was still "moved him to action" by what he saw and heard on his favorite medium, but the constant stream of coverage also "paralyzed him in self-surveillance." In short, the endless news cycle that had enveloped countless Americans over the years was now also enveloping Trump. And just as its fractured, splintered, and conflict-driven imagery was now part and parcel of his cynical worldview, it was also now the cynical reality of most of his followers.[102]

Another media book to appear late in the Trump presidency was Eric Alterman's *Lying in State: Why Presidents Lie—And Why Trump Is Worse* (2020). An historian and critic of the American media, Alterman took as his singular focus the forty-fifth president's habit of exaggeration and untruthfulness, placing it in a broader historical context: "Presidents who do not lie to the nation have been the exception, not the rule." Alterman offered evidence for his assertion by examining a lengthy list of various presidential liars, from earliest times to President Obama, a man less apt to tell "demonstrable untruths" but who could still shade the truth when it benefited his policies. If lying while in the presidency had been the norm, however, Trump while in office had perfected the art form. While most past presidents had told lies that were "more or less tethered to reality," Trump appeared willing to forgo even this minimum accommodation to the truth. "His ability to lie without concern for credibility is both shocking and gruesomely impressive," said Alterman.[103]

Why had Trump been so successful in elevating the art form? Clearly, personal inclination and a lifetime of exaggeration and outright lying were factors. But so too, as Alterman saw it, was a news media culture that until recently had been all too complicitous in indulging or even shielding presidential lies—Woodrow Wilson's claims about his health, FDR's statements about his war aims, or JFK's dismissal of his extramarital affairs, George W. Bush's unqualified assertions about Iraqi weapons of mass destruction: "It was the media's willingness to embrace the culture of dishonesty that helped to open the door for a president openly contemptuous of the media—and the truth itself."[104] Certainly, there were legacy media outlets, notably the *New York Times* and the *Washington Post*, that had broken with long-standing policy and began using the word "lie" in their news coverage or employing fact-checking, occasionally in real time on their websites. And some of these same news outlets were, of course, criticized for their change of editorial policy. But other mainstream news outlets remained reluctant to employ the label, or worse were complicit in promulgating Trump's exaggerated or outright false statements. This was an abrogation of the traditional journalistic mission, chided Alterman, who feared the slippery slope to authoritarianism: "Donald Trump knows, as most tyrants do, that without the accountability the media provide, almost anything can be justified."[105]

For Trump's critics, perhaps no media outlet was more responsible for his rise and continued untruths than Rupert Murdoch's Fox News. Prior to his candidacy, during it, and as president, the network, these critics say, gave Trump a nearly unlimited platform on which to air his grievances, make false claims, and promote conspiracies, all of which had the cumulative effect of further dividing an already polarized nation. In essential ways, this is the thesis at the heart of former CNN chief media correspondent Brian Stelter's *Hoax: Donald Trump, Fox News, And the Dangerous Distortion of Truth* (2020). Reissued with updated material in 2021, following Trump's election loss and the January 6 Capitol Hill riot, the book traces a relationship that would not only change contemporary politics but Americans' relation to the truth.

Much of Stelter's early Fox history is by now familiar. In hiring the late political consultant and former CNBC president Roger Ailes to launch the Fox News Channel, Murdoch was intent on establishing a conservative alternative to CNN, a favorite target of those on the right. In contrast to CNN's alleged liberal bias, Fox would instead offer "balanced and unbiased coverage," as Ailes put it in his founding mission statement. Relatively few were drawn at first to the new cable network: at its launch on October 7, 1996, it did not have many subscribers, and none in the major media markets of New York and Los Angeles. By the 2000 presidential election pitting a Texas governor against a sitting vice president, though, the channel's subscribers had swelled to fifty-six million nationwide, marking the largest increase in viewership among the big three cable news television networks.[106] A key to the channel's success was the doubt cast on the reliability of its rivals, Stelter points out: "Disbelief of, and disdain for, the news media was the cornerstone of the Fox's business model in 1996." Expressed most forcefully on the opinion side of things, this attitude not only helped to build a loyal audience and huge profits but also became "the cornerstone of Trump's presidency."[107]

The COVID-19 pandemic was a high-profile example of this dynamic. "He [Trump] deliberately played down the crisis—and Fox was there to help him," Stelter writes. In later January 2020, for instance, Trump was asked by Fox financial journalist Maria Bartiromo whether Americans had any cause for worry. "We're in great shape," responded the president.

Even after he imposed a partial travel ban from China on January 31, he clung to this narrative for almost the next month and a half, abetted by some of the channel's prime-time superstars, who believed the virus threat was being overstated by liberal media and its allies for the purposes of wounding Trump. On March 22, another Fox host surveyed the growing number of states in various stages of shut down and cautioned officials not to let the cure be worse than the disease. Several hours later, on Twitter, Trump reposted in kind: "WE CANNOT LET THE CURE BE WORSE THAN THE PROBLEM ITSELF." The seeming orchestrated messaging had a clear effect on how the Fox audience viewed the pandemic: "Poll after poll showed that Fox viewers were less concerned about the virus than avid consumers of other news sources"[108]

In the final chapter of his reissued and updated book, Stelter discusses events that post-dated its initial release. The largest share of his narrative focuses on the 2020 election—and its ironic effect on Fox News. In a curious twist of fate, the very network that had done so much to propel Trump to the presidency would soon incur his wrath. The instigator was Fox's election desk, an independent, data-driven operation. On the eve of November 3, it was the first to place the key state of Arizona in the win column of Democratic contender Joe Biden. Trump's path to the presidency had now very much narrowed "and his ploys to lie his way into a second term were weakened considerably." Loyal Fox viewers pushed back, incensed that their network had betrayed their candidate, but the network had no choice but to stick to its projection, lest it seem unprofessional and incompetent. Soon other networks followed Fox's lead. A few days later, Fox also had to follow along when CNN and other networks projected a Biden win in Pennsylvania, thereby signaling Trump's defeat. Suddenly, as one distraught Fox producer put it, the network was "bleeding eyeballs," with once loyal viewers setting out in search of more reliably pro-Trump outlets, such as Newsmax.[109]

The Fox network now faced an unfamiliar dilemma: its news department dutifully continued to report Biden's election victory, but many of its commentators seemed intent on stoking voter doubt and mistrust. (At least two later became targets of lawsuits by two of the leading voting-machine manufacturers.[110]) Meanwhile, under pressure from the Murdochs, the news CEO and her management team were testing various strategies to win back disgruntled Fox audience members. Eventually, these strategies would largely succeed. But there was a fallout from the post-election Fox commentary that perhaps not even the network's leaders could have seen coming. Convinced the election had been stolen, some of Trump's most ardent supporters participated in what Stelter describes as "an act of domestic terrorism against the United States." The January 6 insurrection had multiple causes, it now seems clear from the evidence uncovered by the US House Select Committee to Investigate the January 6th Attack. But what seems equally clear is that it may not have happened at all, as contrarian conservative and military historian Max Boot has said, if Fox News "and all the rest had not been spreading poisonous lies about the election."[111]

CONCLUSION

The teeming richness of recent media criticism appears to spring from several sources. Certainly, contemporary critics have been able to draw on, and respond to, an impressive history of existing criticism. From Walter Lippmann's *Public Affairs* to Noam Chomsky's propaganda model, past media commentators have pointed to many of the salient themes, often testing their theories of how a democratic press should operate against the major events of their day. In many ways, their intellectual example has set the standard for those who have succeeded them. Contemporary criticism has also benefited from its diversity. If in the past white males largely dominated the genre, and indeed much of journalism, the number of recent articles, books, and broadcast commentaries by women, people of color, members of the LGBTQ community, and other historically marginalized critics has raised new issues, while examining long-standing ones through unique lenses. Finally, today's media criticism has been made richer by its wide-ranging political perspectives, from various shades of conservatism to center-left liberalism to progressivism.

These perspectives have resulted in agreement on some issues but disagreement on many others. For older conservative critics like Bernard Goldberg, Brent Bozell, Mark Levin, and Sharyl Attkisson, the charge of liberal bias, first articulated by the earliest messengers of the right, still resonates. In their different ways, they have framed a critique of a mainstream news media that too often champions liberal ideas and causes, while ignoring or denigrating conservative ones. As they see it, the volatile Trump era exacerbated these default tendencies, causing many in the media to drop any pretense of balance or evenhandedness. Younger conservative critics have pushed this critique even further, charging that the establishment media during the Trump era and after have dropped all pretense of impartiality and become a virtual propaganda arm of the Democratic party and other elitists. In the more extreme version of this view, the establishment media has been a willing participant in propagating a worldwide globalist conspiracy, the very one that Donald Trump so successfully demonized during his election campaign.[112] In response, these critics champion countermeasures, including the call for visionaries on the populist right to create bolder alternatives to establishment news sources.

Today's progressive critics are also suspicious of globalists and call for alternative news sources, albeit with a different agenda. For them, the priority is an independent press, free of global corporate entanglements, that will serve the public's agenda and not that of the rich and powerful. Following the Trump era, the progressive project has become ever more urgent, since in many ways the media backslid during this period, focusing even more intently on spectacle and profit margins and less on underlying issues of social and economic justice. For many leading progressive critics, the only viable long-term solution to this unfortunate drift is a public- and government-supported media. In emphasizing the public good over the corporate good, such media would not only report on what now goes largely unreported but would lay the groundwork for a fairer, more equitable, and perhaps postcapitalist democracy.

This is a bridge too far for many center-left critics. While they agree with those further to their left that news outlets too often put profits before the common good and concentrate on scandal, spectacle, and trivia, as they so often did during the Trump presidency, liberal commentators are as a rule hesitant to call for deep structural changes, either to the existing media system or to the society at large. Reformers by political allegiance and often personal inclination, they tend to view the status quo as stubborn but remediable. Some, like veteran media critic Alex Jones, have even made clear their view that a profitable bottom line is the best guarantor of accountable journalism. For those like Jones—and indeed for younger commentators like Mike Taibbi—a return to verities like accountability, objectivity, and perseverance would benefit not only the profession but also democracy itself.

Each of these critiques has its merits—and each, it almost goes without saying, has its weaknesses. If, for instance, conservative critics are correct that too many mainstream news outlets embrace social causes that skew left, whether out of internal "woke" lobbying or external coercion, they are less alert to how much of their own project is directed to promoting an alternative and sometimes dangerous right-wing agenda. Similarly, if progressive media analysts accurately depict the market constraints that not only impede independent journalism but a more democratic and free society, they too often arrive at a gauzy vision of some postcapitalist utopia, buttressed by a noncommercial, government-supported media, that seems more aspirational than probable. Finally, if liberal critics are right to draw attention to the devolving journalistic values of the commercial press—its tendency in particular to frame complex issues in simple either/or terms conflict—such critics may be naïve in thinking that traditional values stand any chance of being reinstated without a compelling market reason to do so.

Bracketing all these concerns is a still larger question: how can the institution of the American press—and the society in which it operates—function at a time of widespread skepticism, a time when so many Americans seem unwilling or unable to embrace a shared reality about subjects of common concern such as climate change, a worldwide pandemic, and the machinery and results of elections? The answer raises a dark specter: for if consensus is the bedrock of democracy, and mutually agreed-upon truths the substratum of consensus, then a riven society distrustful of fact-based journalism, a key source of information about the world, seems doomed to embrace not only another model of comprehending reality but another form of governance.

In true authoritarian systems, of course, both ways of knowing and ways of being governed come together more often than not in the person of the supreme leader, who elides all political and epistemic quandaries by simply proclaiming what the law and truth is.[113] America is not yet that kind of system. But those who would condemn the press rather than seek to reform it are shutting their eyes to history.

NOTES

1. Candace Owens, *How Black America Can Make Its Second Escape from the Democrat Plantation* (New York: Threshold, 2020), 155, 157.

2. Alex Marlow, *Breaking the News: Exposing the Establishment Media's Hidden Deals and Secret Corruption* (New York: Threshold, 2021), vii.

3. Robert McChesney, *Blowing the Roof off the Twenty-First Century: Media, Politics, and the Struggle for Post-Capitalist Democracy* (New York: Monthly Review Press, 2014), 10.

4. Among Goodman's books in this area are *Breaking the Sound Barrier* (2009); *The Silenced Majority: Stories of Uprisings, Occupations, Resistance, and Hope* (2012); *Standing Up to the Madness: Ordinary Heroes in Extraordinary Times* (2014); and *Democracy Now!:Twenty Years Covering the Movements Changing America* (2016).

5. A representative sampling of these authors includes Abigail Martin, "Media Democracy in Action," in *Censored 2012:The Top 25 Censored Stories of 2010–11* (2012), ed. Mickey Huff; Mickey Huff, *The United States of Distraction: Media Manipulation in Post-Truth America* (And What We Can Do about It) (2019); Anita Sarkeesian and Katherine Ross, "Your Humanity Is in Another Castle: Terror Dreams and the Harassment of Women," in *The State of Play: Creators and Critics on Video Game Culture* (2015), eds. Daniel Goldberg and Linus Larsson; and Adrienne Shaw, *Gaming at the Edge: Sexuality and Gender at the Margins of Gamer Culture* (2014).

6. Jill Abramson, *Merchants of Truth: The Business of News and the Fight for Facts* (New York: Simon & Schuster, 2019), 387.

7. On Rusher's influence, see, for example, David Rusk, *If Not Us, Who?:William Rusher, National Review, and the Conservative Movement* (Wilmington: ISI Books, 2011); also, see above, chapter 5, 171–72.

8. Nicole Hemmer, *Messengers of the Right: Conservative Media and the Transformation of American Politics* (Philadelphia: University of Pennsylvania, 2016), xii, xiii, xiv. Hemmer takes up her story in the Ronald Reagan era in her later book *Partisans: The Conservative Revolutionaries Who Remade American Politics in the 1990s* (New York: Basic Books, 2022).

9. Brent Bozell, *And That's the Way It Isn't: A Reference Guide to Media Bias*, ed. Brent H. Baker (Alexandria, VA: Media Research Center, 1990), acknowledgements, n.p.

10. Ibid., 64, 66, 71.

11. L. Brent Bozell, *Weapons of Mass Distortion: The Coming Meltdown of the Liberal Media* (New York: Crown Forum, 2014).

12. See, for example, "Where Americans Go for News," Pew Research Center, June 8, 2004, https://www.pewresearch.org/politics/2004/06/08/i-where -americans-go-for-news/.

13. Feeling marginalized after being replaced as anchor of the *CBS Evening News*, Dan Rather quit the network on June 19, 2006.

14. Bozell, *Weapons*, introduction, 1.

15. Ibid., 76.

16. Ibid., 85, 93.

17. Ibid., 162, 2007.

18. See, Michael M. Grynbaum, "Fox News Drops 'Fair and Balanced' Motto," *New York Times,* June 14, 2017, https://www.nytimes.com/2017/06/14/business/media/fox-news-fair-and-balanced.html.

19. Bernard Goldberg, *Bias*: *A CBS Insider Exposes How the Media Distort the News* (Washington, DC: Regnery, 2001), 30.

20. Ibid., 22.

21. Ibid., 22, 119.

22. See Sharyl Attkisson and Don R. Vaughan, *Writing Right for Broadcast and Internet News* (Boston: Allyn & Bacon, 2002).

23. Dylan Byers, "The Rights Loses Its Hero at CBS," *Politico*, March 11, 2004, https://www.politico.com/story/2014/03/sharyl-attkisson-leaves-cbs-104498.

24. Sharyl Attkisson, *Stonewalled*: *My Fight for Truth against the Forces of Obstruction, Intimidation, and Harassment in Obama's Washington* (New York: Harper, 2014), 19, 352.

25. Howard Kurtz, *Donald Trump, the Press, and the War over Truth* (Washington, DC: Regnery, 2018), 4.

26. Ibid., 4–6.

27. Ibid., 270–71.

28. In between this book and his previous one, he had written a book, with a co-author, about press attempts to hide "the truth" about Hillary Clinton. See L. Brent Bozell, III, with Tim Graham, *Whitewash: What the Media Won't Tell You about Hillary Clinton, But Conservatives Will* (New York: Crown Forum, 2007), 12.

29. L. Brent Bozell, III, with Tim Graham, *Unmasked: Big Media's War against Trump* (West Palm Beach: Humanix Books, 2019), xxv.

30. Ibid., xxvii.

31. Ibid., 42, 51, 111.

32. Ibid., xxvi.

33. Mark Levin, *Unfreedom of the Press* (New York: Threshold Editions, 2019), 3.

34. Sharyl Attkisson, *Slanted: How the News Media Taught Us to Love Censorship and Hate Journalism* (New York: Harper Collins, 2020), 2, 7.

35. Owens, *Blackout*, 9, 160, 166. According to different assessments, Trump overstated his role in lowering Black unemployment. See, for example, Hope Yen, "AP Fact Check: Trump Exaggerates His Role in Black Job Gains," Associated Press, July 28, 2019, https://apnews.com/article/donald-trump-busi

ness-politics-ap-fact-check-f78f4205f474482db8bb8fa7a5ebfa27; also, Charisse Jones, "Under Donald Trump, Blacks Continue to Trail Whites in Employment, Home Ownership," *USA Today*, October 23, 2020, https://www.usatoday.com /story/money/2020/10/23/trump-blacks-trump-best-president-black-people-since -lincoln/3742081001/.

36. Marlow, *Breaking*, ix

37. Ibid., 60–75, 83.

38. Ibid., 173.

39. Quoted in Jennifer Rubin, "A Bulwark against Trump and Trumpism," *Washington Post*, January 8, 2019, https://www.washingtonpost.com/opinions /2019/01/08/bulwark-against-trump-trumpianism/.

40. Charles J. Sykes, *How the Right Lost Its Mind* (New York: St. Martin's Press, 2017), xiv.

41. Ibid., 107, 109.

42. Ibid., 66, 133. Fox News's Sean Hannity, for example, has been estimated to be worth $250 million, with an annual salary as of 2020 of $40 million. See "Sean Hannity Net Worth," CelebrityNetWorth, https://www.celebritynetworth .com/richest-politicians/republicans/sean-hannity-net-worth/.

43. Sykes, *How the Right,* 85.

44. Ibid., 82.

45. Ibid., xiv, 229, 230.

46. Jeff Cohen, *Cable News Confidential*: *My Misadventures in Corporate Media*. Foreword by Jim Hightower (Sausalito: Polipoint, 2006), 1, 6.

47. Ibid., 59.

48. Ibid., 2.

49. Ibid., 201–3.

50. Robert McChesney, *Rich Media, Poor Democracy: Communication Policies in Dubious Times*, with a new preface by the author (1999; repr., New York: The New Press, 2015), xxxvii–xxviii.

51. Robert W. McChesney, *The Problem of the Media: U.S. Communication Policies in the 21st Century* (New York: Monthly Review Press, 2004), 7, 8, 19.

52. Ibid., 57, 65–73, 97.

53. Robert W. McChesney, *The Death and Life of American Journalism: The Media Revolution That Will Begin the World Again* (Philadelphia: Nation Books, 2010), xiii.

54. Among the western European countries with robust state-supported media are United Kingdom, Sweden, Netherlands, Germany, Denmark, Italy, France, and Spain. See Katerina Eva Masta, "Across Western Europe, Public News Media Are Widely Used and Trusted Sources of News," Pew Research Center, June

8, 2018, https://www.pewresearch.org/fact-tank/2018/06/08/western-europe-pub
lic-news-media-widely-used-and-trusted/.

55. Robert W. McChesney, *Blowing the Roof Off the Twenty-First Century:
Media, Politics, and the Struggle for Post-Capitalist Democracy* (New York:
Monthly Review Press, 2014), 51–61.

56. In an earlier book, he argued how digital media would remain mired in the
existing political economy until "enlightened public investments" unleashed its
journalistic and other potential. See Robert W. McChesney, *Digital Disconnect:
How Capitalism Is Turning the Internet against Democracy* (New York: The
New Press, 2013), 232.

57. McChesney, *Blowing*, 227.

58. Ibid., 229–30.

59. Ibid., 235–36.

60. See Project Censored: The News That Didn't Make the News, website,
https://www.projectcensored.org/.

61. Amy Goodman, with David Goodman, *The Exception to the Rulers:
Exposing Oily Politicians, War Profiters, and the Media That Love Them* (New
York: Hyperion, 2004), 4.

62. Amy Goodman and David Goodman, *Static: Government Liars, Media
Cheerleaders, and the People Who Fight Back* (New York: Hachette, 2006), 80.

63. Ibid., 306.

64. Amy Goodman and David Goodman, *Standing Up to the Madness: Ordinary Heroes in Extraordinary Times* (New York: Hyperion, 2008), ix–x.

65. Amy Goodman, *Breaking the Sound Barrier*, with a foreword by Bill
Moyers, edited by Denis Moynihan (Chicago: Haymarket, 2009), vii–x.

66. Amy Goodman and Denis Moynihan, *The Silenced Majority: Stories
of Uprisings, Occupations, Resistance and Hope*, with a foreword by Michael
Moore (Chicago: Haymarket, 2012).

67. Amy Goodman, with David Goodman and Denis Moynihan, *Democracy
Now!: Twenty Years Covering Movements Changing America* (New York: Simon
& Schuster, 2016), 347.

68. Ahmad Abuznaid, "What We've Seen in Sheikh Jarrah Is a Microcosm of
What We've Experienced for the Last 70+ Years," interview by Janine Jackson,
Counterspin, May 11, 2021, https://fair.org/home/what-weve-seen-in-sheikh
-jarrah-is-a-microcosm-of-what-weve-experienced-for-the-last-70-years/.

69. "History of Project Censored," Project Censored, accessed August 11,
2021, https://www.projectcensored.org/more-about-project-censored/.

70. *Project Censored's State of the Free Press 2021*, eds., Mickey Huff and
Andy Lee Roth, foreword by Mike Taibbi (New York: Seven Stories Press, 2020).

71. Benjamin Neimark, Oliver Belcher, and Patrick Bigger, "U.S. Military Is a Bigger Polluter Than as Many As 140 countries—Shrinking This War Machine Is a Must," *The Conversation*, June 24, 2019, https://theconversation.com/us-military-is-a-bigger-polluter-than-as-many-as-140-countries-shrinking-this-war-machine-is-a-must-119269.

72. Mickey Huff and Nolan Higdon, *The United States of Distraction: Media Manipulation in Post-Truth America (And What We Can Do about It)*, with a foreword by Ralph Nader (San Francisco: City Lights Books, 2019), 22, 25.

73. Ibid., 148.

74. Ibid., 166, 177.

75. James Fallows, *How the Media Undermine American Democracy*, with a new afterword (1996; repr., New York: Vintage, 1997), 52, 288.

76. Ibid., 3.

77. There is a shelf's worth of books on public journalism. Two of the earliest and most influential are David "Buzz" Merritt, *Public Journalism and Public Life: Why Telling the News Is Not Enough*, 2nd ed. (New York: Routledge, 1997) and Jay Rosen, *What Are Journalists For?* (New Haven: Yale University Press, 1999).

78. Quoted in Fallows, *How the Media Undermine*, 263.

79. Ibid., 285.

80. Alex S. Jones, *The Future of the News That Feeds Democracy* (New York: Oxford University Press, 2009), xvii.

81. Ibid., xix, 3, 199.

82. Ibid., 84.

83. Ibid., 222.

84. Abramson, *Merchants*, 69.

85. Marc Tracy, "Digital Revenue Exceeds Print for the 1st Time for the New York Times Company," *New York Times*, August 5, 2020, https://www.nytimes.com/2020/08/05/business/media/nyt-earnings-q2.html.

86. Abramson, *Merchants*, 387, 390.

87. Ibid., 387.

88. "2018 Pulitzer Prizes Journalism"; "2019 Pulitzer Prizes Journalism," The Pulitzer Prizes, https://www.pulitzer.org/winners/david-barstow-susanne-craig-and-russ-buettner-new-york-times; and "2020 Pulitzer Prizes Journalism," The Pulitzer Prizes, https://www.pulitzer.org/prize-winners-by-year/2020.

89. Eric Deggans, *Race-Baiter: How the Media Wield Dangerous Words and Divides a Nation* (New York: Palgrave-Macmillan, 2012), 13, 39.

90. See "Geraldo Rivera: Trayvon Martin's Hoodie Is as Much Responsible for His Death as George Zimmerman," *Fox & Friends*, March 23, 2012, https://video.foxnews.com/v/1525652570001#sp=show-clips; also, "Bill O'Reilly: The

Trayvon Martin Murder Case and Why It Is Important," Fox News, originally published July 2, 2012, https://www.foxnews.com/transcript/bill-oreilly-the -trayvon-martin-murder-case-and-why-it-is-important.

91. Deggans, *Race-Baiter*, 29.

92. Mike Taibbi, *Hate Inc.: Why Today's Media Makes Us Despise One Another* (New York: OR Books 2019), 5, 6.

93. Ibid., 39.

94. Ibid., 259, 294.

95. Matt Taibbi, *Insane Clown President: Dispatches from the 2016 Circus* (New York: Spiegel & Grau, 2017), xxviii.

96. See, for example, Tom Huddleston Jr., "CBS Chief: Trump's Success Is 'Damn Good' For the Network," *Fortune*, March 1, 2016, https://fortune .com/2016/03/01/les-moonves-cbs-trump/.

97. Taibbi, *Insane Clown President*, xxv.

98. Brooke Gladstone, *The Trouble with Reality: A Rumination on Moral Panic in Our Time* (New York: Workman, 2017), 52.

99. Ibid., 103.

100. James Poniewozik, *Audience of One: Donald Trump, Television, and the Fracturing of American* (New York: Liveright, 2019), xvii.

101. See, for example, Peter Grier, "Donald Trump: Genuine 'Birther' or just Furthering His Personal Brand?" *Christian Science Monitor*, March 28, 2011, https://www.csmonitor.com/USA/Politics/The-Vote/2011/0328/Donald-Trump -Genuine-birther-or-just-furthering-his-personal-brand.

102. Poniewozik, *Audience of One*, 237, 271.

103. Eric Alterman, *Lying in State: Why Presidents Lie—And Why Trump Is Worse* (New York: Basic Books, 2020), 1, 5, 219.

104. Ibid., 11.

105. Ibid., 311.

106. Wikipedia, "History of Fox News," last updated August 10, 2021, https:// en.wikipedia.org/wiki/History_of_Fox_News.

107. Brian Stelter, *Hoax: Donald Trump, Fox News, and the Dangerous Distortion of Truth* (2020; repr., New York: One Signal, 2021), 95.

108. Ibid., 310, 315.

109. Ibid., 349, 366. In fact, fewer than thirty thousand selected viewers jumped ship.

110. See Stephen Battaglio, "Voting Software Maker Smartmatic Sues Fox News And Its Anchors for $2.7 Billion," *Los Angeles Times*, February 4, 2021, https://www.latimes.com/entertainment-arts/business/story/2021-02-04/voting -software-smartmatic-sues-fox-news-anchors-27-billion-election. A second suit

by another vending machine maker was filed the next month. See Michael M. Grynbaum and Jonah E. Bromwich, "Fox News Faces Second Defamation Suit over Election Coverage, *New York Times*, March 26, 2021, https://www.nytimes .com/2021/03/26/business/media/fox-news-defamation-suit-dominion.html.

111. Quoted in Stelter, *Hoax,* 373.

112. Liam Stack, "Globalism: A Far-Right Conspiracy Theory Buoyed by Trump," *New York Times*, November 14, 2016, https://www.nytimes.com /2016/11/15/us/politics/globalism-right-trump.html.

113. See, for example, Benjamin Carter Hett, *The Death of Democracy: Hitler's Rise to Power and the Downfall of the Weimar Republic* (2018; repr., New York: St. Martin's Griffin, 2019), 197–201.

Epilogue

The Once and Future Critics

If the last hundred years or so of press criticism have taught us anything, it is that certain themes have stubbornly persisted. That lesson should come as no surprise, given some of the continuities in both the news media and American society itself. But the fact that concerns raised more than a century ago are still being debated today surely says something about how fraught and resistant to change they really are. Consider, for example, the issue of commercialism and the news.

As we have seen, some of the earliest press critics reacted in alarm to the new commercial model, refined by the penny press and later exploited by the yellow press. To these critics, journalism over time had simply become too dependent on circulation and advertising, in the process favoring entertainment over news values. Over the years, one version or another of this critique has shown up in the analyses of a whole series of critics, from George Seldes to James Fallows. And the critique continues today: after tracing the long history of America's battle for media democracy, for instance, one recent scholar put the matter bluntly: "This analysis reaches the uncomfortable conclusion that the current commercial model for media is not adequately serving democracy." The scholar concluded by urging various "stake-holding constituencies to begin pushing for structural alternatives."[1]

Consider, too, the trend of media consolidation. Early on, several critics, including, of course, George Seldes, pointed to the growing power of certain press titans. It was journalist-turned-press critic Ben Bagdikian, though, who made media concentration his special focus. In the various editions of *The Media Monopoly*, as we have seen, he documented in sometimes feverish detail the salient effects of this phenomenon, including the loss of news outlets serving local communities. In his own important if controversial work, critic Noam Chomsky cited Bagdikian's key research appreciatively. But for Chomsky and the radical critics who followed him, it was not the mass media alone, or even principally, that set the national docket. It was, rather, the broader corporate and political economy to which the mass media was too often beholden. For such critics, more worrying still was that within this broader economy, the real power over public messaging was narrowly held. It enabled a select elite to decide which news served their economic and political interests and which did not.

Issues like these are almost sure to occupy future press critics. And these issues will remain relevant, it seems fair to say, precisely because addressing them would take either difficult-to-enact reforms or something approaching a media or societal upheaval. Just as likely, though, critics both today and in the future will need to contend with a host of newer issues—or, at the least, a set of older ones that have taken on greater urgency in a new media landscape. Just what these issues will be inevitably calls for speculation. Still, big topics certainly loom.

THE (UNCERTAIN) ECONOMICS OF JOURNALISM

Beyond the issue of commercialism, the related one of how future journalism will be funded remains fraught. The basic question is seemingly straightforward: which of the several models—publicly funded, family-owned, subsidized, grant-funded, subscription-supported, or of course, advertising-supported—will best ensure journalism's long-term survival, while at the same time supporting innovation and best practices? In fact, the question is anything but straightforward: Any reasonable answer depends on multiple variables, including the type of news organization, competition from other media, prevailing market conditions, technological innovations, changes in consumer habits and tastes, and the like.

Many of these variables are illustrated in the roller-coaster saga of the modern national newspaper. In many ways, the nation's leading newspapers reached a sort of golden age beginning in the later 1960s.[2] Increasingly critical coverage of the Vietnam War helped to drive circulation—as did the publication of the Pentagon Papers in the early 1970s and the

Watergate investigation after that. On Ben Bagdikian's *Washington Post*, as we have seen, competition with the *New York Times* was at this point fierce, resulting in Pulitzer Prizes for each paper between 1972 and 1973. But it was not only the economics of big journalism on the rise. These decades were also good ones for the *image* of journalism—and for the "reporter as truth seeking hero."[3]

A challenge to the traditional business model was, however, gathering steam: Gradually, or suddenly for those who had turned a blind eye to it, younger and even middle-age readers were abandoning print for free digital content, while advertisers were discovering a variety of new online platforms on which to sell their wares. Both the *Times* and *Post* hemorrhaged money, as both circulation and advertising revenue plummeted. Many other big papers folded or were acquired by private equity firms. Eventually, both the *Times* and *Post* took steps to right themselves, as former *Times* executive Jill Abramson chronicles in *Merchants of Truth*. Pay walls and more digital content certainly helped. And so did, as we have seen, the public's media-driven obsession with Donald J. Trump.

How long this economic viability will last is anyone's guess. Meanwhile, other problems persist: local newspapers continue to struggle, with all the attendant problems of neighborhood and regional coverage that that gives rise to; TV news consumption is erratic, even on cable; and younger consumers are relying on their digital devices for headline news.[4] Given all this, will the commercial model hold as journalism's linchpin? Or are more state-supported news media the best guarantors of such journalism, as Robert McChesney and other progressive critics have argued? Or is some form of a hybrid model—one that perhaps fuses noncommercial funding with an entrepreneurial mindset—the wave of the future?[5] Press critics will almost certainly mull these options, taking into account as they often do not only the economics of journalism but also its mission.

THE FIRST AMENDMENT AND ITS DISCONTENTS

Also sure to vex critics in the years ahead are issues centering on the First Amendment. In this regard, some commentators have pointed to the importance of the 2019 defamation suit brought against the *New York Times* by Sarah Palin, the former Alaska governor and GOP vice-presidential candidate.[6] Though dismissed in early 2022 even before jury deliberations ended, the case nevertheless raised unsettling First Amendment concerns for news organizations, along with the fear that similar suits might follow. Of special concern is that one of these suits could prompt a conservative-leaning Supreme Court to review the landmark decision *New York Times Co. v Sullivan*. Pivotal in deciding defamation claims, the decision requires public officials who allege defamation to prove intentional malice.[7] Though some commentators believe a reversal of *New York Times Co. v Sullivan* is "unlikely," they nevertheless worry that "the application of the . . . malice standard could be significantly limited in practice."[8] If that should happen, the extent of traditional press protections will almost certainly be tested and debated.

The First Amendment is also likely to be tested around matters of free speech. Is the amendment a guarantor of democracy by protecting free speech? Or in the process of allegedly protecting free speech, does the First Amendment actually undermine democracy by providing cover for increasingly false, incendiary, and nihilistic speech? Further complicating these questions is the set of libertarian assumptions, codified in past Supreme Court decisions, that informs modern thinking about free speech. At the core of this thinking is the belief that the free market-place of ideas—in which people or organizations with contending views engage in unrestricted competition—is the surest way to weed out error and discover truth. In the end, as free-speech proponents like Elon Musk see it, good ideas inevitably drive out bad ones, thereby strengthening democratic society. But is this always the case? In a provocative (and ironically titled) essay in the *New York Times*, "Free Speech Will Save Our Democracy," author and attorney Emily Bazelon weighed in on this highly fraught question.[9]

In considering the libertarian claim that the truth will always out, Bazelon offers evidence of a countertradition. She explains that, while artfully disguising their projects behind the banner of free speech, "demagogic leaders or movements can use propaganda" or, in modern parlance disinformation, to further their often-undemocratic aims. In other words, "a crude authoritarian censors free speech. A clever one invokes it to play a trick." And the grab bag of such tricks, she reminds us, is large. Constitutionally protected disinformation can distort facts and turn a group into an ugly and dangerous mob. It can also inject alternate facts and half-truths into the national bloodstream, making rational conversation near impossible. And perhaps most insidious of all, it can flood the airwaves and cyberspace with such confusing and contradictory statements that even well-meaning citizens throw up their hands in disgust and take "refuge in cynicism," as Hannah Arendt phrases it in *The Origins of Totalitarianism.*[10]

Under these circumstances, is the absolutist view of the First Amendment really up to the task of preserving democracy? Or in order to preserve democracy, do we need to do a better job of imposing rational limits on free speech, by, for instance, agreeing on commonsensical rules of discourse in the chaotic online environment? Freedom of the press raises related questions: do we continue to champion greater freedom of the press in the hope that good and well-sourced reporting will drive out fake reporting? Or does it not "really matter how much freedom journalists have if no one believes them" anyway, as David E. McCraw suggests in *Truth in Our Times: Inside the Fight for Press Freedom in the Age of Alternative Facts* (2019)?[11] These are difficult questions certainly, and ones sure to be part of the critical conversation in the years to come.

THE EPISTEMOLOGY WARS

In many ways, the debate over the First Amendment is part of an even broader conversation: the ongoing epistemic struggle over what constitutes knowledge. In a timely *National Affairs* essay several years ago that was subsequently expanded into a book, journalist Jonathan Rauch identified the contending sides in this struggle: the "constitution of knowledge" versus "troll epistemology."[12]

By the first term, Rauch was not referring to public consensus on core propositions. Indeed, as he sees it, such a consensus is difficult and perhaps not even desirable. The more essential meaning of the constitution of knowledge is, as he employed the term, a certain socially derived agreement "on the *method* of validating propositions." Put another way, while we as a society may neither believe the same things nor be expected to, we must nevertheless agree at minimum on a set of rules that enable us to distinguish truth from falsehood. In an enlightened democratic society, in which falsehood is permitted but not privileged, such epistemological

rules are typically incorporated into the best practices of a set of professional networks—scientific, legal, medical, academic, and journalistic. In
the case of journalism, for instance, the defining characteristic "is professional editing, and its institutional home is the newsroom, which curates
and checks stories, trains reporters, organizes complex investigations, in-
culcates professional ethics, and more."[13] When these minimum norms are
followed, a certain form of knowledge accumulates and is disseminated
to the larger society.

Troll epistemology, by contrast, tosses a bomb into this orderly social
process, as Rauch explains:

> By insisting that all the fact checkers and hypothesis testers out there are
> phonies, trolls discredit the very possibility of a socially validated real-
> ity, and open the door to tribal knowledge, personal knowledge, partisan
> knowledge, and other manifestations of epistemic anarchy. By spreading
> lies and disinformation on an industrial scale, they sow confusion about
> what might or might not be true, and about who can be relied on to discern
> the difference, and about whether there *is* any difference. By being willing
> to say anything, they exploit shock and outrage to seize attention and hijack
> the public conversation.[14]

All this poses a clear dilemma for those who continue to play by the
normal rules. For in calling out the trolls or in defending the constitution
of knowledge, the champions of truth risk a counterattack, which in turn
further poisons the public conversation.

Rauch is properly alert to the charge of overstatement. It is not the
case, he says, that trolls are always wrong—never identify a real bias in
mainstream media or discover a flaw in how the scientific establishment
or government bureaucracies operate. They do. But even when they do,
their default response is "to trash the institutions" rather than "to remedi-
ate the defects," thereby exacerbating the general atmosphere of distrust
and cynicism. At their best, those participating in the constitution of
knowledge operate differently, remediating defects within their respective
institutions when such defects come to light, as has sometimes been the
case in journalism.[15] Not all knowledge-based institutions are so inclined,
of course. Some like academia, as Rauch sees it, have frequently assumed
a more defensive crouch, dismissing even well-formulated criticism out of
an instinct for self-protection.[16] But such a self-protective posture simply

plays into troll anarchism, into the idea that all is bunk. Here, then, is yet another set of issues sure to be debated in the years ahead.

WOKENESS IS ALL

Finally, there is the charged and complicated issue of wokeness and the media. A good starting point for its consideration is a *New York Times Magazine* special issue published in August 2019.

In that issue, conceived by then *Times* staff writer Nikole Hannah-Jones, who also wrote the introductory essay, most of the some one hundred pages were devoted to a group of essays, photos, poems, and fiction on the history of Blacks in America. Published in the year that marked the "400th anniversary of the beginning of American slavery," the special issue was planned as the opening salvo in an even broader initiative known as the "1619 Project," which set for itself an ambitious aim: "to reframe the country's history by placing the consequences of slavery and the contributions of black Americans at the very center of our national narrative."[17] To accompany the magazine, *Times* editors also assembled a mix of other printed matter, along with a multi-episode audio series. Eventually, in association with the Pulitzer Center, they went on to develop "The 1619 Project Curriculum," an assortment of materials, listening guides, booklists, and historical timelines designed to offer students a different perspective on US history.[18]

The 1619 Project garnered praise in many quarters and its share of awards. Writing in the *Columbia Journalism Review* (August 15, 2019), for instance, journalist Alexandra Neason applauded the project, and Hannah-Jones specifically, for correcting the historical record, in particular the lapses of both women's profession: "For generations, journalism has papered over slavery's impact, at times openly advocating the white supremacist ideologies that enabled the founders of the United States to justify treating human beings as property fit only for forced labor." Neason was especially critical of how the media "had insisted on slavery as a historical fact, rather than a present-day influence." The *Times* project had righted that error, she believed, by conceiving Black enslavement not as an artifact of the past but, four hundred years later, as a living presence.[19] The day before, in *Fortune Magazine*, senior editor Ellen McGirt had followed a similar line of praise, noting that the project "serves as a dramatic and necessary corrective to the fundamental lie of the American origin story."[20] The following year, in May, the Pulitzer Center selected Hannah-Jones as the 2020 winner of its Pulitzer Prize for Commentary.[21] And several months later, the Arthur L. Carter Journalism Institute, at New York University, placed the "1619 Project" eighth on its list of "The Top Ten Works of Journalism of the Past decade." Ta-Nehisi Coates's "The Case for Reparations," which had appeared in *The Atlantic* in 2014, led the list.[22]

The *Times* project also came in for its share of criticism. In a letter in December 2019 to the *Times*, for example, five prominent historians, including Sean Wilentz of Princeton University, applauded the project's efforts to raise "profound, unsettling questions about slavery and the nation's past and present." But the group also voiced its deep concern over the project's many factual errors and what appeared to be "a displacement of historical understanding by ideology." Especially egregious, the historians said, was the assertion "that founders declared the colonies' independence of Britain 'in order to ensure slavery would continue.'" This was a false claim, they charged, not validated by any project evidence or statement. The historians ended by urging the *Times* "to issue prominent corrections of all the errors and distortions," including in any curriculum materials to be distributed.[23]

Magazine editor, Jake Silverstein, thanked the historians for their appraisal, offered his and Hannah-Jones's defense of their fact-checking process, and politely refused the historians' request.[24] About a month later, in a follow-up in the *Atlantic* to his original letter, Wilentz, the Princeton historian, again praised the project for its ambition and worthy goals but reiterated his dismay over the project's distortions. He also called the *Times* and Silverstein to task for their reluctance to correct these distortions: "No effort to educate the public in order to advance social justice can afford to dispense with a respect for basic facts." Wilentz then proceeded to correct the corrected record.[25]

Political reaction to the 1619 Project was also swift. On the extreme right, the criticism was merciless, often veering into character attacks. In *Breaking the News*, for instance, Breitbart editor Alex Marlow, one of the contemporary media critics profiled in chapter 8, dedicated a portion of his broader chapter on the *Times* ("Mob Rule Media: The *New York*

Times in the Age of Woke") to the 1619 Project. After charging that its "vision of America is diametrically opposed to America's most fundamental collective beliefs about our origins and purpose," Marlow went after Hannah-Jones herself: "[She] is a racist conspiracy theorist with a victim complex who embraces violence, publishes glaring falsehoods, and hates America. She directs all her passion toward pushing her narratives with semi-fictional 'journalism.'"[26]

More moderate conservatives were less heated but also faulted the project. In the *National Review*, for example, editor Rich Lowry engaged in a running debate with Hannah-Jones over, among other things, the nature of American exceptionalism—that is, whether the nation was unique *because* of its peculiar history of slavery or in spite of it. In her introductory essay, said Lowry, Hannah-Jones had seemed to be making the former case, which he found flawed. Yes, said Lowry, slavery on these shores was horrific—as he had emphasized in his own writing. It did not follow, though, that "we were exceptional *because* of slavery." Racialized slavery had predated both the Europeans and the colonists, and it was, in fact, "Africans who captured other Africans," marched them coastward to be sold at auction to European slavers, and were indirectly responsible for the ugly Middle Passage to America. When it came to slavery, in short, "colonial America was hardly an island unto itself." And while nothing about this historical qualification was exculpatory, Lowry insisted, it did suggest a cautionary lesson: if American history is viewed only through the lens of slavery, the nation's struggle over time to be a better society, guided by worthy if flawed ideals, risked being permanently erased from the public consciousness.[27]

Even Hannah-Jones's then colleague on the *New York Times*, conservative columnist Bret Stephens, certainly no one's idea of an alt-right flamethrower, weighed in. Like others, Stephens admired the project's ambition, worthy goals, and powerful accompanying imagery. And he disputed, too, the widely held idea in certain circles that the project's essayists and other commentators, including Hannah-Jones, had rejected American values. Still, in his column, Stephens was concerned that, in attempting to reframe the nation's historical narrative, project authors had overreached. "Journalists are, most often, in the business of writing the first rough draft of history," he noted "not trying to have the last word on it." Further on in his column, he expanded on his point, partially echoing a comment about "ideology" that the five historians had made in their letter to the *Times*:

> Monocausality—whether it's the clash of economic classes, the hidden hand of the market, or white supremacy and its consequences—has always been a seductive way of looking at the world. It has always been a simplistic one, too. The world is complex. So are people and their motives. The job of journalism is to take account of that complexity, not simplify it out of existence through the adoption of some ideological orthodoxy.

Such displays of orthodoxy, Stephens said, simply offered added fuel to the flamethrowers, who perhaps hated the paper of record worst of all: "Through its overreach, the 1619 Project has given the critics of *The Times* a gift."[28]

Criticism of the 1619 Project also came in from the populist left. In her provocatively titled book, *Bad News: How Woke Media Is Undermining Democracy* (2021), for example, Batya Ungar-Sargon argued that the 1619 Project and initiatives like it are part of a relatively recent journalistic preoccupation with race in America. The former opinion editor of the *Forward*, a digital publication aimed at a Jewish audience, and currently the deputy opinion editor of *Newsweek*, Ungar-Sargon did not deny "the history or the lingering presence of racism in America." Beyond the disproportionate incarceration rates, the unequal treatment at the hands of the police, the history of redlining in housing, the continuing segregation of the nation's schools, and the ongoing intergenerational poverty, she pointed to the intensifying problem of hate, especially during the presidency of Donald Trump. As agenda setters, the news media had cause, indeed the obligation, to cover "issues of institutional racism" wherever they occur.[29]

But the liberal press had fallen short in this effort, Ungar-Sargon, argued. Instead of addressing institutional racism in all its facets, the press instead took it upon itself to mainstream "a moral panic around *the very idea of race.*" This view of things saw racism as "baked into the DNA of America"—as in many ways "the DNA of America." But such totalistic thinking was misguided, Ungar-Sargon argued, not only out of line with the facts but an excuse that allowed the liberal national media to skirt and even help to perpetuate a more quantifiable problem:

a growing economic inequality that "afflicts working-class people and poor people *of all races*."[30]

How did this journalistic myopia occur? Among other culprits, Ungar-Sargon claimed, was the changing status of the profession. Time was, she wrote, when much of journalism comprised a ragtag group of misfits, not especially well educated, with no real formal training in reporting, and above all poorly paid. If reporters wrote with a special affinity for the people they covered, it was largely because their own backgrounds were not so different. Even those who became the stars of the profession—muckrakers like Ida Tarbell, Upton Sinclair, Will Irvin—often came from marginal economic backgrounds that enabled them to write as passionately as they did. Immigrant publisher Joseph Pulitzer had himself survived a hardscrabble background, returning nearly broke to New York City after serving in the Civil Way and forced to sleep on the streets, among other places. These memories remained seared in him for the rest of his life, motivating his crusading journalism and later, after the purchase of the *New York World*, a desire to make the poor not only his subjects but his readers.[31]

In contrast, said Ungar-Sargon, today's journalists are, at least at the elite level, a different breed. Many come from affluent backgrounds, have been educated at top schools, and are well paid, especially in network and cable news. They are, in short, solid representatives of, and believers in, the American meritocracy, a system in which people with the right education, skill, and achievement advance in the social hierarchy. At the same time, by dint of their education and liberal leanings, many are also idealistic, and therein lies their dilemma: How does one reconcile membership in the meritocracy with compassion for those who are, by definition, excluded from it? The answer, Ungar-Sargon claimed, was by inflaming "a moral panic around race": "Wokeness provided the perfect ideology for affluent, liberal whites who didn't truly want systemic change if it meant their children would have to sacrifice their own status, but who still wanted to feel like the heroes of a story about social justice."[32]

As a remedy, she urged the liberal media to pursue a new version of journalism—or, more accurately, to return to an older one. This is a journalism "that *exposes* the class divide, rather than concealing it," one that, in the clever formulation of early-twentieth-century journalist and humorist Finley Peter Dunne, comforts the afflicted, and afflicts the comfortable. And if such a project needs to be waged on behalf of the poor, it also needs to be undertaken on behalf of democracy itself, "which simply cannot survive when power is concentrated in the hands of so few, thanks in no small part to journalists."[33]

Certainly, Ungar-Sargon has made a compelling argument about journalistic priorities. There is little doubt that inequality in America is an ongoing problem. And just as surely, anything that compels journalists outside their often self-isolating bubble is all for the good. It also seems clear, at least based on past history, that the sort of systemic exposés that Ungar-Sargon argues for can lead to needed reforms, if not always structural change.

Still, such a journalistic call to arms will leave at least some unconvinced. A left-populist who thinks that the right-populists have successfully hijacked a grab bag of white working-class resentments, Ungar-Sargon seems wedded to a view of history as a clash of economic classes. And perhaps it is. But in redefining the journalistic mission in this way, does she also risk forcing members of the profession into another journalistic straightjacket, much as she blames the newly woke media of doing?

Whatever the actual case, press critics now and in the future will almost certainly debate this and many of the other questions raised above. Such is, after all, the nature of criticism, and perhaps as close as we will get to a definition of *its* core mission. Equally likely, the most insightful and persuasive critics will continue their fight not just for a free press but for a free society. It is an ongoing struggle, to be sure, but our progress toward that society is perhaps the best gauge we have of whether publishers, editors, and reporters are actually doing their jobs.

NOTES

1. Victor Pickard, *America's Battle for Media Democracy: The Triumph of Corporate Libertarianism and the Future of Media Reform* (New York: Cambridge, 2015), 230.

2. See "History of Ownership Consolidation," Research Reports, March 3, 2017, Dirks, Van Essen & April, http://www.dirksvanessen.com/articles/view/223/history-of-ownership-consolidation-/; also, Matthew Pressman, *On Press: The Liberal Values That Shaped the News* (Cambridge: Harvard, 2018), 1–22.

3. Jacob Weisberg, "Bad News: Can Democracy Survive If the Media Fail?" A review of *On Press: How Liberal Values That Shaped the News*, by Matthew Pressman; *Breaking News: The Remaking of Journalism and Why It Matters Now*, by Alan Rusbridger; and *Merchants of Truth: The Business of News and the Fight for Facts*, by Jill Abramson, *Foreign Affairs*, September/October, 2019, https://www.foreignaffairs.com/reviews/review-essay/2019-08-12/bad-news.

4. See Ted Johnson, "Cable News Network Viewership Continued to Drop in April vs 2020; Fox News Tops Primetime and Total Day," Deadline, April 27, 2021, https://deadline.com/2021/04/cable-news-viewership-drops-across -the-board-in-april-1234745199/; also, Elisa Shearer, "More Than Eight-In-Ten Americans Get News from Digital Devices," Pew Research Center, January 12, 2021, https://www.pewresearch.org/fact-tank/2021/01/12/more-than-eight -in-ten-americans-get-news-from-digital-devices/.

5. Weisberg, "Bad News."

6. In her suit, Palin claimed that the paper had defamed her when its 2017 editorial asserted a link between one of her political ads and two earlier mass shootings, one involving Arizona Representative Gabby Giffords and the second involving Louisiana Representative and then House Majority Whip Steve Scalise. In fact, the Palin ad had imposed bull's-eyes on specific congressional districts, of which Gifford's was one, but not on specific candidates. Alerted to the error, former opinion editor James Bennet immediately corrected it and issued an apology (not required by *Times* policy) but Palin nevertheless sued for defamation, alleging the paper had damaged her reputation. See Jeremy W. Peters, "Judge Says Palin 'Failed to Prove Her Case' against *The Times*," *New York Times*, March 1, 2022, https://www.ny times.com/2022/03/01/business/media/sarah-palin-new-york-times-trial.html.

7. Wikipedia, "*New York Times Co. v. Sullivan*," last modified March 22, 2022, https://en.wikipedia.org/wiki/New_York_Times_Co._v._Sullivan.

8. "Sarah Palin v. New York Times Case Highlights First Amendment Rights for Journalists," News@TheU, University of Miami, February 2022, https:// news.miami.edu/stories/2022/02/sarah-palin-v.-new-york-times-case-highlights -first-amendment-rights-for-journalists.html.

9. Emily Bazelon, "Free Speech Will Save Our Democracy," *New York Times Magazine*, October 8, 2020, 29.

10. Ibid.

11. David E. McCraw, *Truth in Our Times: Inside the Fight for Press Freedom in the Age of Alternative Facts* (New York: All Points, 2019), 275.

12. Jonathan Rauch, "The Constitution of Knowledge," *National Affairs*, no. 49 (Fall 2018), https://www.nationalaffairs.com/publications/detail/the-consti tution-of-knowledge. (Rauch's book of the same name is *The Constitution of Knowledge: A Defense of Truth* [Washington, DC: Brookings, 2021].)

13. Ibid.

14. Ibid.

15. Ibid. See, for example, "Standards and Ethics," *New York Times Company*, https://www.nytco.com/company/standards-ethics/.

16. For a discussion of the underlying issues and an attempt to address them, see, for example, Michael S. Roth, *Safe Enough Spaces: A Pragmatist's Approach to Inclusion, Free Speech, and Political Correctness on College Campuses*, with a new preface (New Haven: Yale, 2019).

17. "The 1619 Project," *New York Times Magazine*, last updated September 4, 2019, https://www.nytimes.com/interactive/2019/08/14/magazine/1619-america -slavery.html.

18. "The 1619 Project Curriculum," Pulitzer Center, accessed October 2, 2021, https://pulitzercenter.org/lesson-plan-grouping/1619-project-curriculum.

19. Alexander Neason, "The 1619 Project and the Stories We Tell about Slavery," *Columbia Journalism Review*, August 15, 2019, https://www.cjr.org /analysis/the-1619-project-nytimes.php.

20. Ellen McGirt, "The *New York Times* Launches the 1619 Project: Race Ahead," *Fortune*, August 14, 2019, https://fortune.com/2019/08/14/the-new -york-times-launches-the-1619-project-raceahead/.

21. "Commentary: Nikole Hannah-Jones of the *New York Times*, "2020 Pulitzer Prizes," The Pulitzer Prizes, https://www.pulitzer.org/prize-winners-by -year/2020.

22. "Top Ten Works of Journalism of the Decade," Arthur L. Carter Journalism Institute, October 14, 2020, New York University, https://journalism.nyu .edu/about-us/news/top-ten-works-of-journalism-of-the-decade/.

23. For a copy of the original letter, see "We Respond to Historians Who Critiqued The 1619 Project," *New York Times Magazine*, December 20, 2019, updated January 19, 2021, https://www.nytimes.com/2019/12/20/magazine/we -respond-to-the-historians-who-critiqued-the-1619-project.html.

24. Ibid.

25. Sean Wilentz, "A Matter of Facts," *Atlantic*, January 22, 2020, https:// www.theatlantic.com/ideas/archive/2020/01/1619-project-new-york-times -wilentz/605152/.

26. Alex Marlow, *Breaking the News: Exposing Establishment Media's Hidden Deals and Secret Corruption* (New York: Threshold, 2021), 67, 71.

27. Rich Lowry, "The Flagrant Distortions and Subtle Lies of the '1619 Project,'" *National Review*, October 7, 2019, https://www.nationalreview .com/2019/10/new-york-times-1619-project-distorts-history-of-slavery/.

28. Bret Stephens, "The 1619 Chronicles," Opinion, *New York Times*, October 9, 2020, https://www.nytimes.com/2020/10/09/opinion/nyt-1619-project-criti

cisms.html. In both the digital version of the original magazine special feature and in the later revised book, *The 1619 Project: A New Origin Story* (2021), Nikole Hannah-Jones quietly corrected some of wording in her opening essay that had been criticized by others. Among those corrections was the insertion of a qualifier to indicate that not all of the colonists had decided to declare their independence from Britain in order "to protect the institution of slavery." Hannah-Jones and project editors also added new essays and additional material to the book itself. See, for example, Rebecca Onion, "The New *1619 Project*," Slate, November 16, 2021, https://slate.com/news-and-politics/2021/11/1619-project -book-review-whats-changed-from-the-original-magazine-issue.html.

29. Batya Ungar-Sargon, *Bad News: How Woke Media Is Undermining Democracy* (New York: Encounter, 2021), 11–12.

30. Ibid., 12

31. Ibid., 30.

32. Ibid., 14–15

33. Ibid., 18.

Further Reading

Anderson, C. W., Downie, Leonard, Jr., et al. *The News Media: What Everyone Needs to Know.* (2016; repr. New York: Oxford, 2016).

Boorstin, Daniel J. *The Image: A Guide to Pseudo Events in America.* With a New Afterword by Douglas Rushkoff (1962; repr. New York: Vintage, 1992).

Borchard, Gregory A. *A Narrative History of the American Press* (2019; repr. New York: Routledge, 2019).

Hemmer, Nicole. *Messengers of the Right: Conservative Media and the Transformation of American Politics* (2016; repr. Philadelphia: University of Pennsylvania, 2018).

———. *Partisans: The Conservative Revolutionaries Who Remade American Politics in the 1990s* (New York: Basic Books, 2022).

Jacobs, Nicholas F., and Milkis, Sidney M., *What Happened to the Vital Center? Presidentialism, Populist Revolt, and the Fracturing of America* (2022; repr. New York: Oxford, 2022).

Klein, Ezra, *Why We Are Polarized* (2020; repr. New York: Avid Reader, an imprint of Simon & Schuster, 2021).

McWhorter, James. *Woke Racism: How a New Religion Has Betrayed Black America* (New York: Portfolio, an imprint of Penguin Random House, 2021).

Radio's Revolution: Don Hollenbeck's CBS Views the News. Edited and with an introduction by Loren Ghiglione (Lincoln: University of Nebraska, 2008).

Rauch, Jonathan. *The Constitution of Knowledge: A Defense of Truth* (Washington, DC: Brookings, 2021.

Schudson, Michael. *Journalism: Why It Matters* (2020; repr. Medford, MA: Polity, 2020).

Sullivan, Margaret, *Ghosting the News: Local Journalism and the Crisis of American Democracy* (2020; repr. New York: Columbia Global Reports, 2020).

Acknowledgments

It is a special pleasure to acknowledge my debts, assorted as they are, to the people who helped to make this book possible. As it was being written, my friends Peter D'Epiro and Nancy Walsh D'Epiro read successive chapters and offered unfailing encouragement along the way. Pete, the author of several well-regarded books on world history and culture, also trained his keen editorial intelligence on my unfolding manuscript, suggesting edits, pointing out sins of omission and commission, and circling stylistic infelicities that I struggled to disagree with. My heartfelt gratitude to you both. Some early chapters were also read by a trio of other friends—my former *Medical Economics* magazine colleague Neil Chesanow and my fellow Indiana University alumnus Bob Klute and his wife Carol Schoeffel. Thank you all.

Several people with whom I proudly share a surname also contributed to my project. To my nephew Zach, thank you for pointing out critics and books who would have otherwise escaped my notice. I'm also grateful to his brother, David, a wonderful filmmaker, who offered me his encouragement and enthusiasm as I moved ahead. I'm grateful, too, to my own brother, Ken, a gifted artist and designer who, beyond his own enthusiasm for the book, suggested ideas for how its theme might be represented visually on the front cover and elsewhere.

For interior art and images, I owe a big debt of gratitude to the following: Rick Goldsmith, of Kovno Communications, who permitted me to use his photos of George Seldes; the Division of Rare and Manuscript Collections, Cornell University, for access to A. J. Liebling images; Clark University, Worcester, Massachusetts, for a photo of Ben Bagdikian; Don Irvine, for a photo of his father; and Eric Deegans, a fellow Indiana

University alumnus, for sending along a photo of himself. In conjunction with the interior epigraphs, I also thank the following: Condé Nast, for a Liebling excerpt from the *New Yorker*; the Bancroft Library, University of California, Berkeley, for an excerpt from a Bagdikian oral history; Regnery Publishing, for permission to quote from Irvine's *Media Mischief and Misdeeds*, 1984; and Frank Bruni, of Duke University, for permission to quote from his 2018 lecture at UC Riverside.

I would also like to thank the staff of Rowman & Littlefield, and in particular Natalie Mandziuk Long. During a period of mounting professional and personal obligations, she managed to champion the book, offer ways to make it better, and finally guide it through to a successful completion. Thank you, Natalie. I am forever in your debt.

Finally, I would like to express my gratitude to my wife, Maria Cornea, who not only encouraged and supported this project from the beginning but gave me both the time and space to complete it. And at a point when the manuscript was nearly complete and some six hundred endnotes needed to be reformatted to accommodate a future electronic edition, she stepped in and with preternatural patience and precision took on the job. For these reasons and others too numerous to list, I dedicate this book to her. I also dedicate it to the memory of my mother and father, Mary and Tony, who started a new life for themselves and their family in the heady and hopeful days after World War II. Inspired as they were by their nation's promise and freedom, I like to think they would have approved of what their son set out to do.

Text Credits

Chapter 1: Excerpt, epigraph, Walter Lippmann, *Public Opinion*, 1922. Public domain.

Chapter 2: Excerpt, epigraph, George Seldes, *Lords of the Press*, 1938. Public domain.

Chapter 3: Epigraph, A. J. Liebling, *The New Yorker*, April 7, 1956. Used by permission of Condé Nast. © Condé Nast.

Chapter 4: Excerpt, epigraph: Ben H. Bagdikian: journalist, media critic, professor and dean emeritus UC Berkeley's Graduate School of Journalism, BANC MSS 2020/104, © The Regents of the University of California, The Oral History Center, The Bancroft Library, University of California, Berkeley.

Chapter 5: Epigraph, *Media Mischief and Misdeeds* by Reed Irvine, © 1985. Used by permission of Regnery Gateway. All Rights Reserved.

Chapter 6: Excerpt(s) [epigraph] from *Amusing Ourselves to Death* by Neil Postman, copyright © 1985 by Neil Postman. Used by permission of Viking Books, an imprint of Penguin Publishing Group, a division of Penguin Random House LLC. All rights reserved.

Chapter 7: Excerpt(s) [epigraph] from *Manufacturing Consent* by Edward S. Herman and Noam Chomsky, copyright © 1988 by Edward S. Herman and Noam Chomsky. Used by permission of Pantheon Books, an imprint of the Knopf Doubleday Publishing Group, a division of Penguin Random House LLC. All rights reserved.

Chapter 8: Excerpt from Hays Press-Enterprise Lecture, May 18, 2018, UC Riverside, Used by permission of Frank Bruni.

Index

CPSIA information can be obtained
at www.ICGtesting.com
Printed in the USA
BVHW081409010223
657047BV00002B/2